Praise for *Data Governance: The Definitive Guide*

We live in a digital world. Whether we realize it or not, we are living in the throes of one of the biggest economic and social revolutions since the Industrial Revolution. It's about transforming traditional business processes—many of them previously nondigital or manual—into processes that will fundamentally change how we live, how we operate our businesses, and how we deliver value to our customers. Data defines, informs, and predicts—it is used to penetrate new markets, control costs, drive revenues, manage risk, and help us discover the world around us. But to realize these benefits, data must be properly managed and stewarded. *Data Governance: The Definitive Guide* walks you through the many facets of data management and data governance—people, process and tools, data ownership, data quality, data protection, privacy and security—and does it in a way that is practical and easy to follow. A must-read for the data professional!

—*John Bottega, president of the EDM Council*

Enterprises are increasingly evolving as insight-driven businesses, putting pressure on data to satisfy new use cases and business ecosystems. Add to this business complexity, market disruption, and demand for speed, and data governance is front and center to make data trusted, secure, and relevant. This is not your grandfather's slow and bureaucratic data governance either. This book shares the secrets into how modern data governance ensures data is the cornerstone to your business resilience, elasticity, speed, and growth opportunity and not an afterthought.

—*Michele Goetz, vice president/principal analyst–business insights at Forrester*

Data governance has evolved from a discipline focused on cost and compliance to one that propels organizations to grow and innovate. Today's data governance solutions can benefit from technological advances that establish a continuous, autonomous, and virtuous cycle. This in turn becomes an ecosystem—a community in which data is used for good, and doing the right thing is also the easy thing. Executives looking to use data as an asset and deliver positive business outcomes need to rethink governance's role and adopt the modern and transformative approach *Data Governance: The Definitive Guide* provides.

—*Jim Cushman, CPO of Collibra*

Data Governance: The Definitive Guide

People, Processes, and Tools to Operationalize Data Trustworthiness

Evren Eryurek, Uri Gilad, Valliappa Lakshmanan, Anita Kibunguchy-Grant, and Jessi Ashdown

Beijing · Boston · Farnham · Sebastopol · Tokyo

Data Governance: The Definitive Guide

by Evren Eryurek, Uri Gilad, Valliappa Lakshmanan, Anita Kibunguchy-Grant, and Jessi Ashdown

Published by O'Reilly Media, Inc., 1005 Gravenstein Highway North, Sebastopol, CA 95472.

O'Reilly books may be purchased for educational, business, or sales promotional use. Online editions are also available for most titles (*http://oreilly.com*). For more information, contact our corporate/institutional sales department: 800-998-9938 or *corporate@oreilly.com*.

Acquisitions Editor: Jessica Haberman	**Indexer:** WordCo Indexing Services, Inc.
Development Editor: Gary O'Brien	**Interior Designer:** David Futato
Production Editor: Kate Galloway	**Cover Designer:** Karen Montgomery
Copyeditor: Piper Editorial Consulting, LLC	**Illustrator:** Kate Dullea
Proofreader: Arthur Johnson	

March 2021:　　　First Edition

Revision History for the First Edition

2021-03-08:　First Release

See *http://oreilly.com/catalog/errata.csp?isbn=9781492063490* for release details.

978-1-492-06349-0

[LSI]

Table of Contents

Preface

In recent years, the ease of moving to the cloud has motivated and energized a fast-growing community of data consumers to collect, capture, store, and analyze data for insights and decision making. For a number of reasons, as adoption of cloud computing continues to grow, information management stakeholders have questions about the potential risks involved in managing their data in the cloud. Evren faced such questions for the first time when he worked in healthcare and had to put in place the processes and technologies to govern data. Now at Google Cloud, Uri and Lak also answer these questions nearly every week and dispense advice on getting value from data, breaking down data silos, preserving anonymity, protecting sensitive information, and improving the trustworthiness of data.

We noticed that GDPR (*https://gdpr.eu/what-is-gdpr*) was what precipitated a sea change in customers' behavior. Some customers even deleted their data, thinking it was the right thing to do. That reaction, more than any other, prompted us to write this book capturing the advice we have provided over the years to Google Cloud customers. If data is the new currency, we do not want enterprises to be scared of it. If the data is locked away or is not trustworthy, it is of no value.

We all pride ourselves on helping Google Cloud customers get value for their technical expenditures. Data is a huge investment, and we felt obligated to provide our customers with the best way to get value from it.

Customers' questions usually involve one of three risk factors:

Securing the data
> Storing data in a public cloud infrastructure might concern large enterprises that typically deploy their systems on-premises and expect tight security. With a significant number of security threats and breaches in the news, organizations are concerned that they might be the next victim. These factors contribute to risk management concerns for protecting against unauthorized access to or exposure of sensitive data, ranging from personally identifiable information (PII) to corporate confidential information, trade secrets, or intellectual property.

Regulations and compliance

There is a growing set of regulations, including the California Consumer Privacy Act (CCPA), the European Union's General Data Protection Regulation (GDPR), and industry-specific standards such as global Legal Entity Identifier (LEI) numbers in the financial industry and ACORD data standards in the insurance industry. Compliance teams responsible for adhering to these regulations and standards may have concerns about oversight and control of data stored in the cloud.

Visibility and control

Data management professionals and data consumers sometimes lack visibility into their own data landscape: which data assets are available, where those assets are located and how and if they can be used, and who has access to the data and whether they *should* have access to it. This uncertainty limits their ability to further leverage their own data to improve productivity or drive business value.

These risk factors clearly highlight the need for increased data assessment, cataloging of metadata, access control management, data quality, and information security as core data governance competencies that the cloud provider should not only provide but also continuously upgrade in a transparent way. In essence, addressing these risks without abandoning the benefits provided by cloud computing has elevated the importance of not only understanding data governance in the cloud, but also knowing what is important. Good data governance can inspire customer trust and lead to vast improvements in customer experience.

Why Your Business Needs Data Governance in the Cloud

As your business generates more data and moves it into the cloud, the dynamics of data management change in a number of fundamental ways. Organizations should take note of the following:

Risk management

There are concerns about potential exposure of sensitive information to unauthorized individuals or systems, security breaches, or known personnel accessing data under the wrong circumstances. Organizations are looking to minimize this risk, so additional forms of protection (such as encryption) to obfuscate the data object's embedded information are required to safeguard the data should a system breach occur. In addition, other tools are required in order to support access management, identify sensitive data assets, and create a policy around their protection.

Data proliferation

The speed at which businesses create, update, and stream their data assets has increased, and while cloud-based platforms are capable of handling increased data velocity, volume, and variety, it is important to introduce controls and mechanisms to rapidly validate the quality aspects of high-bandwidth data streams.

Data management

The need to adopt externally produced data sources and data streams (including paid feeds from third parties) means that you should be prepared not to trust all external data sources. You may need to introduce tools that document data lineage, classification, and metadata to help your employees (data consumers, in particular) to determine data usability based on their knowledge of how the data assets were produced.

Discovery (and data awareness)

Moving data into any kind of data lake (cloud-based or on-premises) runs the risk of losing track of which data assets have been moved, the characteristics of their content, and details about their metadata. The ability, therefore, to assess data asset content and sensitivity (no matter where the data is) becomes very important.

Privacy and compliance

Regulatory compliance demands auditable and measurable standards and procedures that ensure compliance with internal data policies as well as external government regulations. Migrating data to the cloud means that organizations need tools to enforce, monitor, and report compliance, as well as ensure that the right people and services have access and permissions to the right data.

Framework and Best Practices for Data Governance in the Cloud

Given the changing dynamics of data management, how should organizations think about data governance in the cloud, and why is it important? According to *TechTarget*, data governance is

> the overall management of the availability, usability, integrity, and security of data used in an enterprise. A sound data governance program includes a governing body or council, a defined set of procedures and a plan to execute those procedures.[1]

Simply put, data governance encompasses the ways that people, processes and technology can work together to enable auditable compliance with defined and agreed-upon data policies.

---

1 Craig Stedman and Jack Vaughan, "What Is Data Governance and Why Does It Matter?" (*https://oreil.ly/OdvVk*) TechTarget, December 2019. This article was updated in February 2020; the current version no longer includes this quote.

Data Governance Framework

Enterprises need to think about data governance comprehensively, from data intake and ingestion to cataloging, persistence, retention, storage management, sharing, archiving, backup, recovery, loss prevention, disposition, and removal and deletion:

Data discovery and assessment
> Cloud-based environments often offer an economical option for creating and managing data lakes, but the risk remains for ungoverned migration of data assets. This risk represents a potential loss of knowledge of what data assets are in the data lake, what information is contained within each object, and where those data objects originated from. A best practice for data governance in the cloud is data discovery and assessment in order to know what data assets you have. The data discovery and assessment process is used to identify data assets within the cloud environment, and to trace and record each data asset's origin and lineage, what transformations have been applied, and object metadata. (Often this metadata describes the demographic details, such as the name of the creator, the size of the object, the number of records if it is a structured data object, or when it was last updated.)

Data classification and organization
> Properly evaluating a data asset and scanning the content of its different attributes can help categorize the data asset for subsequent organization. This process can also infer whether the object contains sensitive data and, if so, classify it in terms of the level of data sensitivity, such as personal and private data, confidential data, or intellectual property. To implement data governance in the cloud, you'll need to profile and classify sensitive data to determine which governance policies and procedures apply to the data.

Data cataloging and metadata management
> Once your data assets are assessed and classified, it is crucial that you document your learnings so that your communities of data consumers have visibility into your organization's data landscape. You need to maintain a data catalog that contains structural metadata, data object metadata, and the assessment of levels of sensitivity in relation to the governance directives (such as compliance with one or more data privacy regulations). The data catalog not only allows data consumers to view this information but can also serve as part of a reverse index for search and discovery, both by phrase and (given the right ontologies) by concept. It is also important to understand the format of structured and semi-structured data objects and allow your systems to handle these data types differently, as necessary.

Data quality management

Different data consumers may have different data quality requirements, so it's important to provide a means of documenting data quality expectations as well as techniques and tools for supporting the data validation and monitoring process. Data quality management processes include creating controls for validation, enabling quality monitoring and reporting, supporting the triage process for assessing the level of incident severity, enabling root cause analysis and recommendation of remedies to data issues, and data incident tracking. The right processes for data quality management will provide measurably trustworthy data for analysis.

Data access management

There are two aspects of governance for data access. The first aspect is the provisioning of access to available assets. It's important to provide data services that allow data consumers to access their data, and fortunately, most cloud platforms provide methods for developing data services. The second aspect is prevention of improper or unauthorized access. It's important to define identities, groups, and roles and assign access rights to establish a level of managed access. This best practice involves managing access services as well as interoperating with the cloud provider's identity and access management (IAM) services by defining roles, specifying access rights, and managing and allocating access keys to ensure that only authorized and authenticated individuals and systems are able to access data assets according to defined rules.

Auditing

Organizations must be able to assess their systems to make sure that they are working as designed. Monitoring, auditing, and tracking (who did what and when and with what information) helps security teams gather data, identify threats, and act on those threats before they result in business damage or loss. It's important to perform regular audits to check the effectiveness of controls in order to quickly mitigate threats and evaluate overall security health.

Data protection

Despite the efforts of information technology security groups to establish perimeter security as a way to prevent unauthorized individuals from accessing data, perimeter security is not and never has been sufficient for protecting sensitive data. While you might be successful in preventing someone from breaking into your system, you are not protected from an insider security breach or even from exfiltration (data theft). It's important to institute additional methods of data protection—including encryption at rest, encryption in transit, data masking, and permanent deletion—to ensure that exposed data cannot be read.

Operationalizing Data Governance in Your Organization

Technology certainly helps support the data governance principles presented in the preceding section, but data governance goes beyond the selection and implementation of products and tools. The success of a data governance program depends on a combination of:

- *People* to build the business case, develop the operating model, and take on appropriate roles
- *Processes* that operationalize policy development, implementation, and enforcement
- *Technology* used to facilitate the ways that people execute those processes

The following steps are critical in planning, launching, and supporting a data governance program:

1. **Build the business case.** Establish the business case by identifying critical business drivers to justify the effort and investment associated with data governance. Outline perceived data risks (such as the storage of data on cloud-based platforms) and indicate how data governance helps the organization mitigate those risks.

2. **Document guiding principles.** Assert core principles associated with governance and oversight of enterprise data. Document those principles in a data governance charter to present to senior management.

3. **Get management buy-in.** Engage data governance champions and get buy-in from the key senior stakeholders. Present your business case and guiding principles to C-level management for approval.

4. **Develop an operating model.** Once you have management approval, define the data governance roles and responsibilities, and then describe the processes and procedures for the data governance council and data stewardship teams who will define processes for defining and implementing policies as well as reviewing and remediating identified data issues.

5. **Establish a framework for accountability.** Establish a framework for assigning custodianship and responsibility for critical data domains. Make sure there is visibility to the "data owners" across the data landscape. Provide a methodology to ensure that everyone is accountable for contributing to data usability.

6. **Develop taxonomies and ontologies.** There may be a number of governance directives associated with data classification, organization, and—in the case of sensitive information—data protection. To enable your data consumers to comply with those directives, there must be a clear definition of the categories (for organizational structure) and classifications (for assessing data sensitivity).

7. **Assemble the right technology stack.** Once you've assigned data governance roles to your staff and defined and approved your processes and procedures, you should assemble a suite of tools that facilitate ongoing validation of compliance with data policies and accurate compliance reporting.

8. **Establish education and training.** Raise awareness of the value of data governance by developing educational materials highlighting data governance practices and procedures, and the use of supporting technology. Plan for regular training sessions to reinforce good data governance practices.

The Business Benefits of Robust Data Governance

Data security, data protection, data accessibility and usability, data quality, and other aspects of data governance will continue to emerge and grow as critical priorities for organizations. And as more organizations migrate their data assets to the cloud, the need for auditable practices for ensuring data utility will also continue to grow. To address these directives, businesses should frame their data governance practices around three key components:

- A framework that enables *people* to define, agree to, and enforce data policies
- Effective *processes* for control, oversight, and stewardship over all data assets across on-premises systems, cloud storage, and data warehouse platforms
- The right *tools and technologies* for operationalizing data policy compliance

With this framework in mind, an effective data governance strategy and operating model provides a path for organizations to establish control and maintain visibility into their data assets, providing a competitive advantage over their peers. Organizations will likely reap immense benefits as they promote a data-driven culture within their organizations—specifically:

Improved decision making
Better data discovery means that users can find the data they need when they need it, which makes them more efficient. Data-driven decision making plays a huge role in improving business planning within an organization.

Better risk management
A good data governance operating model helps organizations audit their processes more easily so that they reduce the risk of fines, increase customer trust, and improve operations. Downtime can be minimized while productivity still grows.

Regulatory compliance

Increasing governmental regulation has made it even more important for organizations to establish data governance practices. With a good data governance framework, organizations can embrace the changing regulatory environment instead of simply reacting to it.

As you migrate more of your data to the cloud, data governance provides a level of protection against data misuse. At the same time, auditable compliance with defined data policies helps demonstrate to your customers that you protect their private information, alleviating their concerns about information risks.

Who Is This Book For?

The current growth in data is unprecedented and, when coupled with increased regulations and fines, has meant that organizations are forced to look into their data governance plans to make sure that they do not become the next statistic. Therefore, every organization will need to establish an understanding of the data it collects, the liability and regulation associated with that data, and who has access to it. This book is for you if you want to know what that entails, the risks to be aware of, and the considerations to keep in mind.

This book is for anyone who needs to implement the processes or technology that enables data to become trustworthy. This book covers the ways that people, processes, and technology can work together to enable auditable compliance with defined and agreed-upon data policies.

The benefits of data governance are multifaceted, ranging from legal and regulatory compliance to better risk management and the ability to drive top-line revenue and cost savings by creating new products and services. Read this book to learn how to establish control and maintain visibility into your data assets, which will provide you with a competitive advantage over your peers.

Conventions Used in This Book

The following typographical conventions are used in this book:

Italic

Indicates new terms, URLs, email addresses, filenames, and file extensions.

`Constant width`

Used for program listings, as well as within paragraphs to refer to program elements such as variable or function names, databases, data types, environment variables, statements, and keywords.

This element signifies a tip or suggestion.

 This element signifies a general note.

 This element indicates a warning or caution.

O'Reilly Online Learning

 For more than 40 years, *O'Reilly Media* has provided technology and business training, knowledge, and insight to help companies succeed.

Our unique network of experts and innovators share their knowledge and expertise through books, articles, and our online learning platform. O'Reilly's online learning platform gives you on-demand access to live training courses, in-depth learning paths, interactive coding environments, and a vast collection of text and video from O'Reilly and 200+ other publishers. For more information, visit *http://oreilly.com*.

How to Contact Us

Please address comments and questions concerning this book to the publisher:

O'Reilly Media, Inc.
1005 Gravenstein Highway North
Sebastopol, CA 95472
800-998-9938 (in the United States or Canada)
707-829-0515 (international or local)
707-829-0104 (fax)

We have a web page for this book, where we list errata, examples, and any additional information. You can access this page at *https://oreil.ly/data-governance-TDG*.

Email *bookquestions@oreilly.com* to comment or ask technical questions about this book.

For news and information about our books and courses, visit *http://oreilly.com*.

Find us on Facebook: *http://facebook.com/oreilly*

Follow us on Twitter: *http://twitter.com/oreillymedia*

Watch us on YouTube: *http://www.youtube.com/oreillymedia*

Acknowledgments

Thank you to our respective families, teammates, and managers. Gary O'Brien, our editor at O'Reilly, was a force of nature—this book would not exist without his constant prodding and invaluable advice. Thanks also to our technical reviewers for their invaluable suggestions.

CHAPTER 1

What Is Data Governance?

Data governance is, first and foremost, a data management function to ensure the quality, integrity, security, and usability of the data collected by an organization. Data governance needs to be in place from the time a factoid of data is collected or generated until the point in time at which that data is destroyed or archived. Along the way in this full life cycle of the data, data governance focuses on making the data available to all stakeholders in a form that they can readily access. In addition, it must be one they can use in a manner that generates the desired business outcomes (insights, analysis) and conforms to regulatory standards, if relevant. These regulatory standards are often an intersection of industry (e.g., healthcare), government (e.g., privacy), and company (e.g., nonpartisan) rules and codes of behavior. Moreover, data governance needs to ensure that the stakeholders get a high-quality integrated view of all the data within the enterprise. There are many facets to high-quality data—the data needs to be correct, up to date, and consistent. Finally, data governance needs to be in place to ensure that the data is secure, by which we mean that:

- It is accessed only by permitted users in permitted ways
- It is auditable, meaning all accesses, including changes, are logged
- It is compliant with regulations

The purpose of data governance is to enhance trust in the data. Trustworthy data is necessary to enable users to employ enterprise data to support decision making, risk assessment, and management using key performance indicators (KPIs). Using data, you can increase confidence in the decision-making process by showing supporting evidence. The principles of data governance are the same regardless of the size of the enterprise or the quantity of data. However, data governance practitioners will make choices with regard to tools and implementation based on practical considerations driven by the environment within which they operate.

What Data Governance Involves

The advent of big data analytics, powered by the ease of moving to the cloud and the ever-increasing capability and capacity of compute power, has motivated and energized a fast-growing community of data consumers to collect, store, and analyze data for insights and decision making. Nearly every computer application these days is informed by business data. It is not surprising, therefore, that new ideas inevitably involve the analysis of existing data in new ways, as well as the collection of new datasets, whether through new systems or by purchase from external vendors. Does your organization have a mechanism to vet new data analysis techniques and ensure that any data collected is stored securely, that the data collected is of high quality, and that the resulting capabilities accrue to your brand value? While it's tempting to look only toward the future power and possibilities of data collection and big data analytics, data governance is a very real and very important consideration that cannot be ignored. In 2017, *Harvard Business Review* reported that more than 70% of employees have access to data they should not.[1] This is not to say that companies should adopt a defensive posture; it's only to illustrate the importance of governance to prevent data breaches and improper use of the data. Well-governed data can lead to measurable benefits for an organization.

Spotify Creates Discover Weekly

As an example of how well-governed data can lead to measurable benefits to an organization and how the availability of data can completely change an entire industry, consider the Spotify Discover Weekly feature. In the early 2010s, the way most people listened to music was to purchase physical/digital albums and rip them to create custom playlists. These playlists, consisting of songs you owned, was what you listened to.

There was also a large and thriving illegal music-sharing ecosystem that consisted of pirated singles that could be added to your playlists. In an effort to get the pirated music system under control, music labels allowed the sales of digital singles. As the size of people's digital libraries grew, and as internet connections became more reliable, consumers became willing to keep their purchased tracks online and stream them to their audio devices. Music labels were also willing to "rent" out music when it was streamed. Instead of selling the song, the music labels would be paid each time the song was played.

---

1 Leandro DalleMule and Thomas H. Davenport, "What's Your Data Strategy?" (*https://oreil.ly/kBC23*) *Harvard Business Review* (May–June 2017): 112–121.

This was how Spotify (which is now the world's largest music streaming service) got started. It's worth noting that Spotify owes its very existence to data governance. It got started as a way for music labels to get paid for their work—music piracy was decimating the music industry. Spotify's entire business model was built around tracking the songs users played and reimbursing artists for those songs. The ability to prove that its handling of the data was trustworthy is the reason that Spotify became a viable music service in the first place.

The fact that Spotify was keeping tabs on which songs users played meant that it had data on what people listened to. Thus it was now possible for Spotify to recommend new songs to its listeners. Such recommendation algorithms key off of three things:

- Find other songs by the artists you listen to, or songs in the same genre (e.g., 1940s jazz). This is called *content-based recommendation*.
- Find users who like the same songs you do and recommend the songs that those users like. This is called *collaborative filtering*.
- Use models that analyze the raw audio files of songs you like and recommend songs that are similar. The raw audio captures many inherent features, such as the beat. If you tend to like music with a fast beat and with repeating tonal phrases, the algorithm can recommend other songs with a similar structure. This is called *similarity matching*.

At that point, Edward Newett, an engineer at Spotify, had an interesting idea (*https://oreil.ly/3ZQnQ*): instead of recommending songs one at a time, what if Spotify created a playlist of recommendations? And so, every Monday, Spotify would recommend what they thought each individual user would like. This was called Discover Weekly.

Discover Weekly was a huge hit—within a year after its launch, more than 40 million people had used the service and streamed nearly five billion tracks. The deep personalization had worked. The music sounded familiar but was still novel. The service allowed music lovers to discover new titles, and new artists to find audiences, and it gave Spotify's customers an event to look forward to every week.

Spotify was able to use its recommendation algorithm to provide artists and music labels with insights about fans' preferences. It could leverage the recommendation algorithm to expand users' music preferences and introduce novel bands. This extra knowledge and marketing ability has allowed Spotify to negotiate with music publishers from a position of strength.

None of this would have been possible if Spotify had not assured its users that the information about their listening habits was being used in a responsible way to improve their own music-listening experience. European regulators are very protective of the privacy of EU citizens. Spotify, being based in Europe, could not have gotten its recommendation systems off the ground if it had not proven that it had robust privacy controls in place, and that it was ensuring that data scientists could devise algorithms but not breach data that could be tied to individuals.

Discover Weekly illustrates how data, properly governed, can create a well-loved brand and change the power dynamic in an entire industry. Spotify extended its recommendations with Spotify Wrapped, where listeners everywhere get a deep dive into their most memorable listening moments of the year. This is a great way to have people remember and share their most listened-to songs and artists (see Figure 1-1).

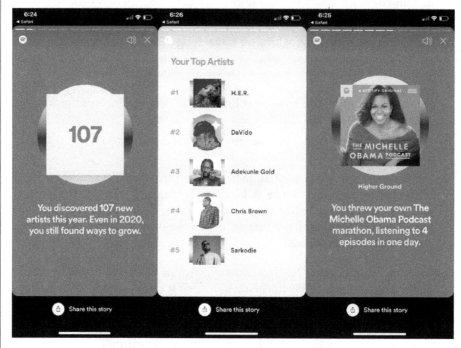

Figure 1-1. Anita Kibunguchy-Grant's 2020 Wrapped playlist

Holistic Approach to Data Governance

Several years ago, when smartphones with GPS sensors were becoming ubiquitous, one of the authors of this book was working on machine learning algorithms to predict the occurence of hail. Machine learning requires labeled data—something that was in short supply at the temporal and spatial resolution the research team needed. Our team hit on the idea of creating a mobile application that would allow citizen scientists to report hail at their location.[2] This was our first encounter with making choices about what data to collect—until then, we had mostly been at the receiving

---

2 This application is the Meteorological Phenomena Identification Near the Ground (mPING) Project (*https://mping.ou.edu*), developed through a partnership between NSSL, the University of Oklahoma, and the Cooperative Institute for Mesoscale Meteorological Studies.

end of whatever data the National Weather Service was collecting. Considering the rudimentary state of information security tools in an academic setting, we decided to forego all personally identifying information and make the reporting totally anonymous, even though this meant that certain types of reported information became somewhat unreliable. Even this anonymous data brought tremendous benefits—we started to evaluate hail algorithms at greater resolutions, and this improved the quality of our forecasts. This new dataset allowed us to calibrate existing datasets, thus enhancing the data quality of other datasets as well. The benefits went beyond data quality and started to accrue toward trustworthiness—involvement of citizen scientists was novel enough that National Public Radio carried a story about the project, emphasizing the anonymous nature of the data collection.[3] The data governance lens had allowed us to carefully think about which report data to collect, improve the quality of enterprise data, enhance the quality of forecasts produced by the National Weather Service, and even contribute to the overall brand of our weather enterprise. This combination of effects—regulatory compliance, better data quality, new business opportunities, and enhanced trustworthiness—was the result of a holistic approach to data governance.

Fast-forward a few years, and now, at Google Cloud, we are all part of a team that builds technology for scalable cloud data warehouses and data lakes. One of the recurring concerns that our enterprise customers have is around what best practices and policies they should put in place to manage the classification, discovery, availability, accessibility, integrity, and security of their data—data governance—and customers approach it with the same sort of apprehension that our small team in academia did.

Yet the tools and capabilities that an enterprise has at its disposal to carry out data governance are quite powerful and diverse. We hope to convince you that you should not be afraid of data governance, and that properly applying data governance can open up new worlds of possibility. While you might initially approach data governance purely from a legal or regulatory compliance standpoint, applying governance policies can drive growth and lower costs.

Enhancing Trust in Data

Ultimately, the purpose of data governance is to build trust in data. Data governance is valuable to the extent that it adds to stakeholders' trust in the data—specifically, in how that data is collected, analyzed, published, or used.

Ensuring trust in data requires that a data governance strategy address three key aspects: *discoverability*, *security*, and *accountability* (see Figure 1-2). Discoverability

---

3 It was on the radio, but you can read about it on NPR's *All Tech Considered* blog (*https://oreil.ly/uWwml*).

itself requires data governance to make technical metadata, lineage information, and a business glossary readily available. In addition, business critical data needs to be correct and complete. Finally, master data management is necessary to guarantee that data is finely classified and thus ensure appropriate protection against inadvertent or malicious changes or leakage. In terms of security, regulatory compliance, management of sensitive data (personally identifiable information, for example), and data security and exfiltration prevention may all be important depending on the business domain and the dataset in question. If discoverability and security are in place, then you can start treating the data itself as a product. At that point, accountability becomes important, and it is necessary to provide an operating model for ownership and accountability around boundaries of data domains.

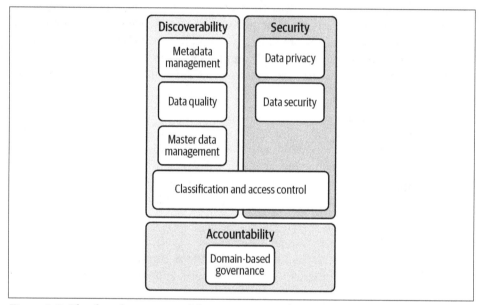

Figure 1-2. The three key aspects of data governance that must be addressed to enhance trust in data

Classification and Access Control

While the purpose of data governance is to increase the trustworthiness of enterprise data so as to derive business benefits, it remains the case that the primary activity associated with data governance involves classification and access control. Therefore, to understand the roles involved in data governance, it is helpful to consider a typical classification and access control setup.

Let's take the case of protecting the human resources information of employees, as shown in Figure 1-3.

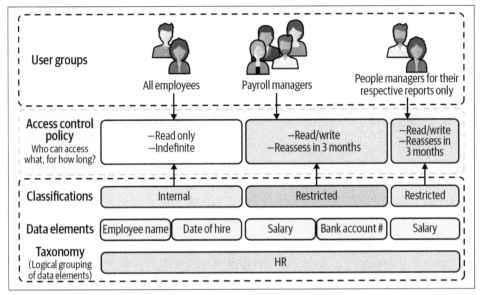

Figure 1-3. Protecting the human resources information of employees

The human resources information includes several data elements: each employee's name, their date of hire, past salary payments, the bank account into which those salary payments were deposited, current salary, etc. Each of these data elements is protected in different ways, depending on the classification level. Potential classification levels might be public (things accessible by people not associated with the enterprise), external (things accessible by partners and vendors with authorized access to the enterprise internal systems), internal (things accessible by any employee of the organization), and restricted. For example, information about each employee's salary payments and which bank account they were deposited into would be restricted to managers in the payroll processing group only. On the other hand, the restrictions could be more dynamic. An employee's current salary might be visible only to their manager, and each manager might be able to see salary information only for their respective reports. The access control policy would specify what users can do when they access the data—whether they can create a new record, or read, update, or delete existing records.

The governance policy is typically specified by the group that is accountable for the data (here, the human resources department)—this group is often referred to as the *governors*. The policy itself might be implemented by the team that operates the database system or application (here, the information technology department), and so changes such as adding users to permitted groups are often carried out by the IT team—hence, members of that team are often referred to as *approvers* or *data stewards*. The people whose actions are being circumscribed or enabled by data governance are often referred to as *users*. In businesses where not all employees have access to enterprise data, the set of employees with access might be called *knowledge workers* to differentiate them from those without access..

Some enterprises default to *open*—for example, when it comes to business data, the domain of authorized users may involve all knowledge workers in the enterprise. Other enterprises default to *closed*—business data may be available only to those with a need to know. Policies such as these are within the purview of the data governance board in the organization—there is no uniquely correct answer on which approach is best.

Data Governance Versus Data Enablement and Data Security

Data governance is often conflated with data enablement and with data security. Those topics intersect but have different emphases:

- Data governance is mostly focused on making data accessible, reachable, and indexed for searching across the relevant constituents, usually the entire organization's knowledge-worker population. This is a crucial part of data governance and will require tools such as a metadata index, a data catalog to "shop for" data. Data governance extends data enablement into including a *workflow* in which data acquisition can take place. Users can search for data by context and description, find the relevant data stores, and ask for access, including the desired use case as justification. An approver (data steward) will need to review the ask, determine whether the ask is justified and whether the data being requested can actually serve the use case, and kick off a process through which the data can be made accessible.

- Data enablement goes further than making data accessible and discoverable; it extends into tooling that allows rapid analysis and processing of the data to answer business-related questions: "how much is the business spending on this topic," "can we optimize this supply chain," and so on. The topic is crucial and requires knowledge of how to work with data, as well as *what the data actually means*—best addressed by including, from the get-go, metadata that describes the data and includes value proposition, origin, lineage, and a contact person who curates and owns the data in question, to allow for further inquiry.

- Data security, which intersects with both data enablement and data governance, is normally thought about as a set of mechanics put in place to prevent and block unauthorized access. Data governance relies on data security mechanics to be in place but goes beyond just prevention of unauthorized access and into policies about the data itself, its transformation according to data class (see Chapter 7), and the ability to prove that the policies set to access and transform the data over time are being complied with. The correct implementation of security mechanics promotes the trust required to share data broadly or "democratize access" to the data.

Why Data Governance Is Becoming More Important

Data governance has been around since there was data to govern, although it was often restricted to IT departments in regulated industries, and to security concerns around specific datasets such as authentication credentials. Even legacy data processing systems needed a way to not only ensure data quality but also control access to data.

Traditionally, data governance was viewed as an IT function that was performed in silos related to data source type. For example, a company's HR data and financial data, typically highly controlled data sources with strictly controlled access and specific usage guidelines, would be controlled by one IT silo, whereas sales data would be in a different, less restrictive silo. Holistic or "centralized" data governance may have existed within some organizations, but the majority of companies viewed data governance as a departmental concern.

Data governance has come into prominence because of the recent introductions of GDPR- (*https://gdpr.eu/what-is-gdpr*) and CCPA-type (*https://oag.ca.gov/privacy/ccpa*) regulations that affect every industry, beyond just healthcare, finance, and a few other regulated industries. There has also been a growing realization about the business value of data. Because of this, the data landscape is vastly different today.

The following are just a few ways in which the topography has changed over time, warranting very different approaches to and methods for data governance.

The Size of Data Is Growing

There is almost no limit to the kinds and amount of data that can now be collected. In a whitepaper published in November 2018, International Data Corporation (*https://www.idc.com/about*) predicts that the global datasphere will balloon to 175 ZB by 2025 (see Figure 1-4).[4]

This rise in data captured via technology, coupled with predictive analyses, results in systems nearly knowing more about today's users than the users themselves.

---

4 David Reinsel, John Gantz, and John Rydning, "The Digitization of the World: From Edge to Core" (*https://oreil.ly/2L1TW*), November 2018.

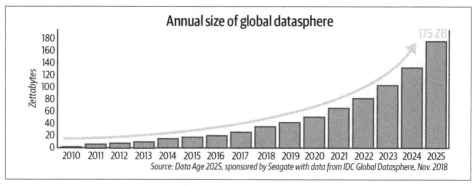

Figure 1-4. The size of the global datasphere is expected to exhibit dramatic growth

The Number of People Working and/or Viewing the Data Has Grown Exponentially

A report by Indeed shows that the demand for data science jobs had jumped 78% between 2015 and 2018.[5] IDC also reports that there are now over five billion people in the world interacting with data, and it projects this number to increase to six billion (nearly 75% of the world's population) in 2025. Companies are obsessed with being able to make "data-driven decisions," requiring an inordinate amount of headcount: from the engineers setting up data pipelines to analysts doing data curation and analyses, and business stakeholders viewing dashboards and reports. The more people working and viewing data, the greater the need for complex systems to manage access, treatment, and usage of data because of the greater chance of misuse of the data.

Methods of Data Collection Have Advanced

No longer must data only be batch processed and loaded for analysis. Companies are leveraging real-time or near real-time streaming data and analytics to provide their customers with better, more personalized engagements. Customers now expect to access products and services wherever they are, over whatever connection they have, and on any device. IDC predicts that this infusion of data into business workflows and personal streams of life will result in nearly 30% of the global datasphere to be real-time by 2025, as shown in Figure 1-5.[6]

---

5 "The Best Jobs in the US: 2019" (*https://oreil.ly/UpU9N*), Indeed, March 19, 2019.

6 Reinsel et al. "The Digitization of the World."

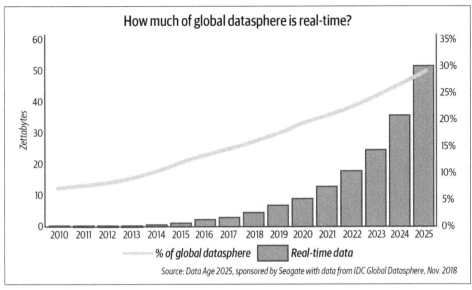

Figure 1-5. More than 25% of the global datasphere will be real-time data by 2025

The advent of streaming, however, while greatly increasing the speed to analytics, also carries with it the potential risk of infiltration, bringing about the need for complex setup and monitoring for protection.

Advanced Data Collection in Sports

It used to be that when you talked about sport statistics, you were talking about relatively coarse-grained data—things like wins and losses. In some sports, you might have information about a player's performance (for example, average number of runs a cricketer gets per inning). However, the quantity and type of data collected in sports has changed dramatically because teams are looking to better understand what levers they can pull to be successful in these highly competitive fields.

It's therefore no surprise that the National Football League (NFL) wanted to better quantify the value of specific plays and actions within a play, which is why it started using league-wide analytics in 2015. If you're not familiar with American football, it is a complex sport, primarily governed by the NFL. The NFL is a professional American football league consisting of 32 teams that are divided equally between the National Football Conference (NFC) and the American Football Conference (AFC).

Traditional metrics such as "yards per carry" or "total rushing yards" can be flawed; recognizing a need to grow its analytics and data collection process, the NFL created Next Gen Stats (NGS). NGS is a league program wherein the pads of every player and official, along with game balls, pylons, and first down chains are all tagged with a radio frequency identification (RFID) chip, which allows for a very robust set of statistics after every game. These statistics constitute real-time data for every player on every play, in every situation, anywhere on the field, including location, speed, acceleration, and velocity (Figure 1-6).

 NFL Big Data Bowl - Plotting Player Position

Python notebook using data from multiple data sources · 10,025 views · 2mo ago

Plotting the field

Using some code that I developed for last year's NFL challenge, this notebook shows how to plot player positions during a play on the football field.

Using matplotlib we can call the `create_football_field` function to create a figure with the football field drawn out. You can then overlay any information from the training data to help visualize how players positions look on the field.

The design is loosely based off of the 1991 video game Techo Super Bowl. A game which I spent many hours playing in my next door neighbor's basement growing up (I wasn't allowed to own a video game console so we had to play at his house).

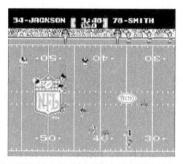

```
import pandas as pd
import numpy as np
import os
import seaborn as sns

import matplotlib.pyplot as plt
import matplotlib.patches as patches
pd.set_option('max_columns', 100)

train = pd.read_csv('../input/nfl-big-data-bowl-2020/train.csv', low_memory=False)
train2021 = pd.read_csv('../input/nfl-big-data-bowl-2021/plays.csv')
```

Figure 1-6. An example of analysis and visualization of the NFL data in Kaggle. Notebook by Rob Mulla (https://oreil.ly/E_XRx)

The types of questions the NFL wanted an answer to included, for example, "What contributes to a successful run play?" It wanted to know whether success depends mostly on the ball carrier who takes the hand off, or on their teammates (by way of blocking), or on the coach (by way of the play call). And could the data even show what part was played by the opposing defense and the actions it took? The NFL would also want to predict how many yards a team might gain on given rushing plays as they happen. Deeper insight into rushing plays ultimately helps teams, media, and fans better understand the skillsets of players and the strategies of coaches.

Because of this, each year the league hosts the NFL's Big Data Bowl, a sports analytics contest that challenges talented members of the analytics community—from college students to professionals—to contribute to the NFL's continuing evolution in the use of advanced analytics.[7] Contestants are asked to analyze and rethink trends and player performance in order to innovate on the way football is played and coached.

This NFL example showcases just how much the methods of data collection have advanced. It's no surprise that this is what's really accelerating the amount of data being generated in the global datasphere.

More Kinds of Data (Including More Sensitive Data) Are Now Being Collected

It's projected that by 2025 every person using technology and generating data will have more than 4,900 digital data engagements per day; that's about about one digital interaction every eighteen seconds (see Figure 1-7).[8]

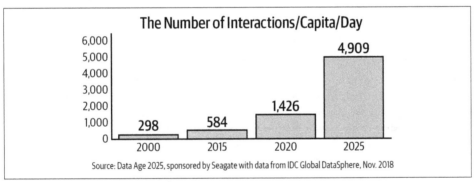

Figure 1-7. By 2025, a person will interact with data-creating technology more than 4,900 times a day

Many of those interactions will include the generation and resulting collection of a myriad of sensitive data such as social security numbers, credit card numbers, names, addresses, and health conditions, to name a few categories. The proliferation of the collection of these extremely sensitive types of data carries with it great customer (and regulator) concern about how that data is used and treated, and who gets to view it.

---

7 Kaggle: NFL Big Data Bowl (*https://oreil.ly/o7lCI*).

8 Reinsel et al. "The Digitization of the World."

The Use Cases for Data Have Expanded

Companies are striving to use data to make better business decisions, coined *data-driven decision making*. They not only are using data internally to drive day-to-day business execution, but are also using data to help their *customers* make better decisions. Amazon is an example of a company doing this via collecting and analyzing items in customers' past purchases, items the customers have viewed, and items in their virtual shopping carts, as well as the items they've ranked/reviewed after purchase, to drive targeted messaging and recommendations for future purchases.

While this Amazon use case makes perfect business sense, there are types of data (sensitive) coupled with specific use cases for that data that are not appropriate (or even legal). For sensitive types of data, it matters not only how that data is treated but also how it's used. For example, employee data may be used/viewed internally by a company's HR department, but it would not be appropriate for that data to be used/viewed by the marketing department.

Use of Data to Make Better Decisions

Many of us enjoy the suggestions our friends and family make for books, movies, music, and so on. Have you noticed how some of these suggestions pop up while you are searching for something online? Here we would like to highlight a few examples that show how use of data resulted in better decisions and better business outcomes.

An example from Safari Books Online (*https://oreil.ly/MKnxp*) shows the use of modern analytics tools to achieve improved sales. Safari Books Online is known for its very large and diverse customer base and for having more than 30,000 books and videos accessible from various platforms. Safari Books Online wanted to unlock value from its massive amounts of usage data, user search results, and trends, and to connect all this data to drive better sales intelligence and higher sales.

The key was to achieve this in near real-time—after all, none of us likes to wait 10 minutes for the results of an online search. In order to provide real-time insights, the Safari Books Online team routinely transferred the usage data corresponding to the content delivery network (CDN) to a cloud native data warehouse to make the information available outside the original silo (see Figure 1-8).

The Safari Books Online team wanted to drill into the data, deliver various dashboards, provide a better user experience, and deliver faster ad hoc queries. Using the new analytics made supporting users much quicker and simpler and achieved higher customer satisfaction. This was because the team could get to relevant information about users (such as their IP addresses, or the title of a book they were querying) in near real-time.

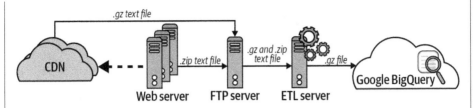

Figure 1-8. Bringing the usage data from content delivery network (CDN) and web application logs into a smart data analytics platform to achieve better data-driven decisions

Achieving better sales intelligence was among the most important use cases for Safari Books Online when it began its journey into data-driven decision making. All the data it had that was once buried, or not even available from its web logs, became sales leads. Assessment of interest among likely readers was integrated into the CRM system and quickly turned into actionable information (see Figure 1-9).

Figure 1-9. A dashboard that is used to monitor titles and trends

Another good example (*https://oreil.ly/3UIse*) is from *California Design Den*, which transformed its decision-making process with data on pricing and inventory management. By leaning on smart analytics platforms, they were able to achieve much faster pricing decisions, sell their inventory, and achieve better profitability.

The ability to aggregate different types of data for decision making (while balancing which data to retain and which to get rid of) is key. Not all data can be valuable for better decision making. It is equally important to guard against biases when you are trying to establish your data-driven decision-making process. You need to define your objectives—maybe set some easy-to-measure goals at first—and create a list of *high-value questions* to which you want to elicit answers. It is OK to go back and revisit your starting point, objectives, and metrics. The answers are to be found in your data, but looking at it from different perspectives will help you decide which data is relevant.

The world is your oyster when it comes to gaining insight from your data. Asking the high-value questions to obtain deeper insights is the essential part of the value chain when it comes to data-driven decision making. Whether you want to drive sales intelligence and increase your revenue, improve support and customer experience, or detect malicious use to prevent operational issues, data-driven decision making is key for any business and any operation, and there are various smart tools out there to help you start taking advantage of your invaluable data.

New Regulations and Laws Around the Treatment of Data

The increase in data and data availability has resulted in the desire and need for regulations on data, data collection, data access, and data use. Some regulations that have been around for quite some time—for example, the Health Insurance Portability and Accountability Act of 1996 (HIPAA), the law protecting the collection and use of personal health data—not only are well known, but companies that have had to comply with them have been doing so for decades—meaning their processes and methodology for treatment of this sensitive data are fairly sophisticated. New regulations, such as the EU's General Data Protection Regulation (GDPR) and the California Consumer Privacy Act (CCPA) in the US, are just two examples of usage and collection controls that apply to myriad companies, for many of whom such governance of data was not baked into their original data architecture strategy. Because of this, companies that have not had to worry about regulatory compliance before have a more difficult time modifying their technology and business processes to maintain compliance with these new regulations.

Ethical Concerns Around the Use of Data

While use cases themselves can fit into the category of ethical use of data, new technology around machine learning and artificial intelligence has spawned new concerns around the ethical use of data.

One recent example from 2018 is that of Elaine Herzberg, who, while wheeling her bike across a street in Tempe, Arizona, was struck and killed by a self-driving car.[9] This incident raised questions about responsibility. Who was responsible for Elaine's

---

9 Aarian Marshall and Alex Davies, "Uber's Self-Driving Car Saw the Woman It Killed, Report Says" (*https://oreil.ly/c9WqC*), *Wired*, May 24, 2018.

death? The person in the driver's seat? The company testing the car's capabilities? The designers of the AI system?

While not deadly, consider the following additional examples:

- In 2014, Amazon developed a recruiting tool for identifying software engineers it might want to hire; however, it was found that the tool discriminated against women. Amazon eventually had to abandon the tool in 2017.
- In 2016, ProPublica analyzed a commercially developed system that was created to help judges make better sentencing decisions by predicting the likelihood that criminals would reoffend, and it found that it was biased against Black people.[10]

Incidents such as these are enormous PR nightmares for companies.

Consequently, regulators have published guidelines on the ethical use of data. For example, EU regulators published a set of seven requirements (*https://oreil.ly/AEaj7*) that must be met for AI systems to be considered trustworthy:

- AI systems should be under human oversight.
- They need to have a fall-back plan in case something goes wrong. They also need to be accurate, reliable, and reproducible.
- They must ensure full respect for privacy and data protection.
- Data, system, and AI business models should be transparent and offer traceability.
- AI systems must avoid unfair bias.
- They must benefit all human beings.
- They must ensure responsibility and accountability.

However, the drive for data-driven decisions, fueled by more data and robust analytics, calls for a necessary consideration of and focus on the ethics of data and data use that goes beyond these regulatory requirements.

Examples of Data Governance in Action

This section takes a closer look at several enterprises and how they were able to derive benefits from their governance efforts. These examples demonstrate that data governance is being used to manage accessibility and security, that it addresses the issue of

---

10 Jonathan Shaw, "Artificial Intelligence and Ethics" (*https://oreil.ly/oglKc*), *Harvard Magazine*, January–February 2019, 44-49, 74.

trust by tackling data quality head-on, and that the governance structure makes these endeavors successful.

Managing Discoverability, Security, and Accountability

In July 2019, Capital One, one of the largest issuers of consumer and small business credit cards, discovered that an outsider had been able to take advantage of a misconfigured web application firewall in its Apache web server. The attacker was able to obtain temporary credentials and access files containing personal information for Capital One customers.[11] The resulting leak of information affected more than 100 million individuals who had applied for Capital One credit cards.

Two aspects of this leak limited the blast radius. First, the leak was of application data sent to Capital One, and so, while the information included names, social security numbers, bank account numbers, and addresses, it did not include log-in credentials that would have allowed the attacker to steal money. Second, the attacker was swiftly caught by the FBI, and the reason for the attacker being caught is why we include this anecdote in this book.

Because the files in question were stored in a public cloud storage bucket where every access to the files was logged, access logs were available to investigators after the fact. They were able to figure out the IP routes and narrow down the source of the attack to a few houses. While misconfigured IT systems that create security vulnerabilities can happen anywhere, attackers who steal admin credentials from on-premises systems will usually cover their tracks by modifying the system access logs. On the public cloud, though, these access logs are not modifiable because the attacker doesn't have access to them.

This incident highlights a handful of lessons:

- Make sure that your data collection is purposeful. In addition, store as narrow a slice of the data as possible. It was fortunate that the data store of credit card applications did not also include the details of the resulting credit card accounts.
- Turn on organizational-level audit logs in your data warehouse. Had this not been done, it would not have been possible to catch the culprit.
- Conduct periodic security audits of all open ports. If this is not done, no alerts will be raised about attempts to get past security safeguards.

---

11 "Information on the Capital One Cyber Incident" (*https://oreil.ly/iNP_N*), Capital One, updated September 23, 2019; Brian Krebs, "What We Can Learn from the Capital One Hack" (*https://oreil.ly/en24B*), *Krebs on Security* (blog), August 2, 2019.

- Apply an additional layer of security to sensitive data within documents. Social security numbers, for example, should have been masked or tokenized using an artificial intelligence service capable of identifying PII data and redacting it.

The fourth best practice is an additional safeguard—arguably, if only absolutely necessary data is collected and stored, there would be no need for masking. However, most organizations have multiple uses of the data, and in some use cases, the decrypted social security number might be needed. In order to do such multi-use effectively, it is necessary to tag or label each attribute based on multiple categories to ensure the appropriate controls and security are placed on it. This tends to be a collaborative effort among many organizations within the company. It is worth noting that systems like these that remove data from consideration come with their own challenges and risks.[12]

As the data collected and retained by enterprises has grown, ensuring that best practices like these are well understood and implemented correctly has become more and more important. Such best practices and the policies and tools to implement them are at the heart of data governance.

Improving Data Quality

Data governance is not just about security breaches. For data to be useful to an organization, it is necessary that the data be trustworthy. The quality of data matters, and much of data governance focuses on ensuring that the integrity of data can be trusted by downstream applications. This is especially hard when data is not owned by your organization and when that data is moving around.

A good example of data governance activities improving data quality comes from the US Coast Guard (USCG). The USCG focuses on maritime search and rescue, ocean spill cleanup, maritime safety, and law enforcement. Our colleague Dom Zippilli was part of the team that proved the data governance concepts and techniques behind what became known as the Authoritative Vessel Identification Service (AVIS). The following sidebar about AVIS is in his words.

---

12 See, for example, the book *Dark Data: Why What You Don't Know Matters* (*https://darkdata.website*) by David Hand (Princeton University Press).

How the US Coast Guard Improved Data Quality

Dom Zippilli

Figure 1-10 illustrates what AVIS looked like when looking at a vessel with no data discrepancies. The data from Automatic Identification Systems (AIS) corresponds well with what was in AVIS, which is best described as "what we think we know" about a ship—an amalgam of information from other USCG systems that handled vessel registration, integration with the International Maritime Organization (IMO), citations, and so on.

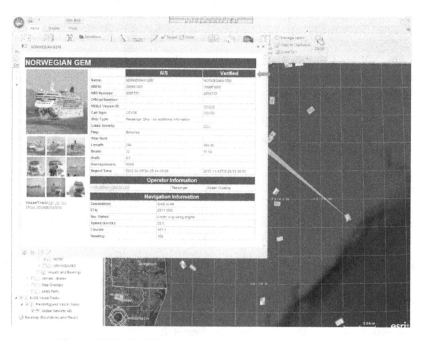

Figure 1-10. What AVIS looked like. Figure courtesy of NAVCEN.

Unfortunately, not all data corresponded this cleanly. Figure 1-11 illustrates a pathological case: no ship image, mismatched name, mismatched Maritime Mobile Service Identity (MMSI), mismatched IMO number, mismatched everything.

	AIS	Verified
Name:	TUG DEBORAH QUINN	DEBORAH QUINN ←
MMSI:	123360000	367432170 ←
IMO Number:	5198366	0991916 ←
Official Number:		274347
MISLE Vessel ID:		71121
Call Sign:	WYA4651	WTC2312 ←
Ship Type:	Vessel Towing	
Class Society:		
Flag:	United States	
Year Built:		
Length:	31	19.60 ←
Beam:	10	8.38 ←
Draft:	4.3	
Discrepancies:	IMO,MMSI,NAME	
Report Time:	2012-02-05T21.39 16-00-00	2011-02-01T00.00-00-00
	Operator Information	
INTENSION TRANSPORTATION COMPANIES LLC		Transportation : Towing
	Navigation Information	
Destination:		
ETA:	10061600	
Nav Status:	Under way using engine	
Speed (knots):	0.0	
Course:	309.5	
Heading:		

Figure 1-11. A pathological case with a lot of inconsistencies between what's tracked in AIS and what's known from an amalgam of other sources. Figure courtesy of NAVCEN.

Such mismatches make knowing which ships are where, and information about those ships, much harder to figure out for USCG in the field. The vessels that cropped up in the AVIS UI were the ones that couldn't be resolved using automated tooling and thus required some human intervention. Automating is nice (and this was almost 10 years ago), but even surfacing the work that had to be done by a human was a *huge* step forward. In almost all cases, the issues were the result of innocent mistakes, but getting things back on track required identifying the issues and reaching out to the maritime community.

The business value of such corrections comes down to maritime domain awareness (MDA), a key part of the USCG's mission. Domain awareness is pretty hard to come by when your data quality is poor. Here are some qualitative examples of how AVIS helped.

For example, imagine a scenario in which a vessel needs to be investigated for some kind of violation, or interdicted for any reason. If that vessel is among many broadcasting with the same MMSI number, our track for that vessel looks like Figure 1-12. This could be even more serious in a search and rescue situation in which we need to locate nearby vessels that could render aid faster than a USCG vessel (cooperation is a major theme of maritime life).

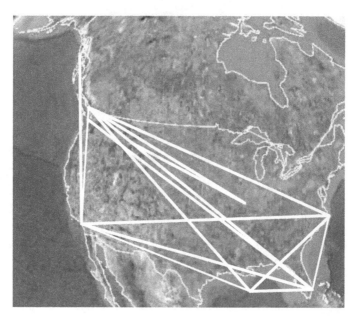

Figure 1-12. Effects of duplicate vehicle id numbers. Figure courtesy of NAVCEN.

Over time, in the pilot program, as shown in Figure 1-13, we saw a drastic reduction in the number of ambiguous vessel tracks received each day. While zero was always the goal, this is by nature a community effort, so it requires constant upkeep.

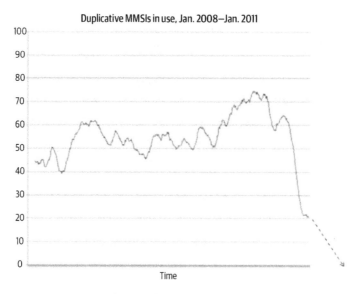

Figure 1-13. Improvements in data quality due to pilot program to correct vessel IDs

The closest I have to a quantitative result (though it doesn't spell out the mission value exactly, as that was expected to be obvious to the reader) is this highlight from a whitepaper that is unfortunately no longer available publicly:

> Over the course of the project, the AVIS team was able to virtually eliminate unidentified and uncorrelated AIS vessel signals broadcasting unregistered MMSI numbers such as 1, 2, 123456789, etc. Specifically, 863 out of 866 vessels were corrected by September 2011, eliminating nearly 100% of incorrect broadcasts.[13]

863 might not seem like a lot, but keep in mind the global merchant fleet is something on the order of 50,000 vessels. So, just for US waters, this is actually a big part of the population, and as you know, it doesn't take a lot of bad data to make all the data useless.

The USCG program is a handy reminder that data quality is something to strive for and constantly be on the watch for. The cleaner the data, the more likely it is to be usable for more critical use cases. In the USCG case, we see this in the usability of the data for search and rescue tasks as well.

The Business Value of Data Governance

Data governance is not solely a control practice. When implemented cohesively, data governance addresses the strategic need to get knowledge workers the insights they require with a clear process to "shop for data." This makes possible the extraction of insights from multiple sources that were previously siloed off within different business units.

In organizations where data governance is a strategic process, knowledge workers can expect to easily find *all* the data required to fulfill their mission, safely apply for access, and be granted access to the data under a simple process with clear timelines and a transparent approval process. Approvers and governors of data can expect to easily pull up a picture of what data is accessible to whom, and what data is "outside" the governance zone of control (and what to do about any discrepancies there). CIOs can expect to be able to review a high-level analysis of the data in the organization in order to holistically review quantifiable metrics such as "total amount of data" or "data out of compliance" and even understand (and mitigate) risks to the organization due to data leakage.

---

13 David Winkler, "AIS Data Quality and the Authoritative Vessel Identification Service (AVIS)" (*https://oreil.ly/ HcGso*) (PowerPoint presentation, National GMDSS Implementation Task Force, Arlington, VA, January 10, 2012).

Fostering Innovation

A good data governance strategy, when set in motion, combines several factors that allow a business to extract more value from the data. Whether the goal is to improve operations, find additional sources of revenue, or even monetize data directly, a data governance strategy is an enabler of various value drivers in enterprises.

A data governance strategy, if working well, is a combination of process (to make data available under governance), people (who manage policies and usher in data access across the organization, breaking silos where needed), and tools that facilitate the above by applying machine learning techniques to categorize data and indexing the data available for discovery.

Data governance ideally will allow all employees in the organization to access all data (subject to a governance process) under a set of governance rules (defined in greater detail below), while preserving the organization's risk posture (i.e., no additional exposure or risks are introduced due to making data accessible under a governance strategy). Since the risk posture is maintained and possibly even improved with the additional controls data governance brings, one could argue there is only an upside to making data accessible. Giving all knowledge workers access to data, in a governed manner, can foster innovation by allowing individuals to rapidly prototype answers to questions based on the data that exists within the organization. This can lead to better decision making, better opportunity discovery, and a more productive organization overall.

The quality of the data available is another way to ascertain whether governance is well implemented in the organization. A part of data governance is a well-understood way to codify and inherit a "quality signal" on the data. This signal should tell potential data users and analysts whether the data was curated, whether it was normalized or missing, whether corrupt data was removed, and potentially how trustworthy the source for the data is. Quality signals are crucial when making decisions on potential uses of the data; for example, within machine learning training datasets.

The Tension Between Data Governance and Democratizing Data Analysis

Very often, complete data democratization is thought of as conflicting with data governance. This conflict is not necessarily an axiom. Data democratization, in its most extreme interpretation, can mean that all analysts or knowledge workers can access all data, whatever class it may belong to. The access described here makes a modern organization uncomfortable when you consider specific examples, such as employee data (e.g., salaries) and customer data (e.g., customer names and addresses). Clearly, only specific people should be able to access data of the aforementioned types, and they should do so only within their specific job-related responsibilities.

Data governance is actually an enabler here, solving this tension. The key concept to keep in mind is that there are two layers to the data: the data itself (e.g., salaries) and the metadata (data about the data—e.g., "I have a table that contains salaries, but I won't tell you anything further").

With data governance, you can accomplish three things:

- Access a metadata catalog, which includes an index of all the data managed (full democratization, in a way) and allows you to search for the *existence* of certain data. A good data catalog also includes certain access control rules that limit the bounds of the search (for example, I will be able to search "sales-related data," but "HR" is out of my purview completely, and therefore even HR-metadata is inaccessible to me).

- Govern access to the data, which includes an acquisition process (described above) and a way to adhere to the principle of least access: once access is requested, provide access limited to the boundaries of the specific resource; don't overshare.

- Independently of the other steps, make an "audit trail" available to the data access request, the data access approval cycle, and the approver (data steward), as well as to all the subsequent access operations. This audit trail is data itself and therefore must comply with data governance.

In a way, data governance becomes the facility where you can enable data democratization, allowing more of your data to be accessible to more of the knowledge employee population, and therefore be an accelerator to the business in making the use of data easier and faster.

Business outcomes, such as visibility into all parts of a supply chain, understanding of customer behavior on every online asset, tracking the success of a multipronged campaign, and the resulting customer journeys, are becoming more and more possible. Under governance, different business units will be able to pull data together, analyze it to achieve deeper insight, and react quickly to both local and global changes.

Manage Risk (Theft, Misuse, Data Corruption)

The key concerns CIOs and responsible data stewards have had for a long time (and this has not changed with the advent of big data analytics) have always been: *What are my risk factors, what is my mitigation plan, and what is the potential damage?*

CIOs have been using these concerns to assign resources based on the answer to those questions. Data governance comes to provide a set of tools, processes, and positions for personnel to manage the risk to data, among other topics presented therein (for example, data efficiency, or getting value from data). Those risks include:

Theft

Data theft is a concern in those organizations where data is either the product or a key factor in generating value. Theft of data about parts, suppliers, or price in an electronics manufacturer supply chain can cause a crippling blow to the business if competition uses that information to negotiate with those very same suppliers, or to derive a product roadmap from the supply-chain information. Theft of a customer list can be very damaging to any organization. Setting data governance around information that the organization considers to be sensitive can encourage confidence in the sharing of surrounding data, aggregates, and so on, contributing to business efficiency and breaking down barriers to sharing and reusing data.

Misuse

Misuse is often the unknowing use of data in a way that's different from the purpose it was collected for—sometimes to support the wrong conclusions. This is often a result of a lack of information about the data source, its quality, or even what it means. There is sometimes malicious misuse of data as well, meaning that information gathered with consent for benign purposes is used for other unintended and sometimes nefarious purposes. An example is AT&T's payout to the FCC in 2015 (*https://oreil.ly/cC4OY*), after its call center employees were found to have disclosed consumers' personal information to third parties for financial gain. Data governance can protect against misuse with several layers. First, establish trust before sharing data. Another way to protect against misuse is declarative—declare the source of the data within the container, the way it was collected, and what it was intended for. Finally, limiting the length of time for which data is accessible can prevent possible misuse. This does not mean placing a lid on the data and making it inaccessible. Remember, the fact that the data exists should be shared alongside its purpose and description—which should make data democratization a reality.

Data corruption

Data corruption is an insidious risk because it is hard to detect and hard to protect against. The risk materializes when deriving operational business conclusions from corrupt (and therefore incorrect) data. Data corruption often occurs outside of data governance control and can be due to errors on data ingest, joining "clean" data with corrupt data (creating a new, corrupt product). Partial data, autocorrected to include some default values, can be misinterpeted, for example, as curated data. Data governance can step into the fray here and allow recording, even at the structured data column level, of the processes and lineage of the data, and the level of confidence, or quality, of the top-level source of the data.

Regulatory Compliance

Data governance is often leveraged when a set of regulations are applicable to the business, and specifically to the data the business processes. Regulations are, in essence, policies that must be adhered to in order to play within the business environment the organization operates in. GDPR is often referred to as an example regulation around data. This is because, among other things, GDPR mandates a separation of (European citizens') personal data from other data, and treatment of that data in a different way, especially around data that can be used to identify a person. This manuscript does not intend to go into the specifics of GDPR.

Regulation will usually refer to one or more of the following specifics:

- Fine-grained access control
- Data retention and data deletion
- Audit logging
- Sensitive data classes

Let's discuss these one by one.

Regulation around fine-grained access control

Access control is already an established topic that relates to security most of all. *Fine-grained* access control adds the following considerations to access control:

When providing access, are you providing access to the right size of container?
This means making sure you provide the minimal size of the container of the data (table, dataset, etc.) that includes the requested information. In structured storage this will most commonly be a single table, rather than the whole dataset or project-wide permission.

When providing access, are you providing the right level of access?
Different levels of access to data are possible. A common access pattern is being able to either read the data or write the data, but there are additional levels: you can choose to allow a contributor to append (but possibly not change) the data, or an editor may have access to modify or even delete data. In addition, consider protected systems in which some data is transformed on access. You could redact certain columns (e.g., US social security numbers, which serve as a national ID) to expose just the last four digits, or coarsen GPS coordinates to city and country. A useful way to share data without exposing too much is to tokenize (encrypt) the data with symmetric (reversible) encryption such that key data values (for example, a person's ID) preserve uniqueness (and thus you can count how many distinct persons you have in your dataset) without being exposed to the specific details of a person's ID.

All the levels of access mentioned here should be considered (read/write/delete/ update and redact/mask/tokenize).

When providing access, for how long should access remain open?
Remember that access is usually requested for a reason (a specific project must be completed), and permissions granted should not "dangle" without appropriate justification. The regulator will be asking "who has access to what," and thus limiting the number of personnel who have access to a certain class of data will make sense and can prove efficient.

Data retention and data deletion

A significant body of regulation deals with the deletion and the preservation of data. A requirement to preserve data for a set period, and no less than that period, is common. For example, in the case of financial transaction regulations, it is not uncommon to find a requirement that all business transaction information be kept for a duration of as much as seven years to allow financial fraud investigators to backtrack.

Conversely, an organization may want to limit the time it retains certain information, allowing it to draw quick conclusions while limiting liability. For example, having constantly up-to-date information about the location of all delivery trucks is useful for making rapid decisions about "just-in-time" pickups and deliveries, but it becomes a liability if you maintain that information over a period of time and can, in theory, plot a picture of the location of a specific delivery driver over the course of several weeks.

Audit logging

Being able to bring up audit logs for a regulator is useful as evidence that policies are complied with. You cannot present data that has been deleted, but you can show an audit trail of the means by which the data was created, manipulated, shared (and with whom), accessed (and by whom), and later expired or deleted. The auditor will be able to verify that policies are being adhered to. Audit logs can serve as a useful forensic tool as well.

To be useful for data governance purposes, audit logs need to be immutable, write-only (unchangeable by internal or external parties), and preserved, by themselves, for a lengthy period—as long as the most demanding data preservation policy (and beyond that, in order to show the data being deleted).

Audit logs need to include information not only about data and data operations by themselves but also about operations that happen around the data management facility. Policy changes need to be logged, and data schema changes need to be logged. Permission management and permission changes need to be logged, and the logging information should contain not only the subject of the change (be it a data container or a person to be granted permission) but also the originator of the action (the administrator or the service process that initiated the activity).

Sensitive data classes

Very often, a regulator will determine that a class of data should be treated differently than other data. This is the heart of the regulation that is most commonly concerned with a group of protected people, or a kind of activity. The regulator will be using legal language (e.g., personally identifiable data about European Union residents, or "financial transaction history"). It will be up to the organization to correctly identify what portion of that data it actually processes, and how this data compares to the data stored in structured or unstructured storage. For structured data it is sometimes easier to bind a data class into a set of columns (PII is stored in these columns) and tag the columns so that certain policies apply to these columns specifically, including access and retention. This supports the principles of fine-grained access control as well as adhering to the regulation about the data (not the data store or the personnel manipulating that data).

Considerations for Organizations as They Think About Data Governance

When an organization sits down and begins to define a data governance program and the goals of such a program, it should take into consideration the environment in which it operates. Specifically, it should consider what regulations are relevant and how often these change, whether or not a cloud deployment makes sense for the organization, and what expertise is required from IT and data analysts/owners. We discuss these factors next.

Changing regulations and compliance needs

In past years, data governance regulations have garnered more attention. With GDPR and CCPA joining the ranks of HIPAA- and PCI-related regulations, the affected organizations are reacting.

The changing regulation environment has meant that organizations need to remain vigilant when it comes to governance. No organization wants to be in the news for getting sued for failing to handle customer information as per a set of regulations. In a world where customer information is very precious, firms need to be careful how they handle customer data. Not only should firms know about existing regulations, but they also need to keep up with any changing mandates or stipulations, as well as any new regulations that might affect how they do business. In addition, changes to technology have also created additional challenges. Machine learning and AI have allowed organizations to predict future outcomes and probabilities. These technologies also create a ton of new datasets as a part of this process. With these new predicted values, how do companies think about governance? Should these new datasets assume the same policies and governance that the original datasets had, or should they have their own set of policies for governance? Who should have access to this data? How long should it be retained for? These are all questions that need to be considered and answered.

Data accumulation and organization growth

With infrastructure cost rapidly decreasing, and organizations growing both organically and through acquisition of additional business units (with their own data stores), the topic of data accumulation, and how to properly react to quickly amassing large amounts of data, becomes important. With data accumulation, an organization is collecting more data from more sources and for more purposes.

Big data is a term you will keep hearing, and it alludes to the vast amounts of data (structured and unstructured) now collected from connected devices, sensors, social networks, clickstreams, and so on. The volume, variety, and velocity of data has changed and accelerated over the past decade. The effort to manage and even consolidate this data has created data swamps (disorganized and inconsistent collections of data without clear curation) and even more silos—i.e., customers decided to consolidate on System Applications and Products (SAP), and then they decided to consolidate on Hive Metastore, and some consolidated on the cloud, and so on. Given these challenges, knowing what you have and applying governance to this data is complicated, but it's a task that organizations need to undertake. Organizations thought that building a data lake would solve all their issues, but now these data lakes are becoming data swamps with so much data that is impossible to understand and govern. In an environment in which IDC predicts that more than a quarter of the data generated by 2025 will be real-time in nature, how do organizations make sure that they are ready for this changing paradigm?

Moving data to the cloud

Traditionally, all data resided in infrastructure provided and maintained by the organization. This meant the organization had full control over access, and there was no dynamic sharing of resources. With the emergence of cloud computing—which in this context implies cheap but shared infrastructure—organizations need to think about their response and investment in on-premises versus cloud infrastructure.

Many large enterprises still mention that they have no plans to move their core data, or governed data, to the cloud anytime soon. Even though the largest cloud companies have invested money and resources to protect customer data in the cloud, most customers still feel the need to keep this data on-prem. This is understandable, because data breaches in the cloud feel more consequential. The potential for damage, monetary as well as to reputation, explains why enterprises want more transparency in how governance works to protect their data on the cloud. With this pressure, you're seeing cloud companies put more guardrails in place. They need to "show" and "open the hood" to how governance is being implemented, as well as provide controls that not only engender trust among customers, but also put some power into customers' hands. We discuss these topics in Chapter 7.

Data infrastructure expertise

Another consideration for organizations is the sheer complexity of the infrastructure landscape. How do you think about governance in a hybrid and multi-cloud world? Hybrid computing allows organizations to have both on-premise and cloud infrastructure, while multicloud allows organizations to utilize more than one cloud provider. How do you implement governance across the organization when the data resides on-premises and on other clouds? This makes governance complicated and therefore goes beyond the tools used to implement it. When organizations start thinking about the people, the processes, and the tools and define a framework that encompasses these facets, then it becomes a little easier to extend governance across on-prem and in the cloud.

Why Data Governance Is Easier in the Public Cloud

Data governance involves managing risk. The practitioner is always trading off the security inherent in never allowing access to the data against the agility that is possible if data is readily available within the organization to support different types of decisions and products. Regulatory compliance often dictates the minimal requirements for access control, lineage, and retention policies. As we discussed in the previous sections, the implementation of these can be challenging as a result of changing regulations and organic growth.

The public cloud has several features that make data governance easier to implement, monitor, and update. In many cases, these features are unavailable or cost-prohibitive in on-premises systems.

Location

Data locality is mostly relevant for global organizations that store and use data across the globe, but a deeper look into regulation reveals that the situation is not so simple. For example, if, for business reasons, you want to leverage a data center in a central location (say, in the US, next to your potential customers) but your company is a German company, regulation requires that data about employees remains on German soil; thus your data strategy just became more involved.

The need to store user data within sovereign boundaries is an increasingly common regulatory requirement. In 2016, the EU Parliament approved data sovereignty measures within GDPR, wherein the storage and processing of records about EU citizens and residents must be carried out in a manner that follows EU law. Specific classes of data (e.g., health records in Australia, telecommunications metadata in Germany, or payment data in India) may also be subject to data locality regulations; these go beyond mere sovereignty measures by requiring that all data processing and storage occur within the national boundaries. The major public cloud providers offer the ability to store your data in accordance with these regulations. It can be convenient to simply mark a dataset as being within the EU multi-region and know that you have both redundancy (because it's a multi-region) and compliance (because data never leaves the EU). Implementing such a solution in your on-premises data center can be quite difficult, since it can be cost-prohibitive to build data centers in every sovereign location that you wish to do business in and that has locality regulations.

Another reason that location matters is that secure transaction-aware global access matters. As your customers travel or locate their own operations, they will require you to provide access to data and applications wherever they are. This can be difficult if your regulatory compliance begins and ends with colocating applications and data in regional silos. You need the ability to seamlessly apply compliance roles based on users, not just on applications. Running your applications in a public cloud that runs its own private fiber and offers end-to-end physical network security and global time synchronization (not all clouds do this) simplifies the architecture of your applications.

Reduced Surface Area

In heavily regulated industries, there are huge advantages if there is a single "golden" source of truth for datasets, especially for data that requires auditability. Having your enterprise data warehouse (EDW) in a public cloud, particularly in a setting in which you can separate compute from storage and access the data from ephemeral clusters, provides you with the ability to create different data marts for different use cases. These data marts are provided data through views of the EDW that are created on the fly. There is no need to maintain copies, and examination of the views is enough to ensure auditability in terms of data correctness.

In turn, the lack of permanent storage in these data marts greatly simplifies their governance. Since there is no storage, complying with rules around data deletion is trivial at the data mart level. All such rules have to be enforced only at the EDW. Other rules around proper use and control of the data still have to be enforced, of course. That's why we think of this as a reduced surface area, not zero governance.

Ephemeral Compute

In order to have a single source of data and still be able to support enterprise applications, current and future, we need to make sure that the data is not stored within a compute cluster, or scaled in proportion to it. If our business is spiky, or if we require the ability to support interactive or occasional workloads, we will require infinitely scalable and readily burstable compute capability that is separate from storage architecture. This is possible only if our data processing and analytics architecture is serverless and/or clearly separates computes and storage.

Why do we need both data processing and analytics to be serverless? Because the utility of data is often realized only after a series of preparation, cleanup, and intelligence tools are applied to it. All these tools need to support separation of compute and storage and autoscaling in order to realize the benefits of a serverless analytics platform. It is not sufficient just to have a serverless data warehouse or application architecture that is built around serverless functions. You need your tooling frameworks themselves to be serverless. This is available only in the cloud.

Serverless and Powerful

In many enterprises, lack of data is not the problem—it's the availability of tools to process data at scale. Google's mission of organizing the world's information has meant that Google needed to invent data processing methods, including methods to secure and govern the data being processed. Many of these research tools have been hardened through production use at Google and are available on Google Cloud as serverless tools (see Figure 1-14). Equivalents exist on other public clouds as well. For example, the Aurora database on Amazon Web Services (AWS) and Microsoft's Azure Cosmos DB are serverless; S3 on AWS and Azure Cloud Storage are the equivalent of Google Cloud Storage. Similarly, Lambda on AWS and Azure Functions provide the ability to carry out stateless serverless data processing. Elastic Map Reduce (EMR) on AWS and HDInsight on Azure are the equivalent of Google Cloud Dataproc (*https:// cloud.google.com/dataproc*). At the time of writing, serverless stateful processing (Dataflow on Google Cloud) is not yet available on other public clouds, but this will no doubt be remedied over time. These sorts of capabilities are cost-prohibitive to implement on-premises because of the necessity to implement serverless tools in an efficient manner while evening out the load and traffic spikes across thousands of workloads.

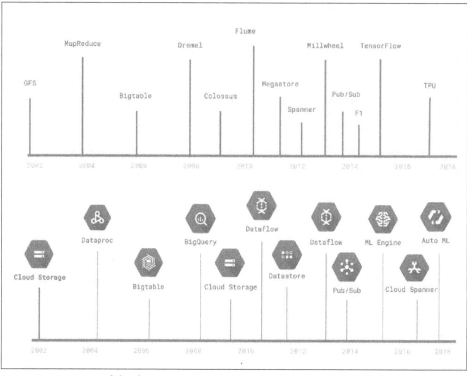

Figure 1-14. Many of the data-processing techniques invented at Google (top panel; see also http://research.google.com/pubs/papers.html (https://oreil.ly/4A7_U)) exist as managed services on Google Cloud (bottom panel).

Labeled Resources

Public cloud providers provide granular resource labeling and tagging in order to support a variety of billing considerations. For example, the organization that owns the data in a data mart may not be the one carrying out (and therefore paying for) the compute. This gives you the ability to implement regulatory compliance on top of the sophisticated labeling and tagging features of these platforms.

These capabilities might include the ability to discover, label, and catalog items (ask your cloud provider whether this is the case). It is important to be able to label resources, not just in terms of identity and access management but also in terms of attributes, such as whether a specific column is considered PII in certain jurisdictions. Then it is possible to apply consistent policies to all such fields everywhere in your enterprise.

Security in a Hybrid World

The last point about having consistent policies that are easily applicable is key. Consistency and a single security pane are key benefits to hosting your enterprise software infrastructure on the cloud. However, such an all-or-nothing approach is unrealistic for most enterprises. If your business operates equipment (handheld devices, video cameras, point-of-sale registers, etc.) "on the edge," it is often necessary to have some of your software infrastructure there as well. Sometimes, as with voting machines, regulatory compliance might require physical control of the equipment being used. Your legacy systems may not be ready to take advantage of the separation of compute and storage that the cloud offers. In these cases, you'd like to continue to operate on-premises. Systems that involve components that live in a public cloud and one other place—in two public clouds, or in a public cloud and on the edge, or a in public cloud and on-premises—are termed *hybrid cloud systems*.

It is possible to greatly expand the purview of your cloud security posture and policies by employing solutions that allow you to control both on-premises and cloud infrastructure using the same tooling. For example, if you have audited an on-premises application and its use of data, it is easier to approve that identical application running in the cloud than it is to reaudit a rewritten application. The cost of entry to this capability is to containerize your applications, and this might be a cost well worth paying for, for the governance benefits alone.

Summary

When discussing a successful data-governance strategy, you must consider more than just the data architecture/data pipeline structure or the tools that perform "governance" tasks. Consideration of the actual humans behind the governance tools as well as the "people processes" put into place is also highly important and should not be discounted. A truly successful governance strategy must address not only the tools involved but the people and processes as well. In Chapters 2 and 3, we will discuss these ingredients of data governance.

In Chapter 4, we take an example corpus of data and consider how data governance is carried out over the entire life cycle of that data; from ingest to preparation and storage, to incorporation into reports, dashboards, and machine learning models, and on to updates and eventual deletion. A key concern here is that data quality is an ongoing concern; new data-processing methods are invented, and business rules change. How to handle the ongoing improvement of data quality is addressed in Chapter 5.

By 2025, more than 25% of enterprise data is expected to be streaming data. In Chapter 6, we address the challenges of governing data that is on the move. Data in flight involves governing data at the source and at the destination, and any aggregations and manipulations that are carried in flight. Data governance also has to address the challenges of late-arriving data and what it means for the correctness of calculations if storage systems are only eventually correct.

In Chapter 7, we delve into data protection and the solutions available for authentication, security, backup, and so on. The best data governance is of no use if monitoring is not carried out and leaks, misuse, and accidents are not discovered early enough to be mitigated. Monitoring is covered in Chapter 8.

Finally, in Chapter 9, we bring together the topics in this book and cover best practices in building a data culture—a culture in which both the user and the opportunity is respected.

One question we often get asked is how Google does data governance internally. In Appendix A, we use Google as an example (one that we know well) of a data governance system, and point out the benefits and challenges of the approaches that Google takes and the ingredients that make it all possible.

CHAPTER 2

Ingredients of Data Governance: Tools

A lot of the tasks related to data governance can benefit from automation. Machine learning tools and automatic policy applications or suggestions can accelerate data governance tasks. In this chapter we will review some of the tools commonly referred to when discussing data governance.

When evaluating a data governance process/system, pay attention to the capabilities mentioned in this chapter. The following discussion concerns tasks and tools that can augment complete end-to-end support for the processes involved in, and the personnel responsible for, data governance organization. We'll dive into the various processes and solutions in more detail in later chapters.

The Enterprise Dictionary

To begin, it is important to understand how an organization works with data and enables data governance. Usually, there is an *enterprise dictionary* or an enterprise *policy book* of some kind.

The first of these documents, the enterprise dictionary, is one that can take many shapes, from a paper document to a tool that encodes or automates certain policies. It is an agreed-upon repository of the information types (*infotypes*) used by the organization—that is, data elements that the organization processes and derives insights from. An infotype will be a piece of information with a singular meaning—"email address" or "street address," for example, or even "salary amount."

In order to refer to individual fields of information and drive a governance policy accordingly, you need to name those pieces of information.

An organization's enterprise dictionary is normally owned by either the legal department (whose focus would be compliance) or the data office (whose focus would be standardization of the data elements used).

In Figure 2-1, you can see examples of infotypes, and a potential organization of those infotypes into organization-specific *data classes* to be used in policy making.

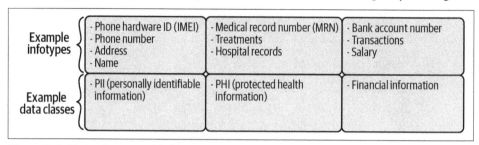

| Example infotypes | - Phone hardware ID (IMEI)
- Phone number
- Address
- Name | - Medical record number (MRN)
- Treatments
- Hospital records | - Bank account number
- Transactions
- Salary |
| Example data classes | - PII (personally identifiable information) | - PHI (protected health information) | - Financial information |

Figure 2-1. Data classes and infotypes

Once the enterprise dictionary is defined, the various individual infotypes within it can be grouped into data classes, and a policy can be defined for each data class. The enterprise dictionary generally contains data classes, policies related to the data classes, and additional metadata. The following sections expand on this.

Data Classes

A good enterprise dictionary will contain a listing of the classes of data the organization processes. Those will be infotypes collected into groups that are treated in a common way from the policy management aspect. For example, an organization will not want to treat "street addresses," "phone numbers," "city, state," and "zip code" differently in a granular manner but must rather be able to set a policy that "all location information for consumers must be accessible only to a privileged group of personnel and be kept only for a maximum of 30 days." This means that the enterprise dictionary we've just described, will actually contain a hierarchy of infotypes—at the *leaf nodes* there will be the individual infotypes (e.g., "address," "email"), and at the *root nodes* you will find a data class, or a sensitivity classification (or sometimes both).

Figure 2-2 shows an example of such a hierarchy from a fictional organization.

Policy tags

Policy tags are tags with access control policies that can be applied to sub-resources, for example, BigQuery columns.

Name ↑	ID	Description
☐ ▼ Restricted	3247623653529953690	Highly Restricted Data
☐ ▼ PHI	4081878655865131464	Patient Health Information
☐ Drug_Details	348889402753783706	Details about a drug perscnbed
☐ NHS_Number	4099447459463431825	Patient ID
☐ Treatment_Details	6587645476172403944	Details about a treatment or condition
☐ ▼ PII	1690556303680165819	Personally identifiable data
☐ Email	5606010836299662298	Email address
☐ IMEI	7077445421065241870	Cellphone hardware ID
☐ IP_Addr	2449414728069309088	IP Address of a session/connection
☐ Personal_Car_VIN	7187828684927708308	Vehicle Identifier
☐ Phone_Num	8401384437536803987	Phone number
☐ SSN	9118232350617909155	US Social Security Number
☐ ▼ Sensitive	5013925770628759512	Sensitive Data
☐ ▼ Financials	358397642325435489	Financial Data
☐ Bank_Account	8370833355300570	International Bank account ID
☐ Credit Card Num	6313828804358283165	Credit Card number
☐ ▼ Unrestricted Data	8097084282273622955	Unrestricted Data, broad access
☐ Car_Details	4696597770432605648	Generic Details about a vehicle

Figure 2-2. A data class hierarchy

In the data class hierarchy detailed in Figure 2-2, you can see how infotypes such as IMEI (cellular device hardware ID), phone number, and IP address are grouped together under personally identifiable information (PII). For this organization, these are easily identifiable automatically, and policies are defined on "all PII data elements." PII is paired with PHI (protected health information (*https://oreil.ly/T1mUo*)) in the "restricted data" category. It is likely that there are further policies defined on all data grouped under the "restricted" heading.

Data classes are usually maintained by a central body within the organization, because policies on "types of data classes" usually affect compliance to regulation.

Some example data classes seen across many organizations are:

PII
> This is data such as name, address, and personal phone number that can be used to uniquely identify a person. For a retailer, this can be a customer list. Other examples include lists of employee data, a list of third-party vendors, and similar information.

Financial information
> This is data such as transactions, salaries, benefits, or any kind of data that can include information of financial value.

Business intellectual property
> This is information related to the success and differentiation of the business.

The variety and kind of data classes will change with the business vertical and interest. The preceding example data classes (PII, financial, business intellectual property) will not work for every organization, and the meaning of data collected and the classification will differ between businesses and between countries. Do note that data classes are a combination of information elements belonging to one topic. For example, a phone number is usually not a data class, but PII (of which phone number is a member) is normally a data class.

The characteristics of a data class are twofold:

- A data class references a set of *policies*: the same retention rules and access rules are required on this data.

- A data class references a set of individual infotypes, as in the example in Figure 2-1.

Data Classes and Policies

Once the data the organization handles is defined in an enterprise dictionary, policies that govern the data classes can be assigned to data across multiple containers. The desired relationship is between a policy (e.g., *access control*, *retention*) and a data class rather than a policy and an individual container. Associating policies with the meaning of data allows for better human understanding ("Analysts cannot access PII" versus "Analysts cannot access column #3 on Table B") and supports scaling to larger amounts of data.

Above, we have discussed the relationship between data classes and policies. Frequently, along with the data class specification, the central data office, or legal, will define an enterprise policy book. An organization needs to be able to answer the question, "What kinds of data do we process?" An enterprise policy book records that. It specifies the data classes the organization uses, the kinds of data that are processed, and how they are processed, and it elaborates on "what are we allowed and not allowed to do" with the data. This is a crucial element in the following respects:

- For compliance, the organization needs to be able to prove to a regulator that it has the right policies in place around the handling of data.
- A regulator will require the organization to submit the policy book, as well as proof (usually from audit logs) of compliance with the policies.
- The regulator will require evidence of procedures to ensure that the policy book is enforced and may even comment on the policies themselves.

We'd like to stress the importance of having a well-thought-out and well-documented enterprise policy book. Not only is it incredibly helpful for understanding, organizing, and enforcing your policies, but it also enables you to quickly and effectively react to changing requirements and regulations. Additionally, it should be noted that having the ability to quickly and easily provide documentation and proof of compliance—not only for external audits but also for internal ones—should not be discounted. Knowing at a glance how your company is doing with its policies and its management of those policies is critical for ensuring a successful and comprehensive governance program. During the course of our research and interviews, many companies expressed their struggles with being able to conduct quick internal audits to know how their governance strategy was going. This often resulted in much time and effort being spent backtracking and documenting policies, how they were enforced, on what data they were attached, and so on. Creating an enterprise policy book and setting yourself up to more easily audit internally (and thus externally) will help you avoid this pain.

To limit liability, risk management, and exposure to legal action, an organization will usually define a maximum (and a minimum) retention rate for data. This is important because during an investigation, certain law enforcement agencies will require certain kinds of data, which the organization must therefore be able to supply. In the case of financial institutions, for example, it is common to find requirements for holding certain kinds of data (e.g., transactions) for a minimum of seven years. Other kinds of data pose a liability: you cannot leak or lose control of data that you don't have.

Another kind of policy will be *access control*. For data, access control goes beyond "yes/no" and into *no access*, *partial access*, or *full access*. Partial access is accessing the data when some bits have been "starred out," or accessing the data after a deterministic encryption transformation, which will still allow acting on distinct values, or grouping by these values, without being exposed to the underlying cleartext. You can think of partial access as a spectrum of access, ranging from zero access to ever-increasing details about the data in question (format only, number of digits only, tokenized rendition, to full access). See Figure 2-3.

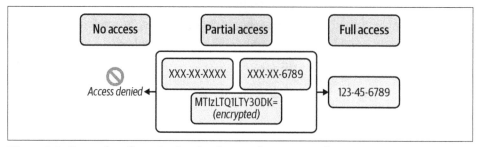

Figure 2-3. Examples of varying levels of access for sensitive data

Normally, a policy book will specify:

- Who (inside or outside the organization) can access a data class
- The retention policy for the data class (how long data is preserved)
- Data residency/locality rules, if applicable
- How the data can be processed (OK/Not OK for analytics, machine learning, etc.)
- Other considerations by the organization

The enterprise policy book—and, with it, the enterprise dictionary—describe the data managed by the organization. Now let's discuss specific tools and functionality that can accelerate data governance work and optimize personnel time.

Per-Use-Case Data Policies

Data can have different meanings and require different policies when the data use case is taken into consideration. An illustrative example might be a furniture manufacturer that collects personal data (names, addresses, contact numbers) in order to ensure delivery. The very same data can potentially be used for marketing purposes, but consent, in most cases, probably has not been granted for the purpose of marketing. However, at the same time, I would very much like that sofa to be delivered to my home, so I want the manufacturer to store the data! The use case, or purpose, of the data access ideally should be an overlay on top of your organizational membership and organizational roles. One way to think about this would be as a "window" through which the analyst can select data, specifying the purpose ahead of time, and potentially moving the data into a different container for that purpose (the marketing database, for example), all with an audit artifact and lineage tracking that will be used for tracking purposes.

Importance of Use Case and Policy Management

Increasingly, as requirements and regulations change to accommodate the new and different types of data that are collected, the use case of data becomes an important aspect of policy management. One of the things that we've heard companies say over and over is that the use case of data needs to be a part of policies—the simple "data class to role-based access type" isn't sufficient. We've given the example of a furniture manufacturer and access to, and usage of, customer address for delivery versus marketing purposes. Another example we've heard about throughout our research is that of a company that has employees who may perform multiple roles. In this case, a simple role-based access policy is inadequate, because these employees may be allowed access to a particular set of data for performing tasks relating to one role but may not have access for tasks relating to a different role. From this you can see how it's more efficient (and effective) to consider access related to what the data will be used for—its use case—rather than only considering infotype/data class and employee role.

Data Classification and Organization

To control the governance of data, it is beneficial to automate, at least in part, the classification of data into, at the very least, infotypes—although an even greater automation is sometimes adopted. A data classifier will look at unstructured data, or even a set of columns in structured data, and infer "what" the data is—e.g., it will identify various representations of phone numbers, bank accounts, addresses, location indicators, and more.

An example classifier would be Google's Cloud Data Loss Prevention (DLP) (*https://cloud.google.com/dlp*). Another classifier is Amazon's Macie service (*https://aws.amazon.com/macie*).

Automation of *data classification* can be accomplished in two main ways:

- Identify data classes on ingest, triggering a classification job on the addition of data sources
- Trigger a data-classification job periodically, reviewing samples of your data

When it is possible, identifying new data sources and classifying them as they are added to the data warehouse is most efficient, but sometimes this is not possible with legacy or federated data.

Upon classifying data, you can do the following, depending on the desired level of automation:

- Tag the data as "belonging to a class" (see "The Enterprise Dictionary" on page 37)
- Automatically (or manually) apply policies that control access to and retention of the data according to the definition of the data class, "purpose," or context for which the data is accessed or manipulated

Data Cataloging and Metadata Management

When talking about data, data classification, and data classes, we need to discuss the *metadata,* or the "information about information"—specifically, where it's stored and what governance controls there are on it. It would be naive to think that metadata obeys the same policies and controls as the underlying data itself. There are many cases, in fact, where this can be a hindrance. Consider, for example, searching in a metadata catalog for a specific table containing customer names. While you may not have access to the table itself, knowing such a table exists is valuable (you can then request access, you can attempt to review the schema and figure out if this table is relevant, and you can avoid creating another iteration of this information if it already exists). Another example is data residency–sensitive information, which must not leave a certain national border, but at the same time that restriction does not necessarily apply to information about the existence of the data itself, which may be relevant in a global search. A final example is information about a listing of phone calls (who called whom, from where, and when), which can be potentially more sensitive than the actual calls themselves, because a call list places certain people at certain locations at certain times.

Crucial to metadata management is a *data catalog,* a tool to manage this metadata. Whereas enterprise data warehouses, such as Google BigQuery, are efficient at processing data, you probably want a tool that spans multiple storage systems to hold the information about the data. This includes where the data is and what technical information is associated with it (table schema, table name, column name, column description)—but you also should allow for the attachment of additional "business" metadata, such as who in the organization owns the data, whether the data is locally generated or externally purchased, whether it relates to production use cases or testing, and so on.

As your data governance strategy grows, you will want to attach the particulars of data governance information to the data in a data catalog: *data class, data quality, sensitivity,* and so on. It is useful to have these dimensions of information schematized, so that you can run a faceted search like "Show me all data of type:table and class:X in the "production" environment".

The data catalog clearly needs to efficiently index all this information and must be able to present it to the users whose permissions allow it, using high-performing search and discovery tooling.

Data Assessment and Profiling

A key step in most insight generation workflows, as you sift through data, is to review that data for outliers. There are many possible reasons for outliers, and best practice is to review before making sweeping/automated decisions. Outliers can be the result of data-entry errors or may just be inconsistent with the rest of the data, but they can also be weak signals or less-represented new segments or patterns. In many cases, you will need to normalize the data for the general case before driving insights. This normalization (keeping or removing outliers) should be done in the context of the business purpose the data is being used for—for example, if you are looking for unusual patterns or not.

The reason for normalizing data is to ensure data quality and consistency (sometimes data entry errors lead to data inconsistencies). Again, this must be done in the context of the business purpose of the data use case. Data quality cannot be performed without a directing business case, because "reviewing transactions" is not the same for a marketing team (which is looking for big/influential customers) and a fraud analysis team (which is looking for provable indications of fraud).

Note that machine learning models, for example, are susceptible to arriving at the wrong conclusions by extracting generalizations from erroneous data. This is also true for many other types of analytics.

Data engineers are usually responsible for producing a report that contains data outliers and other suspected quality issues. Unless the data errors are obviously caused by data entry or data processing, the data errors are fixed/cleansed by data analysts who are part of the organization that owns/produces the data, as previously mentioned. This is done in light of the expected use of the data. However, the data engineers can leverage a programmatic approach in fixing the data errors, as per the data owners' requests and requirements. The data engineers will look for empty fields, out-of-bounds values (e.g., people of ages over 200 or under 0), or just plain errors (a string where a number is expected). There are tools to easily review a sample of the data and make the cleanup process easier, for example, Dataprep (*https://cloud.google.com/data prep*) by Trifacta and Stitch (*https://www.stitchdata.com/*).

These cleanup processes work to ensure that using the data in applications, such as generating a machine learning model, does not result in it being skewed by data outliers. Ideally, data should be profiled in order to detect anomalies per column and make a determination on whether anomalies are making sense in the relevant context (e.g., customers shopping in a physical store outside of store hours are probably an error, while late-night online ordering is very much a reality). The bounds for what kinds of data are acceptable for each field are set, and automated rules prepare and clean up any batch of data, or any event stream, for ingestion. Care must be taken to avoid introducing bias into the data, such as by eliminating outliers where they should not be eliminated.

Data Quality

Data quality is an important parameter in determining the relevant use cases for a data source, as is being able to rely on data for further calculations/inclusions with other datasets. You can identify data quality by looking at the data source—i.e., understanding where it physically came from. (Error-prone human entry? Fuzzy IoT devices optimizing for quantity, not quality? Highly exact mobile app event stream?) Knowing the quality of data sources should guide the decision of whether to join datasets of varying quality, because low-quality data will reduce confidence in higher-quality sources. Data quality management processes include creating controls for validation, enabling quality monitoring and reporting, supporting the triage process for assessing the level of incident severity, enabling root cause analysis and recommendation of remedies to data issues, and data incident tracking.

There should be different confidence levels assigned to different quality datasets. There should also be considerations around allowing (or at least curating) resultant datasets with mixed-quality ancestors. The right processes for data quality management will provide measurably trustworthy data for analysis.

One possible process that can be implemented to improve data quality is a sense of ownership: making sure the business unit responsible for generating the data also owns the quality of that data and does not leave it behind for users downstream. The organization can create a data acceptance process wherein data is not allowed to be used until the owners of the data prove the data is of a quality that passes the organization's quality standards.

Lineage Tracking

Data does not live in a vacuum; it is generated by certain sources, undergoes various transformations, aggregates additionals, and is eventually supporting certain insights. A lot of valuable context is generated from the source of the data and how it was manipulated along the way, which is crucial to track. This is *data lineage*.

Why is lineage tracking important? One reason is understanding the quality of a resulting dashboard/aggregate. If that end product was generated from high-quality data, but later the information is merged into lower-quality data, that leads to a different interpretation of the dashboard. Another example will be viewing, in a holistic manner, the movement of a sensitive data class across the organization data scape, to make sure sensitive data is not inadvertently exposed into unauthorized containers.

Lineage tracking should be able, first and foremost, to present a calculation on the resultant metrics, such as "quality," or on whether or not the data was "tainted" with sensitive information. And later it must be able to present a graphical "graph" of the data traversal itself. This graph is very useful for debugging purposes but is less so for other purposes.

Lineage Tracking and Time/Cost

When describing how lineage tracking—especially doing so visually—is so important, companies have often referred to the level of effort they have to put into debugging and troubleshooting. They have stated how much time is spent not on fixing problems or errors but just on trying to find out if there are any errors or problems at all. We have heard time and time again that better tracking (e.g., notifications about what's going on and when things are "on fire" and should be looked at) not only would help solve issues better but also would save valuable time—and thus expense—in the long run. Often when lineage is talked about, the focus is on knowing where data came from and where it's going to, but there is also value in visually seeing/knowing when and where something breaks and being able to take immediate action on it.

Lineage tracking is also important when thinking about explaining decisions later on. By identifying input information into a decision-making algorithm (think about a neural net, or a machine learning model), you can rationalize later why some business decisions (e.g., loan approval) were made in a certain way in the past and will be made in a certain way in the future. By making business decisions explainable (past transactions explaining a current decision) and keeping this information transparent to the data users, you practice good data governance.

This also brings up the importance of the temporal dimension of lineage. The more sophisticated solutions track lineage across time—tracking not only what the current inputs to a dashboard are but also what those inputs were in the past, and how the landscape has evolved.

Key Management and Encryption

One consideration when storing data in any kind of system is whether to store it in a plain-text format or whether to encrypt it. Data encryption provides another layer of protection (beyond protecting all data traffic itself), as only the systems or users that have the keys can derive meaning from the data. There are several implementations of data encryptions:

- Data encryption where the underlying storage can access the key. This allows the underlying storage system to effect efficient storage via data compression (encrypted data usually does not compress well). When the data is accessed outside the bounds of the storage system—for example, if a physical disk is taken out of a data center—the data should be unreadable and therefore secure.

- Data encryption where the data is encrypted by a key inaccessible to the storage system, usually managed separately by the customer. This provides protection from a bad actor within the storage provider itself in some cases but results in inefficient storage and performance impact.

- Just-in-time decryption, where, in some cases and for some users, it is useful to decrypt certain data as it is being accessed as a form of access control. In this case, encryption works to protect some data classes (e.g., "customer name") while still allowing insights such as "total aggregate revenues from all customers" or "top 10 customers by revenue," or even identifying subjects who meet some condition, with the option to ask for de-masking of these subjects later via a trouble ticket.

All data in Google Cloud is encrypted by default, both in transit and at rest, ensuring that customer data is always protected from intrusions and attacks. Customers can also choose customer-managed encryption keys (CMEK) using Cloud KMS (*https:// cloud.google.com/kms*), or they can opt for customer-supplied encryption keys (CSEK) when they need more control over their data.

To provide the strongest protections, your encryption options should be native to the cloud platform or data warehouse you choose. The big cloud platforms all have a native key management that usually allows you to perform operations on keys without revealing the actual keys. In this case, there are actually two keys in play:

A data encryption key (DEK)
   This key is used to directly encrypt the data by the storage system.

A key encryption key (KEK)
   This key is used to protect the data encryption key and resides within a protected service, a key management service.

A Sample Key Management Scenario

In the scenario depicted in Figure 2-4, the table on the right is encrypted in chunks using the plain data encryption key.[1] The data encryption key is not stored with the table but instead is stored in a protected form (wrapped) by a striped key encryption key. The key encryption key resides (only) in the key management service.

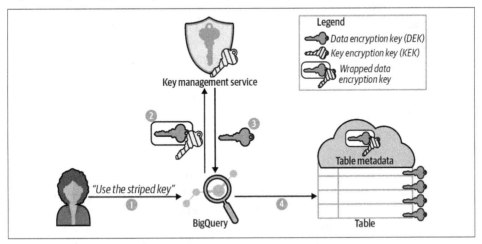

Figure 2-4. Key management scenario

To access the data, a user (or process) follows these steps:

1. The user/process requests the data, instructing the data warehouse (BigQuery) to use the "striped key" to unwrap the data encryption key, basically passing the key ID.

2. BigQuery retrieves the protected DEK from the table metadata and accesses the key management service, supplying the wrapped key.

3. The key management service unwraps the data protection key, while the KEK never leaves the vault of the key management service.

4. BigQuery uses the DEK to access the data and then discards it, never storing it in a persistent manner.

This scenario ensures that the key encryption key never leaves a secure separate store (the KMS) and that the data encryption key never resides on disk—only in memory, and only when needed.

---

1 Protection of data at rest is a broad topic; a good starter book would be *Applied Cryptography* by Bruce Schneier (John Wiley and Sons).

Data Retention and Data Deletion

Another important item in the data governance tool chest is the ability to control how long data is kept—that is, setting maximal and minimal values. There are clear advantages to identifying data that should survive occasional storage space optimization as being more valuable to retain, but setting a maximum amount of time on data retention for a less-valuable data class and automatically deleting it seems less obvious. Consider that retaining PII presents the challenges of proposer disclosure, informed consent, and transparency. Getting rid of PII after a short duration (e.g., retaining location only while on the commute) simplifies the above.

When talking about data retention and data deletion, we're often thinking about them in the context of how to treat sensitive data—that is, whether to retain it, encrypt it, delete it, or handle it some other way. But there are also scenarios around which your governance policies not only can save you from being out of compliance but also can protect you from lost work.

Although it's a bit old, an example that comes to mind around the subject of protection against data deletion is the accidental deletion of the movie *Toy Story 2* in 1998.[2] During the film's production process, Oren Jacob, Pixar's CTO, and Technical Director Galyn Susman were looking at a directory that was holding the assets for several characters when they encountered an error—something along the lines of "directory no longer valid," meaning the location of those characters in the directory had been deleted. During their effort to walk back through the directory to find where the problem occurred, they witnessed, in real time, assets for several of the characters vanish before their eyes.

When all was said and done, an erroneous 10-character command had mistakenly deleted 90% of the movie. They were able to recover most of the movie, but unfortunately about a week's worth of work was lost forever.

You can see from this example that even though sensitive data wasn't leaked or lost, a multitude of data was still accidentally deleted—some of which could never be recovered. We challenge you to consider in your governance program not only how you will deal with and treat sensitive data in terms of where or how long you retain it, and whether or not you delete it, but also how that same program can be implemented on other classes and categories of data that are important for you to back up. While a loss of data may not result in a breach in compliance, it could certainly result in other catastrophic business consequences that, if planned for, will hopefully not happen to you.

---

2 Dan Moshkovich, "Accidental Data Deletion: The Cautionary Tale of *Toy Story 2* and MySpace" (*https://oreil.ly/Gh7sL*), *HubStor* (blog), August 17, 2020.

Case Study: The Importance of Clear Data Retention Rules for Data Governance

A lesson about data retention was learned by a Danish taxi company that actually had a data governance policy in place.[3]

To understand the story, we need a little bit of context about GDPR Article 5 (*https://oreil.ly/2npEa*), the regulation covering treatment of European citizens' data by tech companies. GDPR details the standards that organizations have to follow when processing personal data. These standards state that data must be handled in a way that is transparent to its subject (the European citizen), collected for a specific purpose, and used only for that purpose. GDPR Article 5(1)(c) addresses data minimization by requiring that personal data be limited to what is necessary relative to the purpose for which it is processed. And Article 5(1)(e)—the one that's most relevant to the taxi company example—specifies that data cannot be stored any longer than is necessary for the purposes for which it was gathered.

The Danish taxi company in this example (Figure 2-5) processed taxi ridership data for legitimate purposes, making sure there was a record of every ride, and of the associated fare, for example, for chargeback and accounting purposes.

Figure 2-5. Danish taxis (photo courtesy of Håkan Dahlström, Creative Commons License 2.0 (https://oreil.ly/e-8lF)

The Danish taxi company, as mentioned, had a data retention policy in place: after two years, the data from a taxi ride was made anonymous by deleting the name of the passenger. However, that action did not make the data *completely* anonymous, as multiple additional details were (albeit transparently) collected. These included the geolocation of the taxi ride's start and end and the phone number of the passenger. With these details, even without the name of the passenger, it was easy to identify the

---

3 For more about this case study, see coverage by the law firm Gorrissen Federspiel (*https://oreil.ly/peZ3j*).

passenger, and therefore the company was not in compliance with its own statement of anonymization; thus the data retention policy was actually not effective.

The lesson learned is that considering the business goal of a data retention policy, and whether or not that goal is actually achieved by the policy set in place, is essential. In our case, the taxi company was fined by the European Union and was criticized for the fact that telephone numbers are actually used as unique identifiers within the taxi ride management system.

Workflow Management for Data Acquisition

One of the key workflows tying together all the tools mentioned so far is data acquisition. This workflow usually begins with an analyst seeking data to perform a task. The analyst, through the power of a well-implemented data governance plan, is able to access the data catalog for the organization and, through a multifaceted search query, is able to review relevant data sources. Data acquisition continues with identifying the relevant data source and seeking an access grant to it. The governance controls send the access request to the right authorizing personnel, and access is granted to the relevant data warehouse, enforced through the native controls of that warehouse. This workflow—identifying a task, shopping for relevant data, identifying relevant data, and acquiring access to it—constitutes a data access workflow that is safe. The level of data access requested—that is, access to metadata for search, access to the data itself, querying the data in aggregate—these are all data governance decisions.

IAM—Identity and Access Management

When talking about data acquisition, it's important to detail how access control works. The topic of access control relies on user authentication and, per the user, the authorization of the user to access certain data and the conditions of access.

The objective of authenticating a user is to determine that "you are who you say you are." Any user (and, for that matter, any service or application) operates under a set of permissions and roles tied to the identity of a service. The importance of securely authenticating a user is clear: if I can impersonate a different user, there is a risk of assuming that user's roles and privileges and breaking data governance.

Authentication used to be traditionally accomplished by supplying a password tied to the user requesting access. This method has the obvious drawback that anyone who has somehow gained access to the password can gain access to everything that user has access to. Nowadays, proper authentication requires:

- Something you know—this will be your password or passphrase; it should be hard to guess and changed regularly.

- Something you have—this serves as a second factor of authentication. After providing the right passphrase, a user will be prompted to prove that they have a certain device (a cell phone able to accept single-use codes, a hardware token), adding another layer of security. The underlying assumption is that if you misplace that "object" you would report it promptly, ensuring the token cannot be used by others.

- Something you are—sometimes, for another layer of security, the user will add biometric information to the authentication request: a fingerprint, a facial scan, or something similar.

- Additional context—another oft-used layer of security is ensuring that an authenticated user can access only certain information from within a specific sanctioned application or device, or other conditions. Such additional context often includes:

  — Being able to access corporate information only from corporate hardware (sanctioned and cleared by central IT). This, for example, eliminates the risk of "using the spouse's device to check for email" without enjoying the default corporate anti-malware software installed by default on corporate hardware.

  — Being able to access certain information only during working hours—thus eliminating the risk of personnel using their off-hours time to manipulate sensitive data, maybe when those employees are not in appropriate surroundings or are not alert to risk.

  — Having limited access to sensitive information when not logged in to the corporate network—when using an internet café, for example, and risking network eavesdropping.

The topic of authentication is the cornerstone of access control, and each organization will define its own balance between risk aversion and user-authentication friction. It is a known maxim that the more "hoops" employees have to jump through in order to access data, the more these employees will seek to avoid complexity, leading to shadow IT and information siloing—directions opposed to data governance (data governance seeks to promote data access to all, under proper restrictions). There are detailed volumes written on this topic.[4]

---

4 An example book about identity and access management is *Identity and Access Management* (*https://oreil.ly/qoANU*) by Ertem Osmanoglu (Elsevier Science, Syngress).

User Authorization and Access Management

Once the user is properly authenticated, access is determined by a process of checking whether the user is authorized to access or otherwise perform an operation on the data object in question, be it a table, a dataset, a pipeline, or streaming data.

Data is a rich medium, and sample access policies can be:

- For reading the data directly (performing "select" SQL statement on a table, reading a file).
- For reading or editing the metadata associated with the data. For a table, this would be the schema (the names and types of columns, the table name). For a file, this would be the filename. In addition, metadata also refers to the creation date, update date, and "last read" dates.
- For updating the content, without adding new content.
- For copying the data or exporting it.
- There are also access controls associated with workflows, such as performing an extract-transform-load (ETL) operation to move and reshape the data (replacing rows/columns with others).

We have expanded here on the policies previously mentioned for data classes, which also detail partial-read access—which can be its own authorized function.

It's important to define identities, groups, and roles and assign access rights to establish a level of managed access.

Identity and access management (IAM) should provide role management for every user, with the capability to flexibly add custom roles that group together meaningful permissions relevant to your organization, ensuring that only authorized and authenticated individuals and systems are able to access data assets according to defined rules. Enterprise-scale IAM should also provide context (IP, device, the time the access request is being generated from, and, if possible, use case for access). As good governance results in context-specific role and permission determination before any data access, the IAM system should scale to millions of users, issuing multiple data access requests per second.

Summary

In this chapter, we have gone through the basic ingredients of data governance: the importance of having a policy book containing the data classes managed, and how to clean up the data, secure it, and control access. Now it is time to go beyond the tooling and discuss the importance of the additional ingredients of *people* and *processes* to a successful data governance program.

CHAPTER 3

Ingredients of Data Governance: People and Processes

As mentioned in the preceding chapters, companies want to be able to derive more insights from their data. They want to make "data-driven decisions." Gone are the days of business decisions being based exclusively on intuition or observation. Big data and big data analytics now allow for decisions to be made based on collecting data and extracting patterns and facts from that data.

We have spent much time explaining how this movement into using big data has brought with it a host of considerations around the governance of that data, and we have outlined tools that aid in this process. Tools, however, are not the only factor to evaluate when designing a data governance strategy—the *people* involved and the *process* by which data governance is implemented are key to a *successful* implementation of a data governance strategy.

The people and process are aspects of a data governance strategy that often get overlooked or oversimplified. There is an exceedingly heavier reliance on governance tools, and though tools are getting better and more robust, they are not enough by themselves; *how* the tools are implemented, an understanding of the people using them, and the process set up for their proper use are all critical to governance success as well.

The People: Roles, Responsibilities, and Hats

Many data governance frameworks revolve around a complex interplay of many roles and responsibilities. These frameworks rely heavily on each role playing its part in keeping the well-oiled data governance machine running smoothly.

The problem with this is that most companies are rarely able to exactly or even semi-fully match these frameworks, due to lack of employee skill set or, more commonly, a simple lack of headcount. For this reason, employees working in the information and data space of their company often wear different user *hats*. We use the term *hat* to delineate the difference between an actual *role or job title* and *tasks* that are done. The same person can perform tasks that align with many different roles or wear many different hats as part of their day-to-day job.

User Hats Defined

In Chapter 1, we outlined three broad categories of governors, approvers, and users. Here we will look in depth at the different hats (versus roles) within each category (and expand on an additional category of ancillary hats), the tasks associated with each hat, and finally, the implications and considerations when looking at these hats from a task-oriented perspective versus a role-based approach. In Table 3-1 we've listed out each hat with its respective category and key tasks for quick reference, with more detailed descriptions following.

Table 3-1. Different hats with their respective categories and the tasks associated with them

Hat	Category	Key tasks
Legal	Ancillary	Knows of and communicates legal requirements for compliance
Privacy tsar	Governor	Ensures compliance and oversees company's governance strategy/process
Data owner	Approver (can also be governor)	Physically implements company's governance strategy (e.g., data architecture, tooling, data pipelining, etc.)
Data steward	Governor	Performs categorization and classification of data
Data analyst/data scientist	User	Runs complex data analytics/queries
Business analyst	User	Runs simple data analyses
Customer support specialist	Ancillary (can also be a user)	Views customer data (but does not use this data for any kind of analytical purpose)
C-suite	Ancillary	Funds company's governance strategy
External auditor	Ancillary	Audits a company's compliance with legal regulations

Legal (ancillary)

Contrary to the title of *legal*, this hat may or may not be an actual attorney. This hat includes the tasks of ensuring the company is up to date in terms of compliance with the legal requirements for its data handling and communicating this information internally. Depending on the company, the person with this hat may actually be an attorney (this is especially true for highly regulated companies, which will be covered in depth later) who must have a deep knowledge of the type of data collected and how it's treated to ensure that the company is in compliance in the event of an external audit. Other companies, especially those dealing with sensitive but not highly regulated data, are more likely to simply have someone whose task is to be up to date on regulations and have a deep understanding of which ones apply to the data the company collects.

Privacy tsar (governor)

We chose to title this hat *privacy tsar* because this is a term we use internally at Google, but this hat has also been called *governance manager, director of privacy,* and *director of data governance* in other literature. The key tasks of this hat are those which ensure that the regulations the legal department has deemed appropriate are followed. Additionally, the privacy tsar also generally oversees the entire governance process at the company, which includes defining which governance processes should be followed and how. We will discuss other process approaches later in this chapter. It's important to note that the privacy tsar may or may not have an extremely technical background. On the surface it might seem that this hat would come from a technical background, but depending on the company and the resources it has dedicated to its data governance efforts, these tasks are often performed by people who sit more on the business side of the company rather than on the technical side.

Understanding the movement of people is of utmost importance when it comes to battling COVID-19. Google, a company that processes significant amounts of highly personal data that includes location information, was torn between helping healthcare providers and authorities to battle the deadly pandemic more effectively and preserving the trust of the billions of people worldwide who use Google's services.

Privacy tsar, work example 1: Community mobility reports.   The challenge of preserving privacy while at the same time providing useful, *actionable* data to health authorities required the full attention of Google's privacy tsars, the people entrusted with creating the internal regulations that make sure that technology does not intrude into users' personal data and privacy.

The solution they found was to provide information in an aggregated form, based on anonymized sets of data from only those users who have turned on "location history" in Google's services.[1] This setting is off by default, and users need to "opt in" to enable it. Location information history can always be deleted by the user at any time. In addition, differential privacy (a technique covered in Chapter 7) was further used to identify small groups of users with outlier results and eliminate those groups completely from the provided solution. Another differential privacy technique was employed to add statistical noise to the results; the noise, statistically irrelevant for aggregates, helps ensure that no individual can be tracked back through the data.

---

1 See Google's "Community Mobility Reports" (*https://oreil.ly/HlXej*) for more on this.

The result is a useful set of reports tracking communities and changes in behavior over time. Health officials can then assess whether "stay at home" orders are being complied with, and trace back sources of infection due to people congregating.

In Figure 3-1, we see the results of that work. A sample from the report for San Francisco County shows increased people presence in residential areas (bottom right) but a reduced presence across the board in retail sites, grocery stores, parks, transit stations, and workplaces. Note that no individual location is named, yet the data is useful for health officials in estimating where people congregate. For example, an order about the reopening of retail stores can be considered.

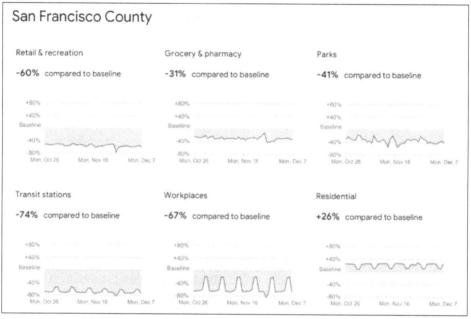

Figure 3-1. Example from the Google mobility reports

Privacy tsar, work example 2: Exposure notifications. An even more daunting task related to COVID-19 is how to safely (from a privacy perspective) inform people about prolonged exposure to a person diagnosed with COVID-19.[2] Because the virus is highly contagious and can be transmitted through the air, identifying exposures and making sure people who were inadvertently exposed to a positively diagnosed person get tested (and isolate themselves if testing positive), is crucial to breaking infection chains and limiting outbreaks. This process is a recognized technique in battling infections

---

2 For more about exposure notifications, see "Exposure Notifications: Using Technology to Help Public Health Authorities Fight COVID 19" (*https://oreil.ly/0HrdE*) and "Privacy: Preserving Contact Tracing" (*https://oreil.ly/5yJQV*).

and is otherwise known as *contact tracing*. Technology can augment this technique by immediately alerting the individual as an alternative to a prolonged phone investigation in which public health authorities question a positively diagnosed individual as to their whereabouts over the incubation period. (Many people cannot accurately identify where they have been over the course of the past few days, nor can everyone easily produce a list of all the people they have interacted with over the course of the past week.)

However, a positive COVID-19 diagnosis is highly personal, and having this information delivered to everyone that a diagnosed person came in contact with is an emotionally loaded process. Furthermore, having your technology do that for you is highly intrusive and will cause resistance to the point of not enabling this technology.

So how does a privacy tsar thread the needle between preserving personal information and privacy and combating a deadly disease?

The solution that was found maintains the principles required to ensure privacy:

- It must be an "opt-in" solution—the people must enable it, and the product provides information to ensure consent is acquired after being informed.
- Since the topic is whether or not the subject was next to a diagnosed person, location information, though it might be useful to health authorities to understand where the incident occurred, is not collected. This is a decision made by the privacy tsar in favor of preserving privacy.
- The information is shared only with public health authorities and not with Google or Apple.

So how does the solution work? Every phone beams a unique yet random and frequently changing identifier to all nearby phones; the phones collect the list of beacons, and this list is matched with anyone who has reported their diagnosis. If your phone was in proximity to the phone of someone who has uploaded a positive diagnosis, the match will be reported to you (see Figure 3-2). Note that the identity of the infected individual is not reported, nor is the specific time and place. Thus the crucial information (you have been near a positively diagnosed individual so get tested!) is shared without sacrificing the privacy of the infected individual.

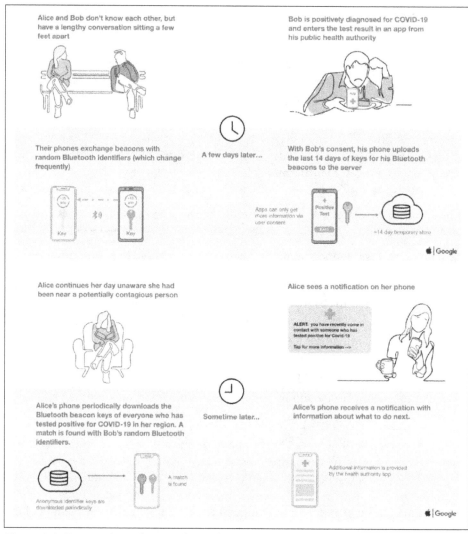

Figure 3-2. Excerpt from the Google/Apple guide to the exposure notification technology

Data owner (approver/governor)

In order for the privacy tsar's governance strategy/process to be realized, the data owner is needed.[3] The tasks of the data owner include physically implementing the

---

3 While "classical literature" on data governance often separates data owners and data custodians (the former residing more on the business side of things, and the latter more on the technical side), during the course of our research and interviews with many companies we found that, in practice, these two "sides of the coin" are often conflated, and the actual tasks of data ownership tend to fall on those with technical expertise.

processes and/or strategies laid out by the privacy tsar. This most often includes the ideation and creation of the data architecture of the company, along with choosing and implementing tooling and data pipeline and storage creation, monitoring, and maintenance—in other words, "owning the data." It's clear from the task descriptions that these must be performed by someone with quite a bit of technical background and expertise; hence people who wear the data owner hat largely are engineers or folks with an engineering background.

Data steward (governor)

When researching data governance, you will find that there is likely to be much weight given to the role of *data steward*, and that's with good reason—the tasks of a data steward include categorization and classification of data. For any sort of governance to be implemented, data must be defined and labeled to clearly identify what the data is: sensitive, restricted, health related, and so on. A large part of the reason we advocate the usage of the term *hats* versus *roles* is exemplified by the fact that it's very rare to find a singular person doing the "role" of data steward in the wild. The act of data "stewardship" is highly, highly manual and extremely time consuming. In fact, one company we spoke to said that for a short while it actually had a "full time" data steward who quit after several months, citing the job as being "completely soul sucking." Because of the manual, time-consuming nature of the role—coupled with the fact that in most cases there is no *dedicated person* to perform stewardship duties—these duties often fall to many different people across the company or to someone who has another role/other duties they perform as well. As such, full data categorization/classification is often not done well, not done fully, or, in the worst cases, just not done at all. This is an important item to note, because without stewardship, governance is incomplete at best. We will cover this in more depth later, but here is where we begin to see a recurring theme when looking at the people and the process. Many of the governance processes that most companies employ right now are undertaken to *get around* the fact that stewardship falls short. As we outlined in Chapter 1, the quick growth and expansion of data collected by companies has resulted in an overwhelm of data, and companies simply don't have the time or headcount to dedicate to being able to categorize, classify, and label ALL of their data, so they create and utilize other methods and strategies to "do their best given the limitations."

Data analyst/data scientist (user)

Data analysts and data scientists are, in general, some of the primary or key users of data within a company and are largely who data governance efforts are for. Companies struggle with governance and security of their data versus the democratization of their data. In order to be data driven, companies must collect and analyze large amounts of data. The more data that can be made available to analysts and scientists, the better—unless of course that data is sensitive and should have limited access.

Therefore, the better the governance execution, the better (and the more safely) analysts or scientists are able to do their job and provide valuable business insights.

Business analyst (user)

While data analysts and data scientists are the main users or consumers of data, there are a few people in the periphery of a company who also use and view data. In moving toward being more data driven, companies have folks who sit on the business side of things who are very interested in the data analyses produced by analysts and scientists. In some companies, data engineers aid in the creation and maintenance of much simpler analytics platforms to aid in "self-service" for business users. More and more business people in companies have questions that they hope crunching some data will help them to answer. Analysts/scientists thus end up fielding many, many inquiries, some of which they simply don't have time to answer. By enabling business users to directly answer some of their own questions, analysts/scientists are able to free up their time to answer more complex analysis questions.

Customer support specialists (user/ancillary)

While a customer support specialist is technically only a "viewer" of data, it's worth noting that there *are* folks with this role who will need access to some sensitive data, even though they don't have any tasks around manipulating that data. In terms of hats, customer support specialists *do* tend to have this as their sole role and are not also doing other things; however, they are consumers of data, and their needs, and how to grant them appropriate access, must be considered and managed by the other hats executing a company's governance strategy.

C-suite (ancillary)

In many companies, members of the C-suite have limited tasks in relation to the actual execution of a data governance strategy. They are nonetheless a critical hat in the grand scheme of governance because they "hold the purse strings." As we mentioned earlier, tools and headcount are critical factors when considering a successful data governance strategy. It thus makes sense that the person who actually *funds* that strategy must understand it and be on board with the funding that makes it a reality.

External auditor (ancillary)

We have included the hat of external auditor in this section despite the fact that external auditors are not within a particular company. Many of the companies we've spoken to have mentioned the importance of the external auditor in their governance strategy. No longer is it good enough to simply be "compliant" with regulations—companies now often need to *prove* their compliance, which has direct implications for the way a governance strategy and process is employed. Oftentimes, companies need to prove who has access to what data as well as all the different locations and permutations of that data (its lineage). While internal tool reporting can generally help with providing proof of compliance, the way that a governance strategy is set up and tended to can help, or hinder, the production of this documentation.

Data Enrichment and Its Importance

As we mentioned at the beginning of this section, one person may wear many hats—that is, perform many of the tasks involved in carrying out a data governance strategy at a company. As can be seen in the list of hats and the (fairly long) list of tasks *within* each hat shown in Table 3-1, it's easy to see how many of these tasks may not be completed well, if at all.

While there are many tasks that are important to successful implementation of a data governance strategy, it could be argued that the most *critical* are data categorization, classification, and labeling. As we pointed out, these tasks are manual and highly time consuming, which means that they rarely get executed fully. There is a saying: "In order to govern data, you must first know what it is." Without proper data enrichment (the process of attaching metadata to data), the central task of the data steward hat, proper data governance falls short. This central task of the data steward is so key, however, that what we commonly see is that the person who wears the data steward hat also often wears the privacy tsar hat as well as the data owner hat, and/or they may even wear a hat in a completely different part of the company (a common one we see is business analyst). Wearing many hats results in a limited amount of tasks that can be done (one person can only do so much!), and most often the majority of the time-consuming task of data enrichment falls off the list.

In the next section we will cover some common governance processes we've observed over the years. One thing to keep in mind while reading through the processes is how the hats play a role in the execution of these processes. We will discuss their interplay later in this chapter.

The Process: Diverse Companies, Diverse Needs and Approaches to Data Governance

It's important to note that in the discussion of the people and processes around data governance, there is no "one size fits all" approach. As mentioned, in this section we will begin to examine some broad company categories, outline their specific concerns, needs, and considerations, and explore how those interplay with a company's approach to data governance.

We'd like to reemphasize the point that there is no "one size fits all" approach to governance; and you need to fit your program to your needs—whether those be mitigated by headcount, the kind of data you collect, your industry, etc. We have seen many governance approaches and frameworks that are somewhat inflexible and thus might be difficult to implement if you don't fit their particular parameters. We hope that through exploration of elements to consider you're able to create a framework for yourself that not only matches your governance needs and goals but also matches where your company is right now, and where you'd like to be in the future.

Legacy

Legacy companies are defined as companies that have been around for quite some time and most certainly have, or have had, legacy on-premises (on-prem) systems—most often many different systems, which bring with them a host of issues. The time and level of effort this work requires often leads to it not being done fully, or simply not being done at all. Further, for consistency (and arguably for the most effective use of data and data analytics), every company should have a *central data dictionary*, defining all data names, classes, and categories that is standardized and used throughout the company. Many legacy companies lack this central data dictionary because their data is spread out through these various on-prem systems. More often than not, these on-prem systems and the data within them are associated with a particular branch or line of business. And that branch, in and of itself, is agnostic of the data that resides in the other lines of the business's systems. As such, there ends up being a dictionary for each system and line of business that may not align to any other line of business or system, which makes cross-system governance and analytics nearly impossible.

A prime example of this would be a large retailer that has a system that houses its online sales and another system that handles its brick-and-mortar sales. In one system the income the company receives from a sale is called "revenue," while in the other system it's simply called "sales." Between the two systems, the same enterprise dictionary is not being used—one can see where this becomes problematic if executives are trying to figure out what the total income for the company is. Analytics are nearly impossible to run when the same data does not have the same metadata vernacular attached. This becomes an even larger issue when considering sensitive data and its treatment. If there is no agreed-upon, company-wide terminology (as outlined in the enterprise dictionary), and if that terminology is not implemented for *all sources* of data, governance is rendered incomplete and ineffective.

The power of the cloud and big data analytics drives many companies to want to migrate their data, or a portion of their data, to the cloud—but the past pain of inconsistent enterprise dictionaries and haphazard governance gives them pause. They don't want to "repeat their past mistakes"; they don't want to simply replicate all of their current issues. While tools can help to right past wrongs, they simply aren't enough. Companies need (and desire) a framework for how to move their data and have it properly governed from the beginning, with the right people working the right process.

Cloud Native/Digital Only

Cloud-native companies (sometimes referred to as *digital only*) are defined as companies who have, and have always had, all of their data stored in the cloud. Not always, but in general, these tend to be much younger companies who have never had on-premises systems and thus have never had to "migrate" their data to a cloud environment. Based on that alone, it's easy to see why cloud-native companies don't face the same issues that legacy companies do.

Despite the fact that cloud-native companies do not have to deal with on-prem systems and the "siloing" of data that often comes along with that, they still may deal with different clouds as well as different storage solutions within and between those clouds that have their own flavor of "siloing." For one, a centralized data dictionary, as we've explored, is already a challenge, and having one that spans multiple clouds is even more daunting. Even if a centralized data dictionary is established, the process and tools (because some clouds require that only certain tools be used) by which data is enriched and governed in each cloud will probably be slightly different. And that is something that hinders consistency (in both process and personnel) and thus hinders effectiveness. Further, even within a cloud, there can be different storage solutions that also may carry with them different structures of data (e.g., files versus tables versus jpegs). These structures can be difficult to attach metadata to, which makes governance additionally difficult.

In terms of cloud—and data governance within clouds specifically—cloud-native companies tend to have better governance and data management processes set up from the beginning. Because of their relatively young "age" in dealing with data, there is often less data overall, and they have more familiarity with some common data-handling best practices. Additionally, cloud-native companies by definition have *all* of their data in the cloud, including their most sensitive data—which means that they've most likely been dealing with the need for governance since the beginning, and they most likely have some processes in place for governing, if not *all* of their data, at least their most sensitive data.

Retail

Retail companies are an interesting category, as not only do they often ingest quite a bit of data from their own stores (or online stores), but they also tend to ingest and utilize quite a bit of third-party data. This presents yet another instance in which data governance is only as good as the process set up for it and the people who are there to execute it. The oft-mentioned importance of creating and implementing a data dictionary applies, as well as having a process around how this third-party data is ingested, where it lands, and how governance can be applied.

One twist that we have not discussed but that very much applies in the case of retail is that of governance beyond simple classification of data. So far we have discussed the importance of classifying data (especially sensitive data) so that it can be known and thus governed appropriately. That governance most often relates to the treatment of and/or access to said data. But data access and data treatment are not the only aspects to consider in some instances; the use case for that data is also important. In the case of retail, there may be a certain class of data—email for example—that was collected for the purpose of sending a customer their receipt from an in-store purchase. In the context (use case) of accessing this data for the purposes of sending a customer a receipt, this is completely acceptable. If, however, one wanted to access this *same* data for the purpose of sending a customer some marketing material around the item they just purchased, this use case would *not* be acceptable unless the customer has given explicit consent for their email to be used for marketing. Now, depending on the employee structure at a company, this problem may not be solvable with simple role-based access controls (fulfillment gets access, marketing does not) if the same employee may cover many different roles. This warrants the need for a more complex process that includes establishing use cases for data classes.

Combo of Legacy and Retail

A particularly interesting use case we've come across in our customer interviews is that of a very large legacy retail company. In business for over 75 years, this company is looking to leverage powerful data analytics tools to help it move toward being a more data-driven company.

The struggle, interestingly, is not only in its old legacy on-prem data-storage systems but also in its internal processes around data and data management.

It currently has its data separated into several data marts, a configuration aimed at distributing responsibility for segments of data: a mart for marketing for in-store sales, for third-party sales, and so on. This, however, has become problematic for the company, as not only is there no "central source of truth" in terms of an enterprise dictionary, but it also cannot run any kind of analytics across its data marts, resulting in duplication of data from one mart to another since analytics can only be run within a mart.

Historically, the company was very focused on keeping all of its data on-prem; however, this view has changed with the increased security that is now available in the cloud, and the company is now looking to migrate all of its data off-premises. Through this migration effort, not only is the company looking to change the basic infrastructure of its data story from a decentralized one (multiple marts) to a centralized one (centralized data warehouse), but it is also using this as an opportunity to restructure its internal processes around data management and governance (see Figure 3-3).

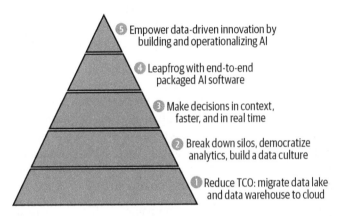

Figure 3-3. *Breaking down data silos by restructuring internal processes is often a key stage after enterprises consolidate their on-premises data into the cloud*

Data centralization enables the company to have one enterprise dictionary that allows for all new data—namely sensitive data—to be quickly marked and treated accordingly. Quick and easy handling of sensitive data also enables quicker and easier access controls (as they need to be applied only once, as opposed to each mart). This not only saves overhead effort but also allows for the implementation of more easy-to-use self-service analytics tools for employees who may not be analysts by trade but, with the right tools and access to data, are able to run simple analytics. This new process, however, is really only good for new incoming data.

This company, like many legacy companies with a lot of historical data, is struggling with how to handle the data it already has stored. It currently has 15 years of data (~25 terabytes) stored on-premises, and while it knows there is a wealth of information there, the time and effort required to migrate, enrich, and curate all this data seems daunting at best, especially when the payoff is not known.

Highly Regulated

Highly regulated companies represent the sector of companies that deal with extremely sensitive data—data that often carries additional compliance requirements beyond the usual handling of sensitive information. Some examples of highly regulated companies would be those dealing with financial, pharmaceutical, or healthcare services.

Highly regulated companies deal with multiple kinds of sensitive data. They have to juggle not only basic data governance best practices but also the additional regulations related to the data they collect and deal in, and they face regular audits to make sure that they are aboveboard and compliant. As a result of this, many highly regulated companies are more sophisticated in their data-governance process. As they've had to deal with compliance related to their data from the get-go, they often have better systems in place to identify and classify their sensitive data and treat it appropriately.

Also, for many of these kinds of companies, their business is based solely around sensitive data, so not only do they tend to have better processes in place from the beginning, but also those processes most often include a more well-funded and sophisticated organization of the people who handle that sensitive data. These companies tend to actually have people dedicated to each of the hats discussed earlier, and that additional headcount, as we pointed out, can be the deciding factor in whether a data-governance strategy is successful or unsuccessful.

One final note about highly regulated companies is that, as a result of the legal requirements they face on the handling of certain data, they can function similarly to legacy companies in that they have difficulty moving off-prem and/or trying out new tools. Any tool that will touch sensitive data under a regulation must meet the standards (fully) of that regulation. As an example, a tool or product in beta may be used by a healthcare company only if it is HIPAA compliant. Many product betas, because they're used for early access and as a way to work out bugs, are not designed to meet the most stringent compliance standards. While the final product may be compliant, the beta generally is not, meaning that highly regulated companies often don't get to experiment with these new tools/products and thus have trouble migrating to new, potentially better tools than the ones they're currently using.

Unique Highly Regulated Organization: Hospital/University

When discussing highly regulated industries, finance and healthcare are the ones most commonly referenced. In our discussions with customers we came across another highly regulated industry that had some unique challenges: hospital/universities. These "companies" are unique in that they collect a lot of clinical data from their hospitals, but they also collect (and produce) a lot of research data through university-sponsored research studies.

Each of these types of data comes with its own specific regulations and standards for research—e.g., HIPAA covers clinical data, and the Institutional Review Board (IRB) protects the rights and welfare of human research subjects recruited to participate in research activities.

One particular hospital/university we spoke to was looking at the use case of being able to run secondary analytics across its clinical and research data. Currently it has two main pipeline solutions for its data: one for clinical and one for research.

For its clinical pipelines, data is stored on-prem in a Clarity data warehouse for each hospital, and only analysts with access to that database are able to run analytics.

For its research pipelines, each "lab" within the university has its own on-prem storage, and again, only analysts with access to that server can run analytics. It can be seen that not only does this structure not allow for secondary analyses to be run across labs, but they also can't be run across clinical and research.

Knowing that there is a wealth of value in these secondary analytics, this hospital/ university decided to migrate a large portion of its clinical and research data to the cloud, to get it all in one central location. In order to do this, however, much needs to be done to make the data comply with healthcare and research regulations. As such, the hospital/university created a specialized team dedicated to this migration effort; that team's role included tasks such as: creating an enterprise dictionary, enriching data, reviewing the presence of sensitive data, reviewing policies attached to data, applying new policies to data, and applying a standardized file structure.

Fortunately for this organization, it was able to secure funding for such an elaborate undertaking, and yet it is still looking at ways to automate its process. Migration and the setup of data in the cloud is but one hurdle—maintaining and managing a data store going forward will require effort as well, and as such, tools that enable automation are top of mind for this organization.

Small Companies

For our purposes, we define a small company as one that has fewer than one thousand employees. One of the benefits of small companies is their smaller employee footprint.

Smaller companies often have small data-analytics teams, which means that there are fewer people who actually need to touch data. This means that there is less risk overall. One of the primary reasons to govern data is to make sure that sensitive data does not fall into the wrong hands. Fewer employees also makes for a much less arduous and less complicated process of setting up and maintaining access controls. As we discussed earlier, access controls and policy management can get increasingly complicated, especially when factors such as use case for data come into play.

Another benefit of a small amount of people touching data is that there is often less proliferation of datasets. Data analysts and scientists, as part of their jobs, create many different views of datasets and joins (combining tables from different dataset sources). This proliferation of data makes it hard to track where the data came from and where it's going to (not to mention who had and now has access). Fewer analysts/

scientists mean fewer datasets/tables/joins, resulting in data that's much easier to track and thus easier to govern.

Large Companies

While there are many more company types, we will end our exploration of broad categories with large companies, defined as companies with more than one thousand employees.

If small companies have the governance benefit of dealing with less data, large companies deal with the reverse, in that they often deal with *a lot* of data. Large companies not only generate a great deal of data themselves but also often deal with a lot of third-party data. This results in immense difficulty in wrapping their arms around it all; they are overwhelmed by the data and often struggle to govern even a portion of it. As such, only some data gets enriched and curated, which means that only some of their data is able to be used to drive insights.

Large companies often put processes in place to limit this overwhelm by choosing only select data to enrich, curate, and thus govern. A common strategy for limiting the data that a data steward must enrich is to select a number of categories and govern only the data that falls within those categories. Another is to only govern known pipelines of data (these are the pipelines consisting of the primary data a company deals with, such as daily sales numbers from a retail store) and to handle "ad hoc" pipeline data (engineers at times are asked to create *new* pipelines to address one-time or infrequent data analysis use cases) only as time allows or if absolutely necessary.

It's easy to see that these strategies (which we will discuss in more depth later) result in a sort of iceberg of data where enriched (*known*), curated data sits at the top, and below that is a mound of data that is, in the main, un-nriched and thus *unknown*. Companies don't know what this data is, which means they can't govern it, and ungoverned data is quite scary. It could be sensitive, it could be noncompliant, and there could be dire consequences if it happens to get leaked. This causes much fear and forces companies with this problem to use strategies to help mitigate their risk.

Not only do large companies deal with copious amounts of data, but they also tend to have a much larger workforce of data analysts, data scientists, and data engineers—all of whom need access to data to do their jobs. More data, plus more people who need access to data, results in much more complicated (and often poorly managed) processes around access control. Access control is generally based on user role, which should determine the data (and only that data) that they need access to. This strategy may seem simple, but it is a difficult process to implement for two main reasons. First, in order to know what data is critical to a particular user's role, data must be known. And we know from previous discussion in this book that the majority of data a company has is unknown. This results in not only the inability to govern (it's impossible to govern what you don't know you have) but also the inability to know what data is appropriate for whom. Data specialists still need to do their job, however, so (too much) access is often granted at the expense of risk. Companies try to offset this risk by creating a "culture of security," which puts the onus on the employee to do the right thing and not expose or misuse potentially sensitive information. Another issue with role-based access is that roles and their ensuing uses for data are not always black and white; the use case for data must also be considered. Depending on the company, a user in the same role may be able to use data for some use cases and not for others (an example being the use case we outlined in the retail section). As touched on Chapter 2, and as will be covered in depth later, the addition of use case as a parameter during policy creation helps to mitigate this issue.

Like legacy companies, large companies often also deal with the issue of having many different storage systems, the majority of which are legacy. Large companies tend to be built up over time, and with time comes more data and more storage systems. We've already discussed how the siloed nature of different storage systems makes governance difficult. Different storage systems naturally create data silos, but large companies have another factor that results in even more complex "silos": acquisitions.

Large companies are sometimes built completely from within, but others become large (or larger) due to acquisitions. When companies acquire other, smaller companies, they also acquire all their data (and its underlying storage), which brings along a whole host of potential problems—primarily, how the acquired company handled its data, as well as its overall governance process and approach. This includes how the company managed its data: its method of data classification, its enterprise dictionary (or lack thereof), its process and methods around access control, and its overall culture of privacy and security. For these reasons, many large companies find it nearly impossible to marry their central governance process with that of their acquisitions, which often results in acquired data sitting in storage and not being used for analytics.

People and Process Together: Considerations, Issues, and Some Successful Strategies

We have now outlined the different people involved in various kinds of companies, as well as some specific processes and approaches utilized by the different company types.

There is obviously a synergy between people and process, of which there are some considerations and issues. We will review several of the issues we've observed, along with outlining a few strategies we have seen in which the right people and process together have resulted in moving toward a successfully implemented data-governance strategy.

Considerations and Issues

This certainly is not an exhaustive list of all the potential issues with implementing a successful data-governance strategy; we are simply highlighting some of the top issues we've observed. We only briefly note the mitigation efforts to combat these issues; the latter half of this text will go into these in much more detail.

"Hats" versus "roles" and company structure

We previously discussed our intentional use of the terms *hats* versus *roles* and the impact that wearing many hats has on the data governance process. To expand on that idea further, an additional issue that arises with hats versus roles is that responsibility and accountability become unclear. When looking at the different kinds of approaches that different companies take to achieve governance, an underlying need is for actual people to take responsibility for the parts of that process. This is easy when it is clearly someone's *job* to conduct a piece of the process, but when the lines between what is and what is not within a person's purview are blurred, these fuzzy lines often result in inadequate work, miscommunication, and overall mismanagement. It's clear that a successful governance strategy will rely not simply on roles but on tasks, and on who is responsible or accountable for these tasks.

Tribal knowledge and subject matter experts (SMEs)

When talking with customers about their pain points with data governance, one of the things we hear over and over again is that they need tools to help their analysts find which datasets are "good," so that when an analyst is searching for data, they know that *this* dataset is of the best quality and is the most useful one for their use case. The companies state that this would help their analysts save time searching for the "right/best" dataset, as well as assisting them in producing better analytics. Currently, through most companies, the way analysts know which datasets they should work with is by word of mouth, or "tribal knowledge." This is an obvious problem for companies because roles change, people move on, etc. Companies request "crowd-sourcing" functionality, such as allowing analysts to comment on or rank datasets to help give them a "usefulness" score for others to see when searching. This suggestion is not without merit but uncovers the larger problems of *findability* and *quality*. Companies are relying on *people* to know the usefulness of a dataset and to transfer that knowledge on to others, yet this strategy is fallible and difficult (if not impossible) to scale. This is where tools that lessen (or negate) the effort placed on a particular user or users aid in the process. A tool that can detectthe most-used datasets and surface these first in a search, for example, can help minimize the reliance on tribal knowledge and SMEs.

Definition of data

Regardless of their type, *all* companies want to be able to collect data that can be used to drive informed business decisions. They are certain that more data, and the analytics that could be run on that data, could result in key insights—insights that have the potential to skyrocket the success of their business. The problem, however, is that in order for data to be used, it must be *known*. It must be known what the letters or numbers or characters in a column of a table mean. And now it must *also* be known whether those numbers, letters, or characters represent information that is sensitive in nature and thus needs to be treated in a specific way. Data enrichment is key to "knowing" data, yet it is largely a manual process. It generally requires actual people to look at each and every piece of data to determine what it is. As we discussed, this process is cumbersome on its own, and it becomes almost impossible when the extra complexity of disparate data storage systems and different data definitions and catalogs are considered. The "impossible" nature of this work in general means that it just never gets done; this leaves companies scrambling to use a few tools and to implement some half strategies to make up for it—and also hoping that educating people on how data *should* be treated and handled will somehow be enough.

Old access methods

Gone are the days of simple access controls—i.e., these users/roles get access and these users/roles do not. Historically, there were not many users or roles who even had the *need* to view or interact with data, which meant that only a small portion of employees in a company needed to be granted access in the first place. In today's data-driven businesses there is the potential for many, many users who may need to touch data in a variety of ways, as seen in the beginning of this chapter. Each hat has different types of tasks that it may need to do in relation to data that requires varying levels of access and security privilege.

We already discussed the problematic nature of unknown data; another layer to that is the implementation of access controls. There is a synergy between knowing which data even *needs* access restrictions (remember, data must be known in order for it to be governed) and knowing what those restrictions should be for what users. As discussed in Chapter 2, there are varying levels of access control, all the way from access to plain text to access to hashed or aggregated data.

A further complication around access is that of the *intent* of the user accessing data. There may be use cases for which access can and should be granted, and other use cases for which access should strictly be denied. A prime example (and one we've heard from more than one company) is a customer's shipping address. Imagine the customer just bought a new couch, and their address was recorded in order to fulfill shipment of that couch. A user working to fulfill shipping orders should undoubtedly get access to this information. Now let's say that the slipcovers for the couch this customer just bought go on sale, and the company would like to send a marketing flyer to the customer to let them know about this sale. It may be the case that the user in the company who handles shipping data also happens to handle marketing data (remember hats?). If the customer has opted OUT of promotional mail, the user in this example would not be able to send the marketing material *even though* they have access to that data. This means that access controls and policies need to be sensitive enough to account not only for a black-and-white "gets access/doesn't get access" rule for a particular user, but also for what *purpose* the user is using the data.

Regulation compliance

Another struggle that companies have is around compliance with regulations. Some regulations, such as those in financial and healthcare industries, have been around for quite a while, and as we pointed out before, companies who deal with these kinds of data tend to have better governance strategies, for two main reasons: one, they've been dealing with these regulations for some time and have built in processes to address them, and two, these regulations are fairly established and don't change much.

The advent of a proliferation of data collection has brought about new regulations such as GDPR and CCPA that aim to protect *all* of a person's data, not just their most sensitive data (i.e., health or financial data). Companies in all types of industries, not just highly regulated ones, now must comply with these new regulations or face serious financial consequences. This is a difficult endeavor for companies that previously did not have regulations to comply with and thus perhaps did not address this during the setting up of their data infrastructure. As an example, one of the main components of GDPR is the "right to be forgotten," or the ability for a person to request that all their data collected by a company be deleted. If the company does not have its data set up to *find* all the permutations of a person's individual data, it will struggle to be compliant. Thus, it can be seen how findability is important not only from the perspective of finding the right data to analyze but also from the perspective of finding the right data to delete.

Case Study: Gaming of Metrics and Its Effect on Data Governance

Be aware of the human element when you assign regulations and compliance. A relevant case study about how, when introducing metrics, you should factor in the human response to these metrics is in Washington, DC's school system. In 2009, Washington, DC introduced a new ranking system called IMPACT through which teachers were assessed and scored. The system, born out of the intention to promote "good" teachers and generally improve education—and, even further, to allow "low scoring" teachers to be dismissed—actually did not achieve the desired result.

The ranking system was based on an algorithm that took into account standardized test scores of students, with the underlying assumption that test scores for students

---

with "good" teachers should show improvement year after year. However, the ranking system did not include social and familial circumstances, nor did it include any kind of feedback or training from a controlled set.

The result of implementing the system was that teachers were let go based only on the results of the standardized tests, and without regard to feedback from administrators. The immediate reaction was that teachers pivoted to focusing on how to pass the standardized tests rather than on the underlying principles of the subjects. This resulted in high scores and advancement for teachers whose students passed the tests, but it did not, sadly, promote excellence among the students.

In fact, in 2018 a city-commissioned investigation revealed that one in three students graduating in 2017 received a diploma despite missing classes. After being challenged, and after a detailed account of the usage of the algorithm and its usefulness had been carried out, the system was eventually "reconsidered" in 2019.[4]

The process lessons here are that, although the motivation (improving teaching, promoting excellent teachers) should have been easily agreed upon by both teachers' unions and the school district administrators, the implementation was lacking. A proper way to introduce a process is to first have a discussion with the affected people. Take feedback to heart and act on it. Run the process for the first time as a trial, with transparent results, open discussion, and a willingness to pivot if it isn't working as intended.

Processes and Strategies with Varying Success

The issues with people and process are many, and we have observed some strategies that have been implemented with varying degrees of success. While we will explore some of these strategies here, the latter part of this book dives deeper into how these strategies (and others) can be implemented to achieve greater data governance success.

Data segregation within storage systems

We've reviewed some of the issues that arise from having multiple data-storage systems; however, some companies use multiple storage systems and even different storage "areas" within the same storage system in an advantageous and systematic way. Their process is to separate curated/known data from uncurated/unknown data. They may do this in a variety of ways, but we have heard two common, prevailing strategies.

---

4 Perry Stein, "Chancellor Pledges to Review D.C.'s Controversial Teacher Evaluation System" (*https://oreil.ly/dsHK3*), *Washington Post*, October 20, 2019.

The first strategy is to keep all uncurated data in an on-prem storage system and to push curated data that can be used for analytics to the cloud. The benefit that companies see in this strategy is that the "blast radius," or the potential for data to be leaked either by mistake or by a bad actor, is greatly diminished if only known, clean, and curated data is moved into a public cloud. To be clear, companies often indicate that it is not their total distrust of cloud security that is the problem (although that can play a role as well); it is their concern that *their own employees* may unwittingly leak data if it's in a public cloud versus an on-prem environment.

Figure 3-4 shows an example of data stored on-premises and in the cloud. As you can see, even though both storage systems have structured datasets, only the cloud dataset has been enriched with metadata and thus has been treated with the appropriate governance controls (hashing in this case). The on-premises dataset, while it has the same information, hasn't been curated or enriched; we don't know just by looking at it that the numbers in the first column are credit card numbers or that the words in the second column are customer names. Once these columns have been curated and the appropriate metadata (credit card number, customer name, etc.) has been attached, we can attach governance controls, so that even if the data gets leaked, it will be the protected version and not plain text.

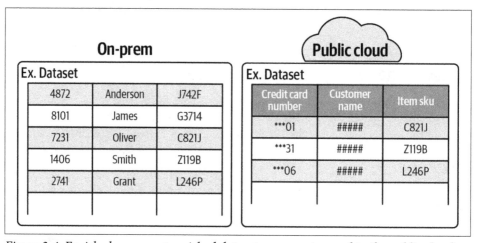

Figure 3-4. Enriched versus not enriched datasets on-premises and in the public cloud

As we've stated, an obvious benefit of this strategy is that if sensitive data resides only on-premises, then if it's leaked or incorrectly accessed, that could only have been done by someone within the company. On the other hand, if that same sensitive data is in a public cloud, it could potentially have been accessed by anyone if leaked or hacked into.

There are a few drawbacks to this strategy, however. One is that when data is segregated this way—some residing on premise and some residing in the cloud—cross-storage analytics are difficult if not impossible to complete. Since one of the main drivers of collecting so much data is being able to run powerful analytics, hindering this seems counterproductive. The other drawback is that segregation also requires upkeep of and attendance to these multiple storage systems and data pipelines, not to mention the creation, maintenance, and enforcement of additional access controls, all of which are difficult to properly manage and stay on top of over time.

The second strategy is similar to the first in that there is a separation between curated and uncurated data, but this is done within the same cloud environment. Companies will create different layers or zones (as can be seen in Table 3-2) within their cloud environment and base access on these; the bottom, uncurated zone may be accessed by only a few users, while the uppermost zone, curated and cleaned (of sensitive data), may be accessed by any user.

Table 3-2. A "data lake" within cloud storage with multiple tiers showing what kind of data resides in each and who has access

	Types of data	Access
Insights zone	Known, enriched, curated, and cleaned data. Data also has likely had governance controls such as encryption, hashing, redaction, etc. *Example: Well-labeled, structured datasets.*	Highest level of access. Most if not all data analysts/scientists and others in a user role.
Staging zone	More known and structured data. Data from multiple sources is likely to be joined here. This is also where data engineers prep data, cleanse it, and get it ready to drop into the insights zone.	More access. Mostly data engineers—those in charge of putting together datasets for analytics.
Raw zone	Any kind of data. Unstructured and uncurated. Could also include things such as videos, text files, etc. *Example: Video files, unstructured datasets*	Very restricted access. Likely a handful of people or just an admin.

Clearly the benefits and drawbacks of this strategy are nearly a reverse of those of the previous strategy. In this strategy, management and upkeep of the storage system, data pipelines, and policies are limited to one system, which makes it far simpler and more streamlined to stay on top of. Analytics are also largely easier to run because they can all be run within one central storage system, as opposed to trying to run them across multiple systems, or dealing with the constant moving of data from one storage system to another for the purposes of analysis.

As we've noted, all data residing within a public cloud does carry the potential drawback of data leaking (whether intentionally or unintentionally) out onto the public internet—a cause for trepidation to be sure.

Data segregation and ownership by line of business

As we've mentioned more than a few times, data enrichment is a key challenge in successful data governance for many reasons, the primary ones being level of effort and lack of accountability/ownership.

One way we've observed companies handle this issue is by segregating their data by line of business. In this strategy, each line of business has dedicated people to do the work of governance on just that data. While this is often not actually delineated by role, each line of business has a deep knowledge of the kind of business it has and handles the ingress and egress of data (pipelines), data enrichment, enforcement/management of access controls and governance policies, and data analysis. Depending on the company size and/or complexities of data within each line of business, these tasks may be handled by just one person, a handful of people, or a large team.

There are several reasons this process tends to be quite successful. The first is that the amount of data any given "team" must wrap its arms around is smaller. Instead of having to look at and manage a company's *entire* data story, the team needs to understand and work on only a portion of it. Not only does this result in less work, but it also allows for deeper knowledge of that data. Deeper knowledge of data has a multitude of advantages, a few being quicker data enrichment and the ability to run quicker, more robust analytics.

The second reason this process is successful is that there is clear, identifiable ownership and accountability for data: there is a specific person (or persons) to go to when something goes wrong or when something needs to change (such as the addition of a new data source or the implementation of a new compliance policy). When there is no clear accountability and responsibility for data, it's easy for that data to be lost or forgotten or worse—mismanaged.

In Figure 3-5, we've tried to show an example flow of different lines of business into a central repository. As you can see, retail store sales, marketing, online sales, and HR not only all feed into the central enterprise data repository in this example, but they are also *fed by* this repository.

To give you an idea of the different key hats and their tasks in each line of business, let's take marketing as an example. In this line of business in our example, we have the hats of data owner, data steward, and business analyst.

The data owner sets up and manages the pipelines in this line of business, along with managing requests for new pipelines and ingestion sources. They also perform the tasks of monitoring, troubleshooting, and fixing any data quality issues that arise, as well as implementing any of the technical aspects of the company's governance policies and strategies.

The data steward is the *subject matter expert* (SME) in this line of business; knowing what data resides here, what it means, how it should be categorized/classed, and what data is sensitive and what isn't. They also serve as the point of contact between their line of business and the central governing body at their company for staying up to date on compliance and regulations, and they're responsible for ensuring that the data in their line of business is in compliance.

Finally, the business analyst is the expert on the business implications for the data in this line of business. They're also responsible for knowing how their data fits into the broader enterprise, and for communicating which data from their line of business should be used in enterprise analytics. In addition, they need to know what additional/new data will need to be collected for this particular line of business to help answer whatever the current or future business questions are.

From this example you can see how each hat has their role and tasks for just this one line of business, and how a breakdown of any of those tasks can result in a less than efficient flow/implementation of a governance program.

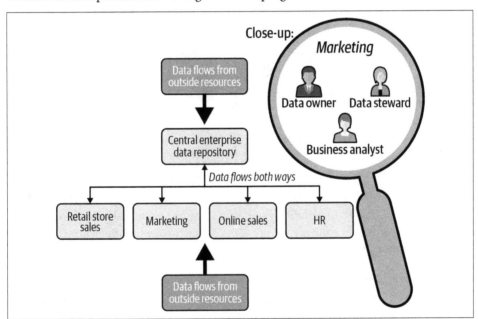

Figure 3-5. Flowchart of an enterprise with four lines of business and their data ingress/ egress, as well as a close-up of one line of business, its key hats

This process, while successful, does come with some pitfalls, however. The primary one is that segregating data by line of business encourages the siloing of data and can, depending on how it's set up, inhibit cross-company analytics.

We recently worked with a large retail company that was dealing with this exact issue.

This large US retailer (with over 350,000 employees), in an effort to better deal with the tremendous amount of data it collects, divided up its data by several lines of business. These included air shipping, ground shipping, retail store sales, and marketing. Having the data separated in this way greatly enabled the company to devote specific data analytics teams to each line of business, whereby it could more quickly enrich its data, allowing it to apply governance policies to aid with CCPA compliance. This strategy, however, created issues when the company began to want to run analytics *across* its different lines of business. To separate its data, the company created infrastructure and storage solutions with data pipelines that fed directly (and only) into one or another line of business. We won't go into too much depth on data pipelines here, but in short, it is a common practice to have data "land" in only one storage solution, because duplicating data and transferring it to additional storage areas is costly and difficult to maintain. Because specific data resided only in one storage area/silo, the company could not run analytics across its lines of business to see what patterns might emerge between, for example, air shipping and retail store sales (Figure 3-6).

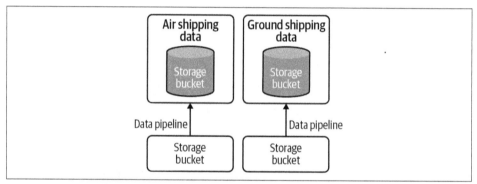

Figure 3-6. The preceding example company's two data silos: air shipping and ground shipping. Each silo has its own data pipeline and stores this data within its own bucket, meaning analytics can be run only within silos unless data from that pipeline is duplicated and piped into another silo.

This process of segregation by line of business to aid with accountability and responsibility is not a bad strategy, and while it's obvious there are pitfalls, there are also ways to make it more successful, which we will cover later in the book.

Creation of "views" of datasets

A classic strategy employed by many companies is to create different "views" of datasets. As seen in Table 3-3, these views are really just different versions of the same dataset and/or table that have sensitive information sanitized or removed.

Table 3-3. Three potentially different types of "views" of data: one plain text, one with sensitive data hashed, and another with sensitive data redacted

Plain text customer name	Hashed customer name	Redacted customer name
Anderson, Dan	Anderson, #####	********
Buchanan, Cynthia	Buchanan, #####	********
Drexel, Frieda	Drexel, #####	********
Harris, Javiar	Harris, #####	********

This strategy is classic (and works) because it allows analytics to easily be run, worry free, by virtually anyone on the "clean" view (the one with sensitive data either hashed or removed). It takes away the risk of access to and usage of sensitive data.

While this strategy works, it is problematic in the long run for several reasons. The first is that it takes quite a bit of effort and manpower to create these views. The clean view has to be manually created by someone who *does* have access to all of the data. They must go in and identify any and all columns, rows, or cells that contain sensitive data and decide how they should be treated: hashed, aggregated, completely removed, etc. They then must create an entirely *new* dataset/table with these treatments in place and make it available to be used for analytics.

The second issue is that new views constantly need to be created as fresher data comes in. This results not only in much time and effort being put into creating "fresh" views but also in a proliferation of datasets/tables that are difficult to manage. Once all these views are created (and re-created), it's hard to know which is the most fresh and should be used. Past datasets/tables often can't be immediately deprecated, as there may be a need down the line for that specific data.

While views have some success and merit in aiding in access controls, we will propose and discuss some strategies we have seen that not only are easier to manage but scale better as a company collects more and more data.

A culture of privacy and security

The final process we'd like to discuss is that of creating a culture of privacy and security. While certainly every company and employee should respect data privacy and security, the ways in which this strategy is thought through and implemented are truly a special ingredient in creating not just a good data governance strategy but a successful one.

We have dedicated an entire chapter to the strategy of building a successful data culture (see Chapter 9), so more on that is to come; however, as a short introduction to the concept, we will note that we have seen companies driven to really look at their data culture and work to implement a new (successful) one because of one (or all) of the following occurring within their organization:

- Their governance/data management tools are not working sufficiently (meaning the tools do not in and of themselves provide all of the governance "functionality" desired by a company).

- People are accessing data they should not be accessing and/or using data in ways that are not appropriate (whether intentionally or not).

- People are not following processes and procedures put into place (again, whether intentionally or not).

- The company knows that governance standards/data compliance are not being met and don't know what else to do, but they hope that educating people on doing the "right thing" will help.

To be sure, throughout this text we have already covered in great detail governance tools, the people involved, and the processes that are/can be followed. This is where the importance of putting all the pieces together can be seen—i.e., tools, people, and process. One or even two pieces are insufficient to achieve a *successful* governance strategy.

As evidenced by the four reasons we've just listed even though a few tools, some people, and several processes are in place, some gaps may still remain.

This is where it must all come together—in a collective *data culture* that encompasses and embodies how the company thinks about and will execute its their governance strategy. That encompasses what tools it will use, what people it will need, and the exact processes that will bring it all together.

Summary

In this chapter, we have reviewed multiple unique considerations regarding the people and process of data governance for different kinds of companies. We've also covered some issues commonly faced by companies, as well as some strategies we've seen implemented with varying success.

From our discussion it should be clear that data governance is not simply an implementation of tools but that the overall process and consideration of the people involved—while it may vary slightly from company to company or industry to industry—is important and necessary for a successful data governance program.

The process for how to think about data, how it should be handled and classified from the beginning, how it continually needs to be (re)classified and (re)categorized, and who will do this work and be responsible for it—*coupled* with the tools that enable these tasks to be done efficiently and effectively—is key, if not mandatory, for successful data governance.

CHAPTER 4

Data Governance over a Data Life Cycle

In previous chapters, we introduced governance, what it means, and the tools and processes that make governance a reality, as well as the people and process aspects of governance. This chapter will bring together those concepts and provide a data life cycle approach to operationalize governance within your organization.

You will learn about a data life cycle, the different phases of a data life cycle, data life cycle management, applying data governance over a data life cycle, crafting a data governance policy, best practices along each life cycle phase, applicable examples, and considerations for implementing governance. For some, this chapter will validate what you already know; for others, it will help you ponder, plant seeds, and consider how these learnings can be applied within your organization. This chapter will introduce and address a lot of concepts that will help you get started on the journey to making governance a reality. Before getting into the detailed aspects of governance, it's important to center our understanding on data life cycle management and what it means for governance.

What Is a Data Life Cycle?

Defining what a data life cycle is should be easy—but in reality, it's quite complex. If you look up the definition of a data life cycle and its phases, you quickly realize that it varies from one author to another, and from one organization to another. There's honestly not one right way to think about the different stages a piece of data goes through; however, we can all agree that each phase that is defined has certain characteristics that are important in distinguishing it from the other phases. And because of these different characteristics within each phase, the way to think about governance will also vary as each piece of data moves through the data life cycle. In this chapter, we will define a data life cycle as the order of stages a piece of data goes through from its initial generation or capture to its eventual archival or deletion at the end of its useful life.

It's important to quickly point out that this definition tries to capture the essence of what happens to a piece of data; however, not all data goes through each phase, and these phases are simply logical dependencies and not actual data flows.

Organizations work with *transactional data* as well as with *analytical data*. In this chapter, we will primarily focus on the analytics data life cycle, from the point when data is ingested into a platform all the way to when it is analyzed, visualized, purged, and archived.

Transactional systems are databases that are optimized to run day-to-day transactional operations. These are fully optimized systems that allow for a high number of concurrent users and transaction types. Even though these systems generate data, most are not optimized to run analytics processes. On the other hand, *analytical systems* are optimized to run analytical processes. These databases store historical data from various sources, including CRM, IOT sensors, logs, transactional data (sales, inventory), and many more. These systems allow data analysts, business analysts, and even executives to run queries and reports against the data stored in the analytic database.

As you can quickly see, transactional data and analytical data can have completely different data life cycles depending on what an organization chooses to do. That said, for many organizations, transactional data is usually moved to an analytics system for analysis and will therefore undergo the phases of a data life cycle that we will outline in the following section.

Proper oversight of data throughout its life cycle is essential for optimizing its usefulness and minimizing the potential for errors. Data governance is at the core of making data work for businesses. Defining this process end-to-end across the data life cycle is needed to operationalize data governance and make it a reality. And because each phase has distinct governance needs, this ultimately helps the mission of data governance.

Phases of a Data Life Cycle

As mentioned earlier, you will see a data life cycle represented in many different ways, and there's no right or wrong answer. Whichever framework you choose to use for your organization has to be the one guiding the processes and procedures you put in place. Each phase of the data life cycle as shown in Figure 4-1 has distinct characteristics. In this section, we will go through each phase of the life cycle as we define it, delve into what each phase means, and walk through the implications for each phase as you think about governance.

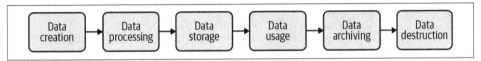

Figure 4-1. Phases of a data life cycle

Data Creation

The first phase of the data life cycle is the creation or capture of data. Data is generated from multiple sources, in different formats such as structured or unstructured data, and in different frequencies (batch or stream). Customers can choose to use existing data connectors, build ETL pipelines, and/or leverage third-party ingestion tools to load data into a data platform or storage system. Metadata—data about data—can also be created and captured in this phase. You will notice *data creation* and *data capture* used interchangeably, mostly because of the source of data. When new data is created, that is referred to as data creation, and when existing data is funneled into a system, it is referred to as data capture.

In Chapter 1, we mentioned that the rate at which data is generated is growing exponentially, with IDC predicting that worldwide data will grow to 175 zettabytes by 2025.[1] This is enormous! Data is typically created in one of these three ways:

Data acquisition
> When an organization acquires data that has been produced by a third-party organization

Data entry
> When new data is manually entered by humans or devices within the organization

Data capture
> When data generated by various devices in an organization, such as IOT sensors, is captured

It's important to mention that each of these ways of generating data offers significant data governance challenges. For example, what are the different checks and balances for data acquired from outside your organization? There are probably contracts and agreements that outline how the enterprise is allowed to use this data and for what purposes. There might also be limitations as to who can access that specific data. All these offer considerations and implications for governance. Later in the chapter, we will look at how to think about governance during this phase, and we will call out the different tools you should think about when designing your governance strategy.

---

1 Andy Patrizio, "IDC: Expect 175 Zettabytes of Data Worldwide by 2025" (*https://oreil.ly/Ug56j*), *Network World*, December 3, 2018.

Data Processing

Once data has been captured, it is then processed, without yet deriving any value from it for the enterprise. This is done prior to its use. *Data processing* is also referred to as *data maintenance*, and this is when data goes through processes such as *integration, cleaning, scrubbing,* or *extract-transform-load* (ETL) to get it ready for storage and eventual analysis.

In this phase, some of the governance implications that you will come across are data lineage, data quality, and data classification. All these have been discussed in much more detail in Chapter 2. To make governance a reality, how do you make sure that as data is being processed, its lineage is tracked and maintained? In addition, checking data quality is very important to make sure you're not missing any important values before storing this data. You should also think about data classification. How are you dealing with sensitive information? What is it? How are you ensuring management of and access to this data so it doesn't get into the wrong hands? Finally, as this data is moving, it needs to be encrypted in transit and then later at rest. There are a lot of governance considerations during this phase. We will delve into these concepts later in the chapter.

Data Storage

The third phase in the data life cycle is *data storage*, where both data and metadata are stored on storage systems and devices with the appropriate levels of protection. Because we're focusing on the analytics data life cycle, a storage system could be a data warehouse, a data mart, or a data lake. Data should be encrypted at rest to protect it from intrusions and attacks. In addition, data needs to be backed up to ensure redundancy in the event of a data loss, accidental deletion, or disaster.

Data Usage

The *data usage* phase is important to understanding how data is consumed within an organization to support the organization's objectives and operations. In this phase, data becomes truly useful and empowers the organization to make informed business decisions when it can be viewed, analyzed, and/or visualized for insights. In this phase, users get to ask all types of questions of the data, via a user interface or business intelligence tools, with the hope of getting "good" answers. This is where the rubber meets the road, especially when confirming whether the governance processes already instituted in previous phases truly work. If data quality is not implemented correctly, the types of answers you receive will be incorrect or might not make too much sense, and this could potentially jeopardize your business operations.

In this phase, data itself may be the product or service that the organization offers. If data is indeed the product, then different governance policies need to be enacted to ensure proper handling of this data.

Because data is consumed by multiple internal and external stakeholders and processes during this phase, proper access management and audits are key. In addition, there might be regulatory or contractual constraints on how data may actually be used, and part of the role of data governance is to ensure that these constraints are observed accordingly.

Data Archiving

In the *data archiving* phase, data is removed from all active production environments and copied to another environment. It is no longer processed, used, or published, but is stored in case it is needed again in an active production environment. Because the volume of data generated is growing, it's inevitable that the volume of archived data grows. In this phase, no maintenance or general usage occurs. A data governance plan should guide the retention of this data and define the length of time it will be stored, including the different controls that will be applied to this data.

Data Destruction

In this final phase, data is destroyed. *Data destruction*, or *purging*, refers to the removal of every copy of data from an organization, typically done from an archive storage location. Even if you wanted to save all your data forever, it's just not feasible. It's very expensive to store data that is not in use, and compliance issues create the need to get rid of data you no longer need. The primary challenge of this phase is ensuring that all the data is properly destroyed and at the right time.

Before destroying any data, it is critical to confirm whether there are any policies in place that would require you to retain the data for a certain period of time. Coming up with the right timeline for this cycle means understanding state and federal regulations, industry standards, and governance policies to ensure that the right steps are taken. You will also need to prove that the purge has been done properly, which ensures that data doesn't consume more resources than necessary at the end of its useful life.

You should now have a solid understanding about the different phases of a data life cycle and what some of the governance implications are. As stated previously, these phases are logical dependencies and not necessarily actual data flows. Some pieces of data might go back and forth between different processing systems before being stored. And some that are stored in a data lake might skip processing altogether and get stored first, and then get processed later. Data does not need to pass through all the phases.

We're sure you've heard the phrase "Rome was not built in a day," but that's really what this data life cycle is trying to do. Applying data governance in an organization is a daunting task and can be very overwhelming. However, if you think about your data within these logical data life cycle phases, implementing governance can be a task that can be broken down into each phase and then thought through and implemented accordingly.

Data Life Cycle Management

Now that you understand the data life cycle, another common term you will run into is *data life cycle management* (DLM). What's interesting is that many authors will refer to data life cycle and data life cycle management interchangeably. Even though there might be a need or desire to bundle them together, it's important to realize that a data life cycle can exist without data life cycle management. DLM, therefore, refers to a comprehensive policy-based approach to manage the flow of data throughout its life cycle, from creation to the time when it becomes obsolete and is purged. When an organization is able to define and organize the life cycle processes and practices into repeatable steps for the company, this refers to DLM. As you start learning about DLM, you will quickly run into a *data management plan*. So let's quickly look at what that means and what it entails.

Data Management Plan

A data management plan (DMP) defines how data will be managed, described, and stored. In addition, it defines standards you will use and how data will be handled and protected throughout its life cycle. You will primarily see data management plans required to drive research projects within institutions, but the concepts of the process are fundamental to implementing governance. Because of this, it's worth us doing a deep dive into them and seeing how these could be applied to implement governance within an organization.

With governance, you will quickly realize that there is no a lack of templates and frameworks—see, for example, the DMPTool from Massachusetts Institute of Technology (*https://oreil.ly/-_Xoc*). You simply need to pick a plan or framework that works for your project and organization and march ahead; there's not one right or wrong way to do it. If you choose to use a data management plan, here is some quick guidance to get you started. The concepts here are much more fundamental than the template or framework, so if you were able to capture these in a document, then you'd be ahead of the curve.

Guidance 1: Identify the data to be captured or collected

Data volume is important to helping you determine infrastructure costs and people time. You need to know how much data you're expecting and the types of data you will be collecting:

Types
> Outline the various types of data you will be collecting. Are they structured or unstructured? This will help determine the right infrastructure to use.

Sources
> Where is the data coming from? Are there restrictions on how this data can be used or manipulated? What are those rules? All of these need to be documented.

Volume
> This can be a little difficult to predict, especially with the exponential growth in data; however, planning for that increase early on and projecting what it could be would set you apart and help you be prepared for the future.

Guidance 2: Define how the data will be organized

Now that you know the type, sources, and volume of data you're collecting, you need to determine how that data will be managed. What tools do you need across the data life cycle? Do you need a data warehouse? Which type, and from which vendor? Or do you need a data lake? Or do you need both? Understanding these implications and what each means will allow you to better define what your governance policies should be. There are many regulations that govern how data can and cannot be used, and understanding them is vital.

Guidance 3: Document a data storage and preservation strategy

Disasters happen, and ensuring that you've adequately prepared for one is very important. How long will a piece of data be accessible, and by whom? How will the data be stored and protected over its life? As we mentioned previously, data purging needs to happen according to the rules set forth. In addition, understanding what your systems' backup and retention policies are, is important.

Guidance 4: Define data policies

It's important to document how data will be managed and shared. Identify the licensing and sharing agreements that pertain to the data you're collecting. Are there restrictions that the organization should adhere to? What are the legal and ethical restrictions on access to and use of sensitive data, for example? Regulations like GDPR and CCPA can easily get confusing and can even become contradictory. In this step, ensure that all the applicable data policies are captured accordingly. This also helps in case you're audited.

Guidance 5: Define roles and responsibilities

Chapter 3 defined roles and responsibilities. With those roles in mind, determine which are the right ones for your organization and what each one means for you. Which teams will be responsible for metadata management and data discovery? Who will ensure governance policies are followed all the way? And there are many more roles that you can define.

A DMP should provide your organization with an easy-to-follow roadmap that will guide others and explain how data will be treated throughout its life cycle. Think of this as a living document that evolves with your organization as new datasets are captured, and as new laws and regulations are enacted.

If this was a data management plan for a research project, it would have included a lot more steps and items for consideration. Those plans tend to be more robust because they guide the entire research project and data end-to-end. We will cover a lot more concepts later in the chapter, so we chose to select items that were easily transferable to creating a governance policy and plan for your organization.

Applying Governance over the Data Life Cycle

We've gone through fundamental concepts thus far; now let's bring everything together and look at how you can apply governance over the data life cycle. Governance needs to bring together people, processes, and technology to govern data throughout its life cycle. In Chapter 2, we outlined a robust set of tools to make governance a reality, and Chapter 3 focused on the people and process side of things. It's important to point out that implementing governance is complicated; there's no easy way to simply apply everything and consider he job done. Most technologies need to be stitched together, and as you can imagine, they're all coming from different vendors with different implementations. You would need to integrate the best-in-class suite of products and services to make things work. Another option is to purchase a fully integrated data platform or governance platform. This is not a trivial task.

Data Governance Framework

Frameworks help you visualize the plan, and there are several frameworks that can help you think about governance across the data life cycle. Figure 4-2 is one such framework in which we highlight all the concepts from Chapter 2, overlaid with the concepts we've discussed in this chapter.

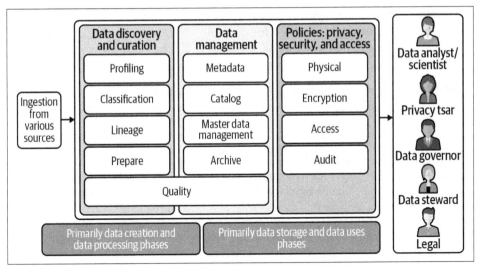

Figure 4-2. Governance over a data life cycle

This framework oversimplifies things to make them easier to understand; it assumes things are linear, from left to right, which is usually not the case. When data is ingested from various sources on the left, this is simply at the point of data creation or capture. That data is then processed and stored, and then it is consumed by the different stakeholders, including data analysts, data engineers, data stewards, and so on.

Data archiving and data destruction are not reflected in this framework because those take place beyond the point when data is used. As we previously outlined, during archiving, data is removed from all active production environments. It is no longer processed, used, or published but is stored in case it is needed again in the future. Destruction is when data comes to the end of its life and is removed according to guidelines and procedures that have been set forth.

One discrepancy that you will quickly notice is that metadata management should be considered from the point of data creation—where enterprises need to discover and curate the data as it's ingested (especially for sensitive data)—to when data is stored and discovered in the applicable storage system. Archiving, even though mentioned within data management, tends to happen when the data's usefulness is done and it is removed from production environments. Though archiving is an important part of governance, this diagram implies that it is taking place in the middle of the data life cycle. That said, it's also possible to have an archiving strategy when data is simply stored in the applicable storage systems, so we cannot completely rule this out.

We want to reiterate that Figure 4-2 provides a logical representation of the phases a piece of data goes through, from left to right, and not necessarily the actual step-by-step flow of the data. There's a lot of back and forth that happens between each phase, and not all pieces of data go through each one of these phases.

Frameworks are good at providing a holistic view of things. However, they are not the be-all, end-all. Make sure whichever framework you select works for your organization and your data.

 We've mentioned it already, but would like to emphasize again the idea of selecting a framework that work for your organization. This can include considerations around the kind of data you collect or work with, as well as what kind of personnel you have dedicated to your data governance efforts. One thing we challenge you to consider is how to take what you have and fit enough framework around it. Take these ideas as laid out (noting that not each step is required or even necessary) and layer on what you have to work with currently as a place to start. More pieces (and people, for that matter) can be added later, but if you focus on at least laying the groundwork—the foundation—you will be in a much better position if or when you *do* have more pieces to add to your framework.

Data Governance in Practice

OpenStreetMap (OSM) (*https://www.openstreetmap.org*) was created by Steve Coast in the UK in 2004 and was inspired by the success of Wikipedia. It is open source, which means it is created by people like you and is free to use under an open license. It was a response to the proliferation of siloed, proprietary international geographical data sources and dozens of mapping software products that didn't talk to each other. OSM has grown significantly to over two million contributors, and what's amazing is that it works. In fact, it works well enough to be the trusted source of data for a number of Fortune 500 companies, including other small and medium-sized businesses. With so many contributors, OSM is successful because it was able to establish data standards early in the process and ensured contributors adhered to them. As you can imagine, a crowdsourced mapping system without a way to standardize contributor data could go wrong very quickly. Defining governance standards can bring value to your organization and provide trusted data for your users.

And now that you have an understanding of the data life cycle with an overlay of the different governance tools, let's delve further into how the different data governance tools we outlined in Chapters 1 and 2 can be applied and used across this life cycle. This section also includes best practices, which can help you start to define your organization's data standards.

Data creation

As previously mentioned, this is the initial phase of the data life cycle, where data is created or captured. During this phase, an organization can choose to capture both the metadata, and the lineage of the data. Metadata describes the data, while the lineage describes the *where* of the data and how it will flow and be transformed and used downstream. Trying to capture these during this initial phase sets you up well for the later phases.

In addition, processes such as classification and profiling can be employed, especially if you're dealing with sensitive data assets. Data should also be encrypted in transit to offer protection from intrusions and attacks. Cloud service providers such as Google Cloud offer encryption in transit and at rest by default.

Define the Type of Data

Establish a set of guidelines for categorizing data that takes into account the sensitivity of the information as well its criticality and value to the organization. Profiling and classifying data helps inform which governance policies and procedures apply to the data.

Data processing

During this phase, data goes through processes such as integration, cleaning, scrubbing, or extract-transform-load (ETL) prior to its use, to get it ready for storage and eventual analysis. It's important that the integrity of the data is preserved during this phase; that is why data quality plays a critical role.

Lineage needs to be captured and tracked here also, to ensure that the end users understand which processes led to which transformation and where the data originated from. We heard this from one user: "It would be nice to have a better understanding of the lineage of data. When finding where a certain column in a table comes from, I need to manually dig through the source code of that table and follow that trail (if I have access). Automate this process." This is a common pain point felt by many, and one in which DLM and governance are critical.

Document Data Quality Expectations

Different data consumers may have different data quality requirements, so it's important to provide a means to document data quality expectations while the data is being captured and processed, as well as techniques and tools for supporting the data's validation and monitoring as it goes through the data life cycle. The right processes for data quality management will provide measurable and trustworthy data for analysis.

Data storage

In this phase, both data and metadata are stored and made ready for analysis. Data should be encrypted at rest to protect it from intrusions and attacks. In addition, data needs to be backed up to ensure redundancy.

Automated Data Protection and Recovery

Because data is stored in storage devices in this phase, find solutions and products that provide automated data protection to ensure that exposed data cannot be read, including encryption at rest, encryption in transit, data masking, and permanent deletion. In addition, implement a robust recovery plan to protect your business when a disaster strikes.

Data usage

In this phase, data is analyzed and consumed for insights and consumed by multiple internal and external stakeholders and processes in the organization. In addition, analyzed data is visualized and used to support the organization's objectives and operations; business intelligence tools play a critical role in this phase.

A data catalog is vital to helping users discover data assets using captured metadata. Privacy, access management, and auditing are paramount at this stage, which ensures that the right people and systems are accessing and sharing the data for analysis. Furthermore, there might be regulatory or contractual constraints on how data may actually be used, and part of the role of data governance is to ensure that these constraints are observed.

Data Access Management

It is important to provide data services that allow data consumers to access their data with ease. Documenting what and how the data will be used, and for what purposes, can help you define identities, groups, and roles and assign access rights to establish a level of managed access. This ensures that only authorized and authenticated individuals and systems are able to access data assets according to defined rules.

Data archiving

In this phase, data is removed from all active production environments. It is no longer processed, used, or published but is stored in case it is needed again in the future. Data classification should guide the retention and disposal method of data.

Automated Data Protection Plan

Beyond being a way to prevent unauthorized individuals from accessing data, perimeter security is not and never has been sufficient for protecting data. The same protections applied in data storage would apply here as well to ensure that exposed data cannot be read, including encryption at rest, data masking, and permanent deletion. In addition, in case of a disaster, or in the event that archive data is needed again in a production environment, it's important to have a well-defined process to revive this data and make it useful.

Data destruction

Finally, data is destroyed, or rather, it is removed from the enterprise at the end of its useful life. Before purging any data, it is critical to confirm whether there are any policies in place that would require you to retain the data for a certain period of time. Data classification should guide the retention and disposal method of data.

Create a Compliance Policy

Coming up with the right timeline for this cycle means understanding state and federal regulations, industry standards, and governance policies and staying up to date on any changes. Doing so helps to ensure that the right steps are taken and that the purge has been done properly. It also ensures that data doesn't consume more resources than necessary at the end of its useful life.

IT stakeholders are urged to revisit the guidelines for destroying data every 12–18 months to ensure compliance, since rules change often.

Example of How Data Moves Through a Data Platform

Here's an example scenario of how data could move through a data platform with the framework in Figure 4-2.

Scenario

Let's say that a business wants to ingest data onto a cloud-data platform, like Google Cloud, AWS, or Azure, and share it with data analysts. This data may include sensitive elements such as US social security numbers, phone numbers, and email addresses. Here are the different pieces it might go through:

1. Business configures an ingestion data pipeline using a batch or streaming service:

    a. Goal: As they move raw data into the platform, it will need to be scanned, classified, and tagged before it can be processed, manipulated, and stored.

    b. Staged ingestion buckets:

        i. Ingest: heavily restricted

        ii. Released: processed data

        iii. Admin quarantine: needs review

2. Data is then scanned and classified for sensitive information such as PII.

3. Some data may be redacted, obfuscated, or anonymized/de-identified. This process may generate new metadata, such as what keys were used for tokenization. This metadata would be captured at this stage.

4. Data is tagged with PII tags/labels.

5. Aspects of data quality can be accessed—that is, are there any missing values, are primary keys in the right format, etc.

6. Start to capture data provenance information for lineage.

7. As data moves between the different services along the life cycle, it is encrypted in transit.

8. Once ingestion and processing are complete, the data will need to be stored in a data warehouse and/or a data lake, where it is encrypted at rest. Backup and recovery processes need to be employed as well, in case of a disaster.

9. While in storage, additional business and technical metadata can be added to the data and cataloged, and users need to be able to discover and find the data.

10. Audit trails need to be captured throughout this data life cycle and made visible as needed. Audits allow you to check the effectiveness of controls in order to quickly mitigate threats and evaluate overall security health.

11. Throughout this process, it is important to ensure that the right people and services have access and permissions to the right data across the data platform using a robust identity and access management (IAM) solution.

12. You need to be able to run analytics and visualize the results for use. In addition to access management, additional privacy, de-identification, and anonymization tools may be employed.

13. Once this data is no longer needed in a production environment, it is archived for a determined period of time to maintain compliance.

14. At the end of its useful life, it is completely removed from the data platform and destroyed.

Case Study: Nike and the 4% Improving Running Shoes

In 2018, Nike launched a new running shoe, and the related advertising campaign claimed that the "Nike Zoom Vaporfly 4%" will make you run 4% faster. While a 4% speed increase does not sound like a lot, over a marathon run that averages to 4–5 hours, this can potentially lead to 10–12 minutes' improvement in the time it takes to finish the race.

The claims were significant and were met with skepticism. A Nike-sponsored study did not help because it was based, by necessity, on a small dataset. Many athletes would pay for an expensive shoe to improve their result by that margin, if the claim were true, but the source of this information (the vendor) sowed doubt. Running an independent scientific experiment to conclude whether or not the claim was true would have been challenging, as this would have required significant investment, and getting the runner(s) to use different kinds of shoes over the same courses in the same conditions to truly eliminate all possible variables and challenges.

Happily, many athletes use a popular record-keeping app called Strava. Strava makes the data publicly available, and many athletes also record the shoes they use when running (Figure 4-3). This created a natural experiment in which you could look over existing data and, with enough data, could potentially tease out patterns.

26.62mi	2:57:01	6:39/mi	94
Distance	Elapsed Time	Pace	Relative Effort

Elevation	909ft	Calories	2,747
Moving Time	2:57:01		

| Garmin Forerunner 735XT | | Shoes: Nike VaporFly 4% (139.0 mi) | |

Figure 4-3. Strava data. Does the Nike Vaporfly make you run 4% faster?

The *New York Times* investigated, collecting half a million real-life performance records from Strava.Keven Quealy and Josh Katz, "Nike Says Its $250 Running Shoes Will Make You Run Much Faster. What If That's Actually True?" (*https://oreil.ly/ox6Vp*) *New York Times*, July 18, 2018. The next step was to determine whether or not the data was useful. While the ideal way would have been to measure runs of identical runners on the same course with different shoes, this was not possible at this scale.

However, the large amount of data did enable the finding of *natural experiments*.[2] This was not a small-scale lab experiment, but an actual account of (admittedly amateur, for the most part) weekend runners reporting and sharing their race results.

The *New York Times* was able to compile 280,000 marathon and 215,000 half marathon results, and then compared running conditions (same races) and concurrent results from the same athletes (different shoes, different races or dates). These comparisons ensured that conditions similar to the ideal experiment were met, and by including knowledge about the races themselves (weather, course layout and difficulty), the data was curated to keep the quality records in while eliminating outliers (less-frequented races, extreme conditions).

The *New York Times* was able to conclude that the Nike shoes were very often part of a more successful run for many runners. The paper pointed out that these results were not gathered through a lab experiment in controlled conditions, but their results were consistent with the Nike-funded study.

This effort would not have been possible without the availability of an open dataset, contributed to freely by runners globally, and preserved and made accessible to researchers. This example of a dataset in which data is made available under a controlled environment (Strava does protect runners' personal data and allows runners full control over how their data is shared, including the ability to opt out and delete their own data) is an excellent example of proper information cycle and data governance.

Operationalizing Data Governance

It's one thing to have a plan, but it's something else to ensure that plan works for your organization. NASA learned things the hard way. In September 1999, after almost 10 months of travel to Mars, the $125-million Mars Climate Orbiter (*https://oreil.ly/2vpu1*) lost communication and then burned and broke into pieces a mere 37 miles away from the planet's surface. The analysis found out that, while NASA had used the metric system, one of its partners had used the International System of Units (SI). This inconsistency was not discovered until it was time to land the orbiter, leading to a complete loss of the satellite. This of course was crushing to the team. After this incident, proper checks and balances were implemented to ensure that something similar did not happen again.

---

2 A natural experiment (*https://oreil.ly/iClKv*) is a situation in which you can identify experimental and control groups determined by factors outside the control of the investigators. In our example here, the runners naturally fell into groups defined by the shoes they wore, rather than being assigned shoes externally. The groups of runners were large enough to qualify for good "experimental" and "control" groups with controlled number of external factors.

Bringing things together so that issues such as the one NASA experienced are caught early and rectified before a disaster happens starts with the creatiion of a data governance policy. A data governance policy is a living, breathing document that provides a set of rules, policies, and guidance for safeguarding an organization's data assets.

What Is a Data Governance Policy?

A data governance policy is a documented set of guidelines for ensuring that an organization's data and information assets are managed consistently and used properly. *A data governance policy is essential in order to implement governance.* The guidelines will include individual policies for data quality, access, security, privacy, and usage, which are paramount for managing data across its life cycle. In addition, data governance policies center on establishing roles and responsibilities for data that include access, disposal, storage, backup, and protection, which should all be familiar concepts. This document helps to bring everything together toward a common goal.

The data governance policy is usually created by a data governance committee or data governance council, which is made up of business executives and other data owners. This policy document defines a clear data governance structure for the executive team, managers, and line workers to follow in their daily operations.

To get started operationalizing governance, a data governance charter template could be useful. Figure 4-4 shows an example template that could help you socialize your ideas across the organization and get the conversation started. Information in this template will funnel directly into your data governance policy.

Use the data governance charter template to kick off the conversation and get your team assembled. Once it has bought into your vision, mission, and goals, that is the team that will help you create and define your governance policy.

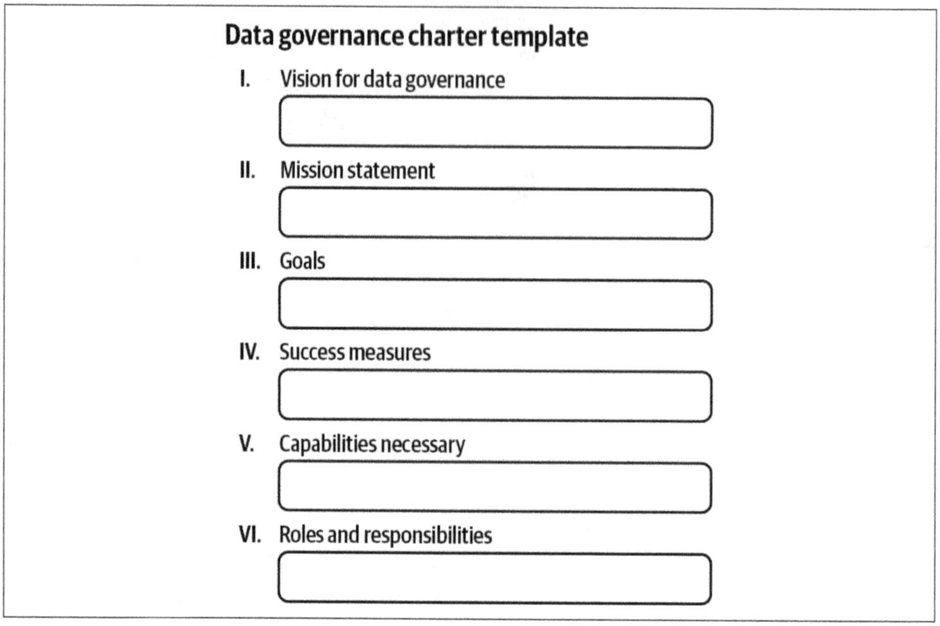

Data governance charter template

I. Vision for data governance

II. Mission statement

III. Goals

IV. Success measures

V. Capabilities necessary

VI. Roles and responsibilities

Figure 4-4. Data governance charter template

Importance of a Data Governance Policy

When you have a business idea and are going to friends to socialize the idea and possibly get them to buy into it, you will quickly run into someone who asks for a business plan. "Do you have a business plan you can share so I can read more about this idea and what your plans are?" A data governance policy allows you to have all the important elements of operationalizing governance documented according to your organization's needs and objectives. It also allows consistency within the organization over a long period of time. It is the document that everyone will refer to when questions and issues arise. It should be reviewed regularly and updated when things in the organization change. You can consider it your business plan—or to another extreme, it can also be your governance bible.

When a data governance policy is well drafted, it will ensure:

- Consistent, efficient, and effective management of the data assets throughout the organization and data life cycle and over time.

- The appropriate level of protection of the organization's data assets based on their value and risk as determined by the data governance committee.

- The appropriate protection and security levels for different categories of data as established by the governance committee.

Developing a Data Governance Policy

A data governance policy is usually authored by the data governance committee or appointed data governance council. This committee will establish comprehensive policies for the data program that outline how data will be collected, stored, used, and protected. The committee will identify risks and regulatory requirements and look into how they will impact or disrupt the business.

Once all the risks and assessments have been identified, the data governance committee will then draft policy guidelines and procedures that will ensure the organization has the data program that was envisioned. When a policy is well written, it helps capture the strategic vision of the data program. The vision for the governance program could be to drive digital transformation for the organization, or possibly to get insights to drive new revenue or even to use data to provide new products or services. Whichever is the case for your organization, the policies drafted should all coalesce toward the articulated vision and mission as outlined in the data governance charter template.

Part of the process of developing a data governance policy is establishing the expectations, wants, and needs of key stakeholders through interviews, meetings, and informal conversations. This will help you get valuable input, but it's also an opportunity to secure additional buy-in for the program.

Data Governance Policy Structure

A well-crafted policy should be unique to your organization's vision, mission, and goals. Don't get hung up on every single piece of information on this template, however; use it more like a guide to help you think things through. With that in mind, your governance policy should address:

Vision and mission for the program
> If you used a data governance charter template as outlined in Figure 4-4 to get buy-in from other stakeholders, that means you already have this information readily available. As mentioned before, the vision for the governance program could be to drive digital transformation for the organization, or to get insights to drive new revenue, or even to use data to provide new products or services.

Policy purpose
> Capture goals for your organization's data governance program, as well as metrics for determining success. The mission and vision of the program should drive the goals and success metrics.

Policy scope
> Document the data assets covered by this governance policy. In addition, inventory the data sources and determine data classifications based on whether data is

sensitive, confidential, or publicly available, along with the levels of security and protection required at the different levels.

Definitions and terms

The data governance policy is usually viewed by stakeholders across the organization who might not be familiar with certain terms. Use this section to document terms and definitions to ensure everyone is on the same page.

Policy principles

Define rules and standards for the governance program you're looking to set up along with the procedures and programs to enforce them. The rules could cover data access (who has access to what data), data usage (how the data will be used and details around what's acceptable), data integration (what transformations the data will undergo), and data integrity (expectations around data quality). Develop best practices to protect data and to ensure regulations and compliance are effectively documented.

Program structure

Define roles and responsibilities (R&Rs), which are positions within the organization that will oversee elements of the governance program. A RACI chart could help you map out who is responsible, who is accountable, who needs to be consulted, and who should be kept informed about changes. Information on governance R&Rs can be found in Chapter 3 of the book.

Policy review

Determine when the policy will be reviewed and updated and how adherence to the policy will be monitored, measured, and remedied.

Further assistance

Document the right people to address questions from the team and other stakeholders.

It's not enough to document a data governance policy as outlined in Figure 4-5, communicating it to all stakeholders is equally important. This could happen through a combination of group meetings and training, one-on-one conversations, recorded training videos, and written communication.

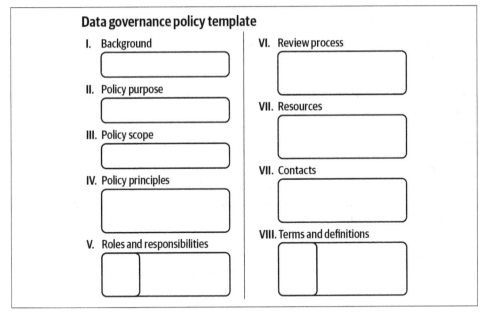

Figure 4-5. Example data governance policy template

In addition, review performance regularly with your data governance team to ensure that you're still on the right track. This also means regularly reviewing your data governance policy to make sure it still reflects the current needs of the organization and program.

Roles and Responsibilities

When operationalizing governance over a data life cycle, you will interact with many stakeholders within the organization, and you will need to bring them together to work on this common goal. While it might be tempting to definitively say which roles do what at which part of the data life cycle, as outlined in Chapter 3, many data governance frameworks revolve around a complex interplay of roles and responsibilities. The reality is that most companies rarely are able to exactly or fully staff governance roles due to lack of employee skill set or, more commonly, a simple lack of headcount. For this reason, employees working in the information and data space of their company often wear different user "hats."

We will not go into detail about roles and responsibilities in this chapter, because they're well outlined in Chapter 3. You still need to define what these look like within your organization and how they will interplay with each other to make governance a reality for you. This will typically be outlined in a RACI matrix describing who is "responsible, accountable, to be consulted, and to be informed" within a certain enforcement, process, policy, or standard.

Step-by-Step Guidance

By this section of the book, you should know that data governance goes beyond the selection and implementation of products and tools. The success of a data governance program depends on the combination of people, processes, and tools all working together to make governance a reality. This section will feel very familiar, because it gathers all the elements discussed in the previous section on data governance policy and puts them in a step-by-step process to show you how to get started. It further double clicks into the concepts as well.

Build the business case

As previously mentioned, data governance takes time and is expensive. If done correctly, it can be automated as part of the application design done at the source with a focus on business value. That said, data governance initiatives will often vary in scope and objectives. Depending on where the initiative is originating from, you need to be able to build a business case that will identify critical business drivers and justify the effort and investment of data governance. It should identify the pain points, outline perceived data risks, and indicate how governance helps the organization mitigate those risks and enable better business outcomes. It's OK to start small, strive for quick wins, and build up ambitions over time. Set clear, measurable, and specific goals. You cannot control what you cannot measure; therefore you need to outline success metrics. The data governance charter template in Figure 4-4 is perfect for helping you get started.

Document guiding principles

Develop and document core principles associated with governance and, of course, associated with the project you're looking to get off the ground. A core principle of your governance strategy could be to make consistent and confident business decisions based on trustworthy data aligned with all the various purposes for the use of the data assets. Another core principle could be to meet regulatory requirements and avoid fines or even to optimize staff effectiveness by providing data assets that meet the desired data quality thresholds. Define principles that are core to your business and project. If you're still new to this area, there are a lot of resources available. If you are looking online, there are several vendor-agnostic, not-for-profit associations, such as the Data Governance Institute (DGI) (*http://www.datagovernance.com*), the Data Management Association (DAMA) (*https://dama.org*), the Data Governance Professionals Organization (DGPO) (*https://dgpo.org*), and the Enterprise Data Management Council (*https://edmcouncil.org*), all of which provide great resources for business, IT, and data professionals dedicated to advancing the discipline of data governance. In addition, identify whether there are any local data governance meetup groups or conferences that you can possibly attend, such as the Data Governance and

Information Quality Conference, DAMA International Events, or a Financial Information Summit.

Get management buy-in

It should be no surprise that without management buy-in, your governance initiative can easily be dead from the get-go. Management controls the big decisions and funding that you need. Outlining important KPIs, and how your plan helps to move them, will get management to be all ears. Engage data governance champions and get buy-in from the key senior stakeholders. Present your business case and guiding principles to C-level management for approval. You need allies on your side to help make the case. And once the project has gotten off the ground, communicate frequently.

Develop an operating model

Once you have management approval, it's time to get to work. How do you integrate this governance plan into the way of doing business in your enterprise? We introduced you to the data governance policy, which can come in very handy during this process. During this stage, define the data governance roles and responsibilities, and then describe the processes and procedures for the data governance council and data stewardship teams who will define processes for defining and implementing policies as well as for reviewing and remediating identified data issues. Leverage the content from the data management policy plan to help you define your operating model. Data governance is a team sport, with deliverables from all parts of the business.

Develop a framework for accountability

As with any project you're looking to bring to market, establishing a framework for assigning custodianship and responsibility for critical data domains is paramount. Define ownership. Make sure there is visibility to the "data owners" across the data landscape. Provide a methodology to ensure that everyone is accountable for contributing to data usability. Refer back to your data management policy, as it probably started to capture some of these dependencies.

Develop taxonomies and ontologies

This is where a lot of the education you've collected thus far comes in handy. Working closely with governance associations, leaning in on your peers, and simply learning about things online will help you with this step. There may be a number of governance directives associated with data classification, organization, and, in the case of sensitive information, data protection. To enable your data consumers to comply with those directives, there must be a clear definition of the categories (for organizational structure) and classifications (for assessing data sensitivity). These should be captured in your data governance policy.

Assemble the right technology stack

Once you've assigned data governance roles to your staff and defined and approved your processes and procedures, you should then assemble a suite of tools that facilitates implementation and ongoing validation of compliance with data policies and accurate compliance reporting. Map infrastructure, architecture, and tools. Your data governance framework must be a sensible part of your enterprise architecture, the IT landscape, and the tools needed. We talked about technology in previous sections, so we won't go into detail about it here. Finding tools and technology that work for you and satisfy the organizational objectives you laid out is what's important.

Establish education and training

As highlighted earlier, for data governance to work, it needs buy-in across the organization. You need to ensure that your organization is keeping up and is still buying into the project you presented. It's therefore important to raise awareness of the value of data governance by developing educational materials highlighting data governance practices, procedures, and the use of supporting technology. Plan for regular training sessions to reinforce good data governance practices. Wherever possible, use business terms, and translate the academic parts of the data governance discipline into meaningful content in the business context.

Considerations for Governance Across a Data Life Cycle

Data governance has been around since there was data to govern, but it was mostly viewed as an IT function. Implementing data governance across the data life cycle is no walk in the park. Here are some considerations you will need to think about as you implement governance in your organization. These should not be surprising to you, because you will quickly notice that they touch on a lot of aspects we introduced in Chapters 1 and 2, as well as in this chapter.

Deployment time

Crafting and setting up governance processes across the data life cycle takes a lot of time, effort, and resources. In this chapter, we have introduced a lot of concepts, ideas, and ways to think about operationalizing governance across the data life cycle, and you can see it gets overwhelming very quickly. There's not a one-size-fits-all solution; you need to identify what is unique about your business and then forge a plan that works for you. Automation can reduce the deployment time compared with hand-coded governance processes. In addition, artificial intelligence is seen as a way to get arms around data governance in the future, especially for things like autodiscovery of sensitive data and metadata management. That means that as you look for solutions in the market, you will need to find out how much automation and integration is built into it, how well it works for your environment and situation, and whether that is the most difficult part of the workflow that could use automation. In a hybrid or even a multi-cloud world, this becomes even more complex and further increases the deployment time.

Complexity and cost

Complexity comes in many forms. In Chapter 1, we talked about how much the data landscape is and about just how quickly data was being produced in the world. Another complexity is a lack of defined industry standards for things like metadata. We touched on this in Chapter 2. In most cases, metadata does not obey the same policies and controls as the underlying data itself, and a lack of standardized metadata specifications means that different products and processes will have different ways of presenting this information. Still another complexity is the sheer amount of tools, processes, and infrastructure needed to make governance a reality. In order to deliver comprehensive governance, organizations must either integrate best-of-breed solutions, which are often complex and very expensive (with high license and maintenance costs), or buy turnkey, integrated solutions, which are expensive and fewer in the market. With this in mind, cloud service providers (CSPs) are building data platforms with all these governance capabilities built in, thus creating a one-stop shop and simplifying the process for customers. As an organization, research and compare the different data platforms provided by CSPs and see which one works for you. Some businesses choose to leave some of their data on-premises; however, for the data that can move to the cloud, these CSPs are now building robust tools and processes to help customers govern their data end-to-end on the platform. In addition, companies such as Informatica, Alation, and Collibra offer governance-specific platforms and products that can be implemented in your organization.

Changing regulation environment

In previous chapters, we've clearly outlined the implications of a constantly changing regulatory environment with the introduction of GDPR and CCPA. We will not go into the same detail here; however, regulations define a lot of what must be done and implemented to ensure governance. They will outline how certain types of data need to be handled and which types of controls need to be in place, and they sometimes will even go as far as outlining what the repercussions are when these things are not complied with. Complying with regulations is absolutely something your organization needs to think about as you implement data governance over the data life cycle.

In our discussions with many different companies, we've heard of two very different philosophies when it comes to considering changes to the regulatory environment. One strategy is to assume that, in the future, the most restrictive regulations that are present now will cascade and be required everywhere (like CCPA being required across the entire US and not just in California), and that ensuring compliance now, even though not required, is a top priority. Conversely, we've also heard the strategy of complying only with what's required right now and dealing with regulations only if they become required. We strongly suggest you take the former approach, because a proper and well-thought-out governance program not only ensures compliance with ever-changing regulations; it also enables many of the other benefits we've outlined thus far, such as better findability, better security, and more accurate analytics from higher-quality data.

Location of data

In order to fully implement governance over a data life cycle, understanding which data is on-premises versus in the cloud is very important. Furthermore, understanding how data will interact with other data along the life cycle does create complexity. In the current paradigm, most organizational data lives both on-premises and in the cloud, and having systems and tools that allow for hybrid and even multicloud scenarios is paramount. In Chapter 1, we talked about why governance is easier in the public cloud—it's primarily because the public cloud has several features that make data governance easier to implement, monitor, and update. In many cases, these features are unavailable or cost-prohibitive in on-premises systems. Data should be protected no matter where it is located, so a viable data life cycle management plan will incorporate governance for all data at all times.

Organizational culture

As you know, culture is one of those intangible things in an organization that plays an important role in how the organization functions. In Chapter 3, we touched on how an organization can create a culture of privacy and security, which allows employees to understand how data should be managed and treated so that they are good stewards of proper data handling and usage. In this section, we're referring to organizational culture, which often dictates what people do and how they behave. Your organization might be free, allowing folks to easily raise questions and concerns, and in such an environment, when something goes wrong, people are more likely to speak up. In organizations in which people are reprimanded for every little thing, they will be more afraid to speak up and report when things are not working or even when things go wrong. In these environments, governance is a little difficult to implement, because without transparency and proper reporting, mistakes are usually not discovered until much later. In the NASA example we provided earlier in this chapter, there were a couple of people within the organization who noticed the discrepancy in the data and even reported it. Their reports were ignored by management, and we all know what happened. Things did not end well for NASA. Remember, instituting governance in an organization is often met with resistance, especially if the organization is accustomed to decentralized operations. Creating an environment in which functions are centralized across the data life cycle simply means that these areas have to adhere to processes that they might not have been used to in the past but that are for the larger good of the organization.

Summary

Data life cycle management is paramount to implementing governance and ensures that useful data is clean, accurate, and readily available to users. In addition, it ensures that your organization remains compliant at all times.

In this chapter, we introduced you to data life cycle management, and how to apply governance over the data life cycle. We then looked into operationalizing governance and how the role of a data governance policy is to ensure that an organization's data and information assets are managed consistently and used properly. Finally, we provided step-by-step guidance for implementing governance and finished with the considerations for governance across the data life cycle, including deployment time, complexity and cost, and organizational culture.

CHAPTER 5

Improving Data Quality

When most people hear the words *data quality*, they think about data that is correct and factual. In data analytics and data governance, data quality has a more nuanced set of qualifiers. Being correct is not enough, if all of the details are not available (e.g., fields in a transaction). Data quality is also measured in the context of a use case, as we will explain. Let's begin by exploring the characteristics of data quality.

What Is Data Quality?

Put simply, data quality is the ranking of certain data according to accuracy, completeness (all columns have values), and timeliness. When you are working with large amounts of data, the data is usually acquired and processed in an automated way. When thinking about data quality, it is good to discuss:

Accuracy
> Whether the data captured was actually correct. For example, an error in data entry causing multiple zeros to be entered ahead of a decimal point, is an accuracy issue. Duplicate data is also an example of inaccurate data.

Completeness
> Whether all records captured were complete—i.e., there are no columns with missing information. If you are managing customer records, for example, make sure you capture or otherwise reconcile a complete customer details record (e.g., name/address/phone number). Missing fields will cause issues if you are looking for customer records in a specific zip code, for example.

Timeliness
> Transactional data is affected by timeliness. The order of events in buying and selling shares, for example, can have an impact on the buyer's available credit. Timeliness also should take into account the fact that some data can get stale.

In addition, the data quality can be affected by outlier values. If you are looking at retail transactions, for example, very large purchase sums are likely indications of data-entry issues (e.g., forgetting a decimal point) and not indicators that revenues went up by two orders of magnitude. This will be an accuracy issue.

Make sure to take all possible values into account. In the above retail example, negative values are likely indications of returns and not "purchasing a product for negative $" and should be accounted for differently (e.g., a possible impact will be the average transaction size—with the purchase and the return each accounting for a single purchase).

Finally, there is the trustworthiness of the source of the data. Not all data sources are equal—there is a difference, for example, between a series of temperature values collected over time from a connected thermometer and a series of human reads of a mercury thermometer collected over time in handwriting. The machine will likely control variables such as the time the sample was taken and will sync to a global atomic clock. The human recording in a notebook will possibly add variance to the time the sample was taken, may smudge the text, or may have hard-to-read handwriting. It is dangerous to take data from both sources and treat them as the same.

Why Is Data Quality Important?

For many organizations, data directly leads to decision making: a credit score compiled from transaction data can lead to a decision by a banker to approve a mortgage. A company share price is instantly computed from the amount offered by multiple buyers and sellers. These kinds of decisions are very often regulated—clear evidence must be collected on credit-related decisions, for example. It is important to the customer and the lender that mortgage decisions are made according to high-quality data. Lack of data quality is the source of lack of trust and of biased, unethical automated decisions being made. A train schedule you cannot trust (based on erroneous or untimely station visits and past performance) can lead to you making decisions about your commute that can potentially result in your always taking your own car, thus negating the very reason for the existence of the mass transit train.

When collecting data from multiple sources or domains, data accuracy and context become a challenge: not only is it possible that the central repository does not have the same understanding of the data as the data sources (e.g., how outliers are defined and how partial data is treated), but it is also possible that data sources do not agree with each other on the meaning of certain values (e.g., how to handle negative values, or how to fill in for missing values). Reconciliation of data meaning can be done by making sure that when a new data source is added, the accuracy, completeness, and timeliness of the data in the data source is examined—sometimes manually—and either described in a way that the data analysts using the resource can use or directly normalized according to the rules in the central repository.

When an error or unexpected data is introduced into the system, there are usually no human curators who will detect and react to it. In a data processing pipeline, each step can introduce and amplify errors in the next steps, until presented to the business user:

- In the data-gathering endpoints, gathering data from low-quality sources which are potentially irrelevant to the business task can, if not eliminated early, cause issues. Consider, for example, mobile ad impressions, or usage details, where some of the data is gathered for an engineering lab source and does not represent real users (and can potentially be very large in volume).
- In the landing zone step, upon normalization/aggregation, the wrong data can be aggregated into a summation and sway the result.
- In the data analytics workload, joining tables of different qualities can introduce unexpected outcomes.

All of the above can be presented in a way such that the business user is kept unaware of decisions/operations happening earlier in the data acquisition chain (see Figure 5-1) and is presented with the wrong data.

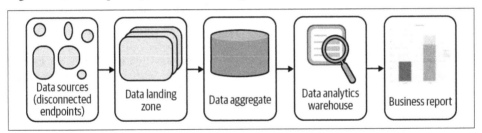

Figure 5-1. Simple data acquisition chain

Any step in the (very simple) chain shown in Figure 5-1 can result in erroneous data, which will eventually drive the wrong business decisions. Let's look at a couple of examples.

In the early days of internet mapping, the mapping provider of the time, a company called MaxMind, was the sole provider of IP addresses to location services. This company made an arguably reasonable decision to have a "default" location right at the center of the United States, in northern Kansas near the Nebraska border. From the time of making this decision until very recently, whenever the service could not find a map location for an IP address, it would provide this default location. The problem with this decision became evident when systems and persons downstream did not realize the meaning of this default, and when illegal activity was detected from "default" (aka unknown) IP addresses—law enforcement would show up at this location in the central US and serve warrants to people who actually live there.[1]

A more current data quality challenge example is within California's collection of COVID-19 cases. California moved from rapid per-county reports to state data (which caused an inconsistency). Later, California moved from "people tested" to "specimens tested" (some people are likely tested more than once, causing another data quality issue), and then in August 2020 the data quality became an even more serious issue

> after a series of errors—among them, a failed link to one of the country's largest testing labs—had led the state to underreport coronavirus cases starting in late July. Counties were forced to comb spreadsheets in search of reliable data, while the state worked to understand the scope of the problem and fix it. A total of 296,000 records were affected.[2]

It took nearly a month to recover from this data-quality issue.

A study performed by Experian and published by MIT Sloan researchers estimates that the cost of bad data (and by that they mean bad, or unmanaged data quality) is around 15–20% of revenue for most companies.[3] The study sampled one hundred "records" (or units of work) from enterprise divisions and then manually calculated the error range of these records. The result was an astonishing error rate of 50%. The Data Warehousing Institute (TDWI) estimated in 2002 that poor data quality costs businesses in the US over $700 billion annually, and since then this figure has grown dramatically. Currently, IBM estimates that the yearly cost of "bad data" is *$3.1 trillion.*[4]

Data Quality in Big Data Analytics

Data warehouses—databases that are used to performing data analytics in petabyte scale—are vulnerable to data quality issues. Typically, to get data in a big data warehouse, you will extract, clean, transform, and integrate data from multiple operational databases to create a comprehensive database. A set of processes termed extract-transform-load (ETL) is used to facilitate construction of data warehouses. The data in the warehouses, though rarely updated, is refreshed periodically and is intended for a read-only mode of operation. The desired use of the data also has an impact on

---

1 Kashmir Hill, "How an Internet Mapping Glitch Turned a Random Kansas Farm into a Digital Hell" (*https://oreil.ly/jX3zM*), *Splinter*, April 10, 2016.

2 Fiona Kelliher and Nico Savidge, "With Data Backlog Cleared, California Coronavirus Cases Officially Decreasing, Newsom Says" (*https://oreil.ly/MLjwe*), *Mercury News*, August 14, 2020.

3 Thomas Redman, "Seizing Opportunity in Data Quality" (*https://oreil.ly/KzIhT*), *MIT Sloan Management Review*, November 27, 2017.

4 IBM, "The Four V's of Big Data" (*https://oreil.ly/N_xH1*), *Big Data & Analytics Hub* (blog).

the kinds of analysis and desired uses of the data. A data warehouse built to support decision making in retail, where transactions are collected hourly and rounded to the nearest five-cent value, has different quality needs than a data warehouse built to support stock trades, where the transaction time needs to be accurate to the microsecond, and values range from microtransactions of below one cent to transactions spanning millions of dollars.

Compared to operational database environments, data warehouses pose additional challenges to data quality. Since data warehouses integrate data from multiple sources, quality issues related to data acquisition, cleaning, transformation, linking, and integration become critical.

 We touched on this earlier, but it's important to keep in mind that proper data quality management not only assists in the ability to run big data analytics but also helps to save on cost and prevent the loss of productivity. The harder it is for analysts to find and use high-quality data, coupled with extra engineering time spent hunting down and solving data issues, the more cost you will incur, and your analytics output will suffer. The downstream effects and cost implications of poorly managed data quality should not be discounted.

Data Quality in AI/ML Models

Of specific note is data quality within AI/ML models. To broadly generalize, machine learning models work by extrapolating from existing data using a model to predict future data (e.g., transaction volume). If the input data has errors within it, the machine learning model will likely amplify these errors. If the machine learning model is used to make predictions, and those predictions are then further input into the model (once acted upon), the predictions become the reality, and the machine learning model becomes compromised because it will generate, by force of a positive feedback loop, more and more errors.

The data available for building machine learning models is usually divided into three nonoverlapping datasets: *training*, *validation*, and *test*. The machine learning model is developed using the training dataset. Next, the validation dataset is used to adjust the model parameters so that overfitting is avoided. Last, the test dataset is used to evaluate the model performance. Errors in one or more datasets can lead to a badly trained machine learning model, which will yield bad output. Note that there is a fine line between cleaning all the errors out manually (which can be cost prohibitive over a large amount of records) and allowing some level of error in a robust model.

Quality Beats Quantity, Even in AI

It is a truth universally acknowledged that an AI product manager in possession of a good idea must be in want of copious amounts of data. The resurgence of AI, starting in around 2014, has been driven by the ability to train ML models on ever-larger datasets. The explosion of smartphones, the rise of ecommerce, and the prevalence of connected devices are some of the trends that have fostered an explosion in the amount of data that a business has available to it when designing new services or optimizing existing ones. With larger datasets comes the ability to use larger and more sophisticated AI models. For example, a typical image classification model now has hundreds of layers, whereas an AI model from the 1990s had only one layer. Such models are practical because of the availability of custom ML hardware like GPUs and TPUs, and the ability to distribute the work across many machines in the public cloud. Thus, any AI product manager with a good idea will be on the hunt to use as much data as possible. The accuracy of the AI model and its ability to represent the real world depends on it being trained with the widest, most representative data possible.

In our effort to gather more data, however, we should be careful to make sure that the collected data is of good quality. A small amount of high-quality data yields much better results than does a large amount of low-quality or outright wrong data. A fascinating example of this second truth (not as universally acknowledged) comes from an effort to reduce the overhead of testing water meters (*https://oreil.ly/7O_YC*) in northern Italy.

The goal was to identify malfunctioning mechanical water meters based on their readings alone. Going out to a site to test a water meter (see Figure 5-2) is pretty expensive; if the team could use AI to identify potential malfunctions from the water readings alone, it would be a huge cost savings. For example, if a water meter ran backwards, or if the amount of water read as being consumed was wholly unreasonable (it was more, perhaps, than the amount of water supplied to the entire neighborhood), we could be sure the meter was faulty. Of course, this also depended on the historical water usage at any meter—a water meter attached to a one-bath house with a small garden would tend to consume a certain amount of water that varies seasonally. A large deviation from this amount would be suspicious.

Figure 5-2. A mechanical water meter of the sort used in Italy, meant to be read by a human looking at the dial. Photo courtesy of Andrevruas, Creative Commons License 3.0 (https://oreil.ly/tHyCu)

The team started out with 15 million readings from 1 million mechanical water meters. This was enough data to train a recurrent neural network (RNN), the fanciest time-series prediction method (with less data, they'd have to settle for something like ARIMA [an autoregressive integrated moving average model]), and so the team got to work. The data was already numeric, so there was no need for any data preprocessing —the team could just feed it into the RNN and do lots of hyperparameter tuning. The idea was that any large differences between what the RNN predicted and what the meter actually read would be attributable to faulty water meters.

How did that go? The team notes:

> Our initial attempts to train a recurrent neural network, without a specific attention to the quality, and to the limitations, of those data used for training, led to unexpected and negative prediction outcomes.[5]

---

5 Marco Roccetti et al., "Is Bigger Always Better? A Controversial Journey to the Center of Machine Learning Design, with Uses and Misuses of Big Data for Predicting Water Meter Failures" (*https://oreil.ly/7O_YC*), *Journal of Big Data* 6, no. 70 (2019).

They went back to the drawing board and looked more closely at those 15 million readings that they had. It turned out that there were two problems with the data: erroneous data and made-up data.

First, some of the data was simply wrong. How could a water meter reading have been wrong? Wouldn't a customer complain? It turns that the process of a water meter reading going to the customer consists of three steps:

1. The mechanical water meter being read by the technician onsite

2. The reading being entered from the technician's logbook into the company ERP system

3. The ERP system calculating the bill

In the case of errors in either data entry, the customer might call to complain, but only the bill was corrected. The water meter readings might still remain wrong! Thus, the AI model was getting trained on wrong data and being told the meters were not faulty. Such wrong data turned out to be about 1% of all observations, which is about the proportion of actually faulty water meters. So, if the meter did return such a bad value, the model was simply tossing a coin—when the historical data did have these wild swings, including negative values, half the time it was because the observation was wrong, and the other half of the time it was because the meter was faulty. The RNN was being trained on noise.

Second, some of the data was simply made up. It costs so much to send a technician out to a site that sometimes past readings were simply extrapolated and a reasonable charge was made to the customer. This was then made up the next time by a true reading. For example, an actual measurement might be made in January, skipped in March, and caught up in May. The value for March wasn't real. Thus the AI model was being trained on data that wasn't real—31% of the "measurements" were actually interpolated values. Further, the readjustments added a lot of noise to the dataset.

After correcting all the billing-related errors and the interpolated values, faulty water meters were detected by the RNN with an accuracy of 85% (a simpler linear regression model would have given them 79%). In order to get there, though, they had to throw away a large percentage of the original data. Quality, in other words, trumped quantity.

A good data governance regime would have been careful to propagate billing corrections back to the original source data and to classify measurements and interpolated values differently. A good data governance regime would have enforced dataset quality from the get-go.

Why Is Data Quality a Part of a Data Governance Program?

To summarize, data quality is absolutely essential when planning a data program. Organizations very often overestimate the quality of the data they have and underestimate the impact of bad data quality. The same program that governs data life cycle, controls, and usage should be leveraged to govern the quality of data (and plan for the impact and response to bad data quality incidents).

Techniques for Data Quality

Having discussed the importance of data quality, let's review a few strategies for cleaning up data, assessing quality, and improving data quality. As a general rule, the earlier in the pipeline that data can be prepared, sanitized, disambiguated, and cleaned, the better. It is important to note, in parallel, that data processing pipelines are not the same for different business purposes/different teams; thus it may be hard to clean up the data upstream, and that task may need to move downstream for the individual teams. There is a balance here: if further down the data analytics pipeline aggregates are performed, causing a coarsening of the data, the crucial meaning needed for cleanup may be lost as discrete values are aggregated. We will highlight three key techniques for data quality: prioritization, annotation, and profiling.

The Importance of Matching Business Case to the Data Use

Participants in a virtual symposium for the Society of Vertebrate Paleontology in October 2020 were baffled by the fact that the transcription, captions, and chat messages in digital Q&A sessions were oddly garbled. After some investigation, a common denominator was determined: the words "bone," "knob," and "jerk"—all very relevant and appropriate when discussing fossils—were banned and made invisible to the participants.[6]

The underlying issue was that the online meeting platform used to power the convention was designed for education and not necessarily for science. While on the surface this does not immediately pose an issue (when you consider teenagers), a built-in "naughty-word filter" seemed to be the culprit.

The filter automatically went over all text data presented in the platform and filtered out certain words considered "not appropriate for school." Words that are *essential* when discussing paleontology, such as, well, "bone," are inappropriate in other settings. To top it off, even "dinosaur" was apparently inappropriate in the business context originally envisioned for the meeting platform.

---

6 Poppy Noor, "Overzealous Profanity Filter Bans Paleontologists from Talking About Bones" (*https://oreil.ly/XHU2z*), *Guardian*, October 16, 2020.

This filtering caused a stir when one researcher found out that "Wang" was one of the banned words, while "Johnson" was not. This issue introduced serious (unintended) bias as both are common surnames as well as slang terms.

At the end of the day, the issue was quickly fixed, and people accepted the error in good humor, laughing at the unintended consequences and sharing them over social media. For the purpose of this book, however, this story presents an important lesson: any system that acts on data (e.g., the data modification system discussed in this sidebar) must be developed with as full a business use case as possible in mind. Clearly, the intended audience is part of the business context, and you obviously cannot treat international science symposium participants like you would treat schoolchildren.

Figure 5-3 drives home the point that data quality must be tied to the specific business case, and it also conveys a more subtle point about data governance. Sharing "banned word lists" between use cases also informs the use case participants of the existence of those other cases as well as of the relevant word lists—not always a desired scenario!

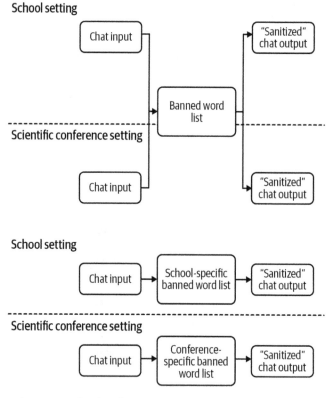

Figure 5-3. Architectures of a chat filter

Scorecard

In your organization, create a scorecard for the data sources. A useful scorecard includes information about the origin of the data and its *accuracy, completeness,* and *timeliness.* This scorecard will be used by data pipeline builders to make decisions about how and where to use the data and for what purpose. More mundane information, such as who is the administrative owner of the data, who asked for it, and so on, can also be useful in a scorecard.

Prioritization

First, *prioritize*—there are different sources of data and different uses for each source. A data source used for prioritizing healthcare actions is very different from a data source used to drive graphics for a lobby "heat map" display. Prioritization should be performed with the eventual business goal in mind. Lineage can help with backtracing the data and repurposing the origin for a different business purpose. By monitoring the lineage of data (more on that in "Lineage Tracking" on page 46) for both its sources as well as its eventual uses—you can prioritize and expend resources on the more critical data sources first.

Annotation

Second, *annotate*—make sure you have a standardized way to attach "quality information" to data sources. Even if you cannot provide a detailed scorecard for each source, being able to attest that "This data has been vetted" or (just as importantly) "This data is not vetted" is valuable, even if there are differences between the datasets and their meaning. As you evolve your data quality program, you can further attach more detailed information to datasets. Begin small, however, and clearly annotate the information at hand so that it does not become "tribal knowledge" and get lost when people in the know move on.

A common technique for annotation can be to "crowdsource" the quality information by allowing people using the data to "vote" on or "star" data according to its quality as they observe it through usage. This allows multiple human eyes on the data, and if you start with a good default (data is normally untrusted) and assign a curator to review data that is highly rated before issuing a quality signal to the rest of the organization, you can effectively practice a fair data quality program. (This is not the only recommendation in this chapter, though!)

Cascading Problems with Tribal Knowledge

While you are certainly very familiar with the struggle of overcoming reliance on tribal knowledge, the following is an interesting use case that further illustrates just how problematic disregarding annotation can be.

We've spoken many times with a healthcare company that is going through a myriad of issues related to lack of annotation and reliance on tribal knowledge. This company is quickly growing and has recently taken in several new acquisitions. Part of the benefit of these acquisitions is the data that they have. This company has the vision of being able to leverage the data from these new acquisitions along with its own data to run some extremely powerful analytics that are sure to have prolific business impact. The company, however, encountered an enormous snag: the enterprise dictionaries, metadata management, and data quality management were anemic or nonexistent at the companies they acquired. The majority of these other companies relied on tribal knowledge, and, post-acquisition, many of the employees who had this knowledge are no longer at the company. This has resulted in most of the acquired data (since it's not properly managed, and no one can know what it is without spending a lot of time and effort to curate it) sitting in storage, just taking up space and not providing any business value whatsoever.

Through this issue the company has come to realize the importance of a centralized governance strategy that it can quickly scale—even for acquisitions—so that in the future this problem hopefully doesn't occur again, or at least such problems can be somewhat mitigated.

Profiling

Data *profiling* begins by generating a data profile: information about a range of data values (e.g., min, max, cardinality), highlighting values that are missing and values that are out-of-bounds (versus the average distribution) data outliers. Reviewing the data profile enables a determination of what are considered legal values (e.g., am I happy with the data outliers, or should I exclude those records?) and of value meaning (e.g., is a negative value in the income column an appropriate value, or should I exclude it?).

We proceed to detail several data profiling and cleanup techniques.

Data deduplication

In a quantitative system, each record should have only one voice. However, there are many cases in which the same record, or the same value, actually gets duplicated, resulting in data quality issues (and potentially in increased cost). Think about a redundant transaction system, where each transaction has an ID, and sometimes the same transaction can appear twice (e.g., due to a transmission issue). Given the ID, you can easily deduplicate the transactions and resolve. But think about a more challenging use case in which you have support cases (a list of customer issues in a ticketing system), each expressed by a user input title. When writing knowledge base articles to address these support cases, it is important to merge different user requests that refer to the same source issue. Since a "user request" is expressed in natural language and can be ambiguous, this is more challenging.

Deduplicating Names and Places

Think of an entity, and it probably needs resolving or disambiguation. Two of the most common entities that you have in datasets are names and addresses. Both of these need to be resolved if you want to deduplicate records. For example, the same person could be addressed as "Dr. Jill Biden," "Jill Biden," or "Mrs. Biden." In all three sets of records, it may be necessary to replace the name by a consistent identifier.

Take, for example, the impact of deduplicating author names in bibliographies, as shown in Figure 5-4. Robert Spence is referenced as Bob Spence and as R. Spence. Combining all these records and replacing the different variants with the canonical version of his name greatly simplifies the set of relationships and makes deriving insights much easier.

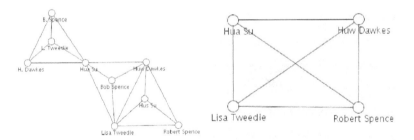

Figure 5-4. Deduplication can dramatically simplify the complexity of a dataset. For example, Lisa Tweedie is also referenced as L. Tweedie. Figure adapted from a paper by Bilgic et al., 2004 (https://oreil.ly/9Dt0t).

For deduplicating names, consider using a tool such as the Google Knowledge Graph Search API (*https://oreil.ly/f7QnZ*), or building one from your set of stakeholders using an open source API such as Akutan (*https://oreil.ly/A4Hp6*).

Similar to names, the same place can be referred to as "the New York Stock Exchange," "11 Wall St," "Wall St. & Broad Street," "Wall and Broad," or any of a myriad number of combinations. If packages are noted as having been delivered to multiple versions of this location, you might want to consolidate them into a canonical representation of the location.

Address resolution of this form is provided by the Google Places API (*https://oreil.ly/ suU1I*) which returns a place ID, a textual identifier that uniquely identifies a place. Place IDs are available for most locations, including businesses, landmarks, parks, and intersections, and will change over time as businesses close or relocate. It can be helpful, therefore, to combine the Places API with the Google Maps Geocoding API (*https://oreil.ly/umbBx*) to yield the actual location in time. Thus, while "the New York Stock Exchange" and "11 Wall Street" yield different place IDs, as shown in Figure 5-5 (after all, the NYSE could relocate!), geocoding them will return the same location.

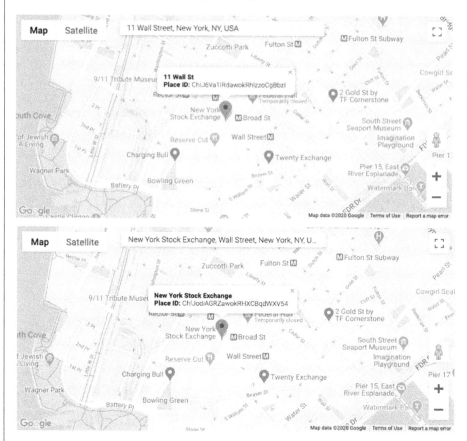

Figure 5-5. The place IDs for "the New York Stock Exchange" and "11 Wall Street" are different from each other but geolocate to the same location

Data outliers

Another tactic is to identify outliers of the data early on and eliminate them. For example, in a system that accepts only natural numbers (the range between 1 and infinity, excluding fractions), such as a house number in a street address book, it would be odd to find negative or fractional numbers, and thus it may make more sense to delete the entire record containing the outlier value rather than manually fixing it. Discretion is advised, as (for example) for 221b Baker Street, the fictional home of Sherlock Holmes. The UK's Royal Mail has had to recognize "221b Baker Street, London" as a real postal address because of all the Sherlock fans expecting it to be genuine! But the mail to 221b redirects to the Sherlock Holmes Museum at 239 Baker Street.

To generalize and scale: when building a dataset, make sure you can determine, for as many fields as possible, the minimum, maximum, and expected values (fractions, negatives, strings, zero...), and include logic to clean up records with unexpected values (or otherwise treat them). These actions are better done early in the processing timeline rather than later, when values have been aggregated or used in machine learning models. It is hard to backtrack/root out issues that are discovered after data has been processed.

Extreme values are not necessarily outliers, and care must be taken there. For example, a perfect SAT score *is* possible; however, in the US the SAT score range is 400–1,600, and values outside this range are suspect. Look at the distribution of the values and how the curve is shaped. The extreme edges of a "bell" curve should be treated differently than a distribution that has two peak clusters.

Consider the example distribution in Figure 5-6 in light of the expected use case of data. In our example, an expected bell curve with a sudden peak at the edge should prompt a more manual investigation and understanding to rule out potential data quality issues. Be wary of automatically dismissing such values without investigating them, as sometimes these outliers are the result not of low-quality data, but of phenomena that should be accounted for in the use case.

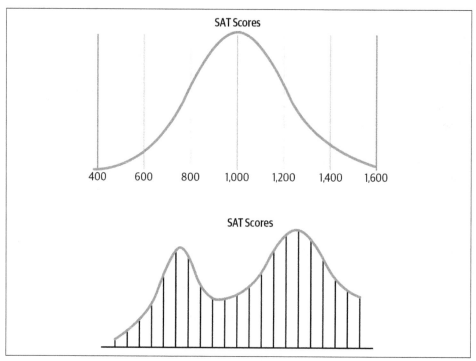

Figure 5-6. Example distributions of data

Lineage tracking

As mentioned earlier, *lineage tracking* for data is a force multiplier. If you can identify source datasets of high quality, you can follow the use of those high-quality sources and express an opinion of the result derivatives. In addition, if you can identify low-quality datasets, you can assume any computed derivative that is a product of one (or more) low-quality source is also a low-quality result—a useful conclusion that should guide the use of the data.

Furthermore, with lineage tracking you can backtrack from high-criticality use cases and results (e.g., dashboards) and learn what data sources are feeding these. At a minimum, you should prioritize the quality assessment of all sources of critical decision-supporting outputs.

This process of monitoring quality by source should not be a one-time thing but should be used every time a new dashboard/end product is set up. And it should be on periodic review, because the benefit of early detection can be significant if managed correctly. The impact of bad data, which can often go unnoticed, has been discussed above.

Data completeness

In some cases, there are data records with missing information, such as a customer record without an address or a transaction without a tracking number. Special consideration should be given to such cases, and an informed decision must be made whether or not to eliminate the records that are incomplete (resulting in "less data" but more "complete" data). Alternatively, if accepting incomplete records, make sure to include an annotation on the dataset indicating that it contains such records and noting which fields are "OK" to be missing and the default values (if any) used as input for those fields that are missing. This is especially important in the case of *merging datasets*.

Merging datasets

During ETL processes, and in general, you should be aware of special values used in the source datasets and make room for them during transformation/aggregation. If one dataset uses "null" to indicate no data and another dataset uses "zero," make sure this information is available to future users. Ensure that the joining process equalizes these two values into one consistent value (either null or zero; they have the same meaning in our example). And of course, record this special new value.

Dataset source quality ranking for conflict resolution

When merging multiple datasets from different vendors, another topic comes to mind: how to react if multiple-source datasets contain the same fields but with certain fields having different values in them. This is a common issue in financial systems, for example, where transactions are collected from multiple sources but sometimes differ in the meaning of special values such as zero, negative 1. One way to resolve that is to attach a ranking to each data source, and, in case of conflict, record the data from the highest-ranked source.

Unexpected Sources for Data and Data Quality

Many a McDonald's fan is disappointed when the ice cream maker in their local branch is broken. In fact, this issue troubled Rashiq, a young McDonald's fan in Germany, so much that he reverse-engineered the McDonald's app, found its API, and discovered a way to figure out whether or not the ice cream maker in a particular branch was operational.

Rashiq tested out the code and later built a site, *mcbroken.com*, that reports on the status of the ice cream makers in every branch on a global scale (Figure 5-7).

---

rashiq
@rashiq

I reverse engineered mcdonald's internal api and I'm currently placing an order worth $18,752 every minute at every mcdonald's in the US to figure out which locations have a broken ice cream machine

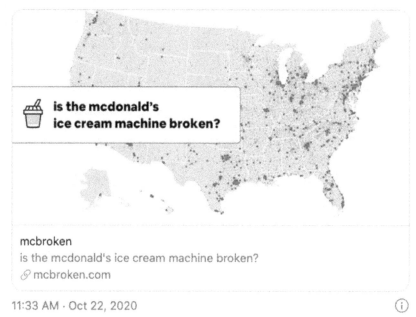

is the mcdonald's
ice cream machine broken?

mcbroken
is the mcdonald's ice cream machine broken?
🔗 mcbroken.com

11:33 AM · Oct 22, 2020

Figure 5-7. Rashiq's Twitter feed

However, there was a downside to Rashiq's code. In order to identify whether or not the ice cream maker was operational, Rashiq had a bot create an ice cream order and add an ice cream to the shopping cart. If that operation was successful, Rashiq would mark the ice cream maker in that branch as "operational." This resulted in thousands of half-completed orders of ice cream at McDonald's locations, globally. Apparently, however, the McDonald's data team was able to control for Rashiq's orders, as evidenced by the reply from McDonald's' director of analytics: "I'm Lovin' It." McDonald's head of communications tweeted a response (Figure 5-8).

Figure 5-8. McDonald's responds to Rashiq's work

Summary

Data quality is making sure that the data's accuracy, completeness, and timeliness are relevant to the business use case in mind. Different types of business use necessitate different levels of the above, and you should strive to keep a scorecard of your data sources when creating an analytics workload composed of descendants of these data sources.

We have reviewed the importance and real-life impact of data quality, through examples of bad data. We have discussed several techniques to improve data quality. If there is one key piece of advice that should be taken into account from this chapter, it is this: for data quality, handle it early, as close to the data source as possible, and monitor resultant products of your data. When repurposing data for a different analytics workload, revisit the sources and see if they are up to the new business task.

CHAPTER 6

Governance of Data in Flight

Data, especially data used for insights via data analytics, is a "living" medium. As data gets collected from multiple sources, it is reshaped, transformed, and molded into various patterns for different use cases: from a standardized "transactions table" to allow for forecasting the next season's business demand, to a dashboard presenting the past yield of a new crop, and more.

Data governance should be consistent across these transformations and allow more efficiency and frictionless security. Data governance should not introduce labor by forcing users to register and annotate new data containers as they work to reshape and collect data for their needs.

This chapter will discuss possible techniques and tools to enable seamless data governance through analysis of data "in flight."

Data Transformations

There are different ways to transform data, all of which impact governance, and we should be aware of these before we dig in deeper. It is common to refer to these processes as extract-transform-load (ETL). This is a generic phrase used to indicate the various stages of moving data between systems.

Extracting data means retrieving it from the source system in which it is stored, e.g., a legacy DB, a file, or the results a web crawler operation. Data extraction is a separate step, as the act of extracting data is a time-consuming retrieval process. It is advantageous to consider the extraction phase as the first step in a pipeline, allowing subsequent steps to operate in batches in parallel to the continued extraction. As data is extracted from the sources, it's useful to perform *data validation*, making sure the values retrieved are "as expected" (that the completeness of records and their accuracy match the expected values; see Chapter 5). If you perform data validation while still operating within the context of the source system, you will be unencumbered by the different computed results performed in later stages, which may be unknown (at this stage), and as you progress, you may lose the context of the source data. In an earlier chapter, we discussed data preparation, which is an example of a data validation process. The data being extracted and validated often lands in a *staging area* not normally accessible to the business users, which is where the data owners and data stewards perform the aforementioned validation checks.

Transforming data usually involves normalization of the data: eliminating outliers, joining from multiple sources into a single record (row), aggregating where relevant, or even splitting a single compound column into multiple columns. Be wary of the fact that any normalization done early, as well as any kind of general purpose cleaning, is also removing information—information whose value may not have been anticipated for a case unknown at the cleaning level. The implications are that you should have the business context in mind when extracting data and that you may need to revisit the source data in case the extraction process removed information needed for a new, unforeseen use case. At this stage, if you are extracting data from a new source, it may be worthwhile to create a scorecard for the source, describing some of the information contexts and those that are potentially not carried over during transformation. See "Scorecard" on page 123 for more about scorecards.

Finally, the load process situates the data into its final destination, usually a data-analytics-capable warehouse such as Google's BigQuery, Snowflake, or Amazon's Redshift.

It is important to note that as data warehousing solutions grew to be more powerful, the transformation process sometimes moved into the data warehousing solution, renaming ETL as ELT.

As data undergoes transformations, it is crucial not only to keep context as expressed by the origin but also to maintain consistency and completeness. Keeping origin context, consistency, and completeness will allow a measure of trustworthiness in the data, which is critical for data governance.

Lineage

Following the discussion of data transformations, it is important to note the role played by data lineage. Lineage, or *provenance*, is the recording of the "path" that data takes as it travels through extract-transform-load, and other movement of data, as new datasets and tables are created, discarded, restored, and generally used throughout the data life cycle. Lineage can be a visual representation of the data origins (creation, transformation, import) and should help answer the questions "Why does this dataset exist?" and "Where did the data come from?"

Why Lineage Is Useful

As data moves around your data lake, it intermingles and interacts with other data from other sources in order to produce *insight*. However, metadata—the information about the data sources and their classification—is at risk of getting lost as data travels. For example, you can potentially ask, for a given data source, "What is the quality of the data coming from that source?" It could be a highly reliable automatic process, or it could be a human-curated/validated dataset. There are other sources that you potentially trust less. As data from different sources intermingle, this information can sometimes be lost. Sometimes it is even desirable to forgo mixing certain data sources in order to preserve authenticity.

In addition to data quality, another common signal potentially available for source data is *sensitivity*. Census information and a recently acquired client phone list are of a certain level of sensitivity, while data scraped off a publicly available web page may be of a different sensitivity.

Thus, data sensitivity and quality, and other information potentially available on the origin, should filter down to the final data products.

The metadata information of the data sources (e.g., sensitivity, quality, whether or not the data contains PII, etc.) can support decisions about whether or not to allow certain data products to mix, whether or not to allow access to that data and to whom, and so on. When mixing data products, you will need to keep track of where the data came from. The business purpose for the data is of particular importance, as the created data products should be useful in achieving that purpose. If the business purpose requires, for example, a certain level of accuracy for time units, make sure the lineage of your data does not coarsen time values as the data is processed. Lineage is therefore crucial for an effective data governance strategy.

How to Collect Lineage

Ideally, your data warehouse or data catalog will have a facility that starts from the data origin and ends with whatever data products, dashboards, or models are used, and that can collect lineage for every transaction along the way. This is far from common, and there will likely be blindspots. You will have to either infer the information that you need on by-products or otherwise manually curate information to close the gap. Once you have this information, depending on how trustworthy it is, you can use it for governance purposes.

As your data grows (and it is common for successful businesses to accumulate data at an exponential rate) it is important to allow more and more automation into the process of lineage collection and to rely less and less on human curation. Automation is important because, as we will see in this chapter, lineage can make a huge difference in data governance, and placing human bottlenecks in the path to governance blocks an organization's ability to make data accessible. Also, a broken chain of lineage (e.g., due to human error) can have a larger impact on derivative data products, as trust becomes harder to come by.

Another way to collect/create lineage information is to connect to the API log for your data warehouse. The API log is expected to contain all SQL jobs and also all programmatic pipelines (R, Python, etc.). If there is a good job audit log, you can use it to create a lineage graph. This allows backtracking table creation statements to the table's predecessors, for example. This is not as effective as just-in-time lineage recording, as it requires backtracking the logs and batch processing. But assuming (not always true!) that you are focusing on lineage within the data warehouse, this method can be extremely useful.

Types of Lineage

The level of granularity of the lineage is important when discussing possible applications for that lineage. Normally, you would want lineage at least in the table/file level—i.e., this table is a product of this process and this other table.

In Figure 6-1, we see a very simple lineage graph of two tables joined by a SQL statement to create a third table.

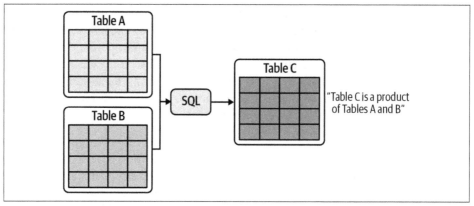

Figure 6-1. Table-level lineage

A column/field-level granularity is more useful: "This table consists of the following columns from this other table and another column from that table." When talking about column-level granularity, you can start to talk about specific types of data being tracked. In structured (tabular) data, a column is normally only a single data type. An example business case would be tracking PII: if you mark at the sources which columns are PII, you can continue tracking this PII as data is moved and new tables are created, and you can confidently answer which tables have PII. In Figure 6-2, two columns from Table A are joined with two columns from Table B to create Table C. If those source columns were "known PII" (as an example), you can use lineage to determine that Table C now contains PII as well.

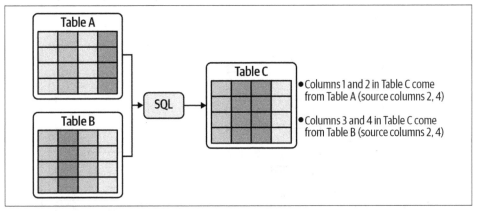

Figure 6-2. Column-level lineage

Row-level lineage allows the expression of information about transactions. Dataset-level lineage allows the expression of coarse information about data sources.

More Granular Access Controls

One of the most common use cases we have heard during our research and interviews is that, while project/file-level access controls work, being able to more granularly control access is highly desired. For example, column-level access control ("Provide access to columns 1–3 and 5–8 of this table but not column 4") allows you to lock down, if you will, a particular column of data and still allow access to the rest of the table.

This method works especially well for tables that contain much usable, relevant analytics data but may also contain some sensitive data. A prime example of this would be a telecommunications company and its retail store transactions. Each retail store's transaction logs not only would contain information about each item purchased, along with date, price, etc., but also would likely contain the purchaser's name (in the event the purchaser is a customer of the telecom company and put the item onto their account). An example system leveraging labels-based (or attribute-based) granular access controls is depicted in Figure 6-3.

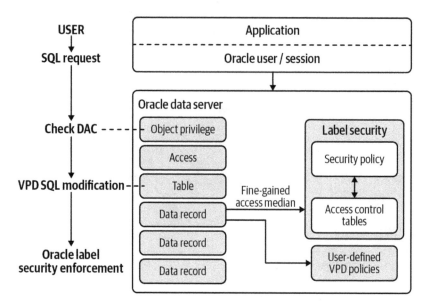

Figure 6-3. Label-based security (https://oreil.ly/z_wP5) in Oracle

An analyst certainly wouldn't need the customer's name or account information, but they would need the other relevant information of item purchased, location, time, price, and so on. Instead of having to either grant full access to this table or rewrite the table with the sensitive information removed, the sensitive column itself can have an access control so that only certain individuals are allowed access, and all others simply see the table with that column removed or redacted/hashed/encrypted in some way.

As we talked about in Chapter 3, most companies do not have enough headcount to support the constant monitoring, tagging, and rewriting of tables to remove or restrict sensitive information. Granular access controls can enable you to get the same result (sensitive information is guarded) while also allowing greater data democratization.

The Fourth Dimension

As data gets created, coarsened, and discarded, it is important to realize that lineage is a temporal state—while a certain table is currently a product of other tables, it is possible that in a previous iteration the very same table was generated out of other data.

Looking at the "state of now" is useful for certain applications, which we will discuss shortly, but it is important to remember that the past versions of certain data objects are relevant to gaining a true understanding of how data is being used and accessed throughout an enterprise. This requires versioning information that needs to be accessible on the object.

How to Govern Data in Flight

Working off the assumption that lineage information is preserved and is reliable to a certain extent, there are key governance applications that rely on lineage.

A common need that gets answered by lineage is debugging or understanding sudden changes in data. Why has a certain dashboard stopped displaying correctly? What data has caused a shift in the accuracy of a certain machine learning algorithm? And so on. Finding from an end product which information feeds into that end product and looking for changes (e.g., a sudden drop in quality, missing fields, unavailability of certain data) could significantly speed up tasks related to end products. Understanding the path and transformations of the data can also help troubleshoot data transformation errors.

Another need that commonly requires at least field-level lineage (and said lineage needs to be reliable) is the ability to infer data-class-level policies. For a certain column that contains PII, I want to mark all future descendants of this column as PII and to effect the same access/retention/masking policies of the source column to the derivatives. You will likely need some algorithmic intelligence that allows you to effect an identical policy if the column is copied precisely and to effect a different (or no) policy if the column contents are nullified as a result of the creation of a derivative.

In Figure 6-4, we see a slightly more involved lineage graph. While the operations performed to create derivatives are marked as "SQL," note that this is not always the case; sometimes there are other ways to transform the data (for example, different scripting languages). As data moves from the external data source into Table D, and as Table D is merged with Table C (the by-product of Tables A and B) and finally presented in a dashboard, you can see how keeping lineage, especially column-level lineage, is important.

For example, a question asked by the business user would be "Who can I show this dashboard to?" Let's say that just one of the sources (Table A, Table B, the external data source) contains PII in one of the columns, and that the desired policy on PII is "available only to full-time employees"; if PII made it into the dashboard, that should effect an access policy on the dashboard itself.

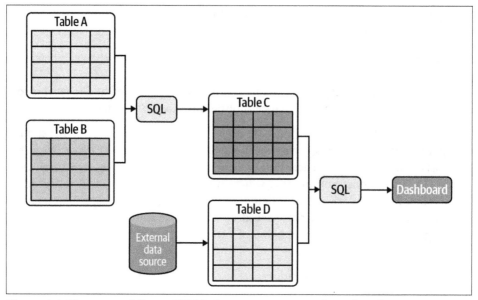

Figure 6-4. Lineage workflow—if Table B contains sensitive data, that data can potentially be found in the dashboard as well

These use cases are rather specific, but broader use cases have been expressed by CIOs and CISOs for a long time:

"Show me all the sensitive data within our data warehouse, and what systems contain sensitive data"
> This is a simple-to-express ask, and with the combination of lineage and the ability to classify data sources, it is much simpler to answer than understanding the multitude of data objects and systems that may be part of an organization's data lake.

"I want to identify certain systems as trusted, and make sure data does not exist in other, less trusted systems without manual oversight"
> This need can be addressed by enforcing egress controls on the trusted systems, a task which is potentially simpler with a good lineage solution. In this way, you can, for example, eliminate data being ingested from unapproved systems, because those sources will show up in the lineage information.

"I need to report and audit all systems that process PII"
> This is a common need in a post-GDPR world, and if you mark all sources of PII, you can leverage the lineage graph to identify where PII gets processed, allowing a new level of control.

Policy Management, Simulation, Monitoring, Change Management

We already provided one example for policy management: *inheritance*. In essence, data governance policies should be derived from the meaning of the data. If in a certain organization we want to govern PII, and PII is defined as all of personal phone numbers, email addresses, and street addresses, these individual infotypes can be automatically detected and associated with the data class. However, scanning a table and determining which columns contain these infotypes is expensive computationally. To correctly identify infotypes, the system will need to sample the relevant columns (without foreknowledge about which columns are sensitive, the entire table will need to be sampled), process those through a pattern matching and/or a machine learning model that will provide a level of confidence as to the underlying infotype, and tag the columns appropriately.

However, this process is made much more efficient if you can just identify the event of a column creation without changing in values from an already-tagged column. This is where lineage comes in.

Another use for lineage information is when data change management is considered. Let's imagine that you want to delete a certain table; or alternatively, you want to change the access policy on a data class; or maybe you want to set up a data-retention control that will coarsen the data over a period of time (for example, change the data from "GPS Coordinates" to city/state after 30 days). With lineage, you can follow the affected data to its end products and analyze the impact of this change. Let's say you limit access to a certain number of fields in a table. You can now see which dashboards or other systems use the data and assess the impact. A desirable result will be highlighting the change in access to end users accessing end products, so a warning could be issued at the time of changing the policy, alerting the administrator to the fact certain users will lose access and potentially even allowing a level of drill down so those users can be inspected and a more informed decision can be made.

Audit, Compliance

We often need to point at lineage information to be able to prove to an auditor or a regulator that a certain end product (machine learning model, dashboard, etc.) was fed into by specific and preapproved transactional information. This is necessary because regulators will want to be able to explain the reasoning behind certain decision-making algorithms and make sure these rely on data that was captured according to the enterprise's charter—for example, making sure loan approvals rely only on specific credit information that was collected according to regulations.

It is increasingly common for regulated organizations to be able to prove that even machine learning models are not biased, that decisions that are derived from data are done so without manipulation, and that there is an unbroken "chain of trust" between properly acquired data sources and the end-user tools (e.g., dashboards, expert systems) that are guiding those decisions. For example, in the credit scenario just described, a decision on a new line of credit must be traced exclusively to a list of transactions from a trusted source, without other influences guiding the decision.

 While it's clearly incredibly important to be able to "prove" compliance in the event of an external audit, these same tools can be used for internal auditing purposes as well. In fact, it's best practice (as we've mentioned several times in earlier chapters) to continually assess and reassess your governance program—how it's going, where it may need to be modified, and how it may or may not need to be updated as regulations and/or business needs change.

Summary

We have seen how collecting data lineage can enable data governance policies, inference, and automation. With a lineage graph, organizations can trace data variations and life cycle, promoting control and allowing a complete picture of the various systems involved in data collection and manipulation. For the business user, governing data while it is "in flight" through lineage allows a measure of trustworthiness to be inherited from trusted sources or trusted processors in the data path. This enriched context of lineage allows matching the right datasets (by sensitivity) to the right people or processes.

While lineage is essentially a technical construct, we should always keep the end business goal in mind. This could be "ensuring decisions are made with high-quality data," in which case we need to show lineage to the result from high-quality sources (and be able to discuss the transformations along the way), or a specific business case such as "tracing sensitive data," as we've already discussed.

The technical lineage and the business lineage use cases discussed here are both important, and we should strive to present the many technical details (e.g., intermediate processing tables) to analysts while at the same time serving a simplified "business view" to the business users.

CHAPTER 7

Data Protection

One of the key concerns of data governance is that of protecting data. Owners of data might be concerned about the potential exposure of sensitive information to individuals or applications without authorization. Leadership might be wary of security breaches or even of known personnel accessing data for the wrong reasons (e.g., to check on the purchase history of a celebrity). Users of the data might be concerned about how the data they rely on has been processed, or whether it has been tampered with.

Data protection has to be carried out at multiple levels to provide defense in depth. It is necessary to protect the physical data centers where the data is stored and the network infrastructure over which that traffic is carried. To do this, it is necessary to plan how authorized personnel and applications will be authenticated and how that authorization will be provisioned. However, it is not enough to simply secure access to the premises and the network—there is risk involved with known personnel accessing data that they are not supposed to be accessing, and these personnel are inside the network. Additional forms of protection such as encryption are required so that even if a security breach happens, the data is obfuscated.

Data protection needs to be agile because new threats and attack vectors continue to materialize.

Planning Protection

A key aspect of data governance is determining the level of protection that needs to be afforded to different types of data assets. Then all of the organization's data assets must be classified into these levels.

For example, at the *planning level*, it might be mandated that data created by the payment-processing system needs to be secured because a malicious actor with access to individual transaction data might be able to make spurious orders and have them billed to the original customer. This will then have to be implemented at the *authentication level* by ensuring that access to any aspect of the payments data is available only to personnel and applications that are recognized as having a role of employee. However, not all data is made available to all employees. Instead, the payments data might be classified at different levels. Only aggregate data by store location, date, inventory, and payment type might be made available to business planners. Access to individual transactions would be authorized only to the payments support team, and even then is granted only for specific transactions on a timed basis, when authorization is provided in the form of a support ticket carrying the customer's approval. Given this, it is necessary to ensure that exfiltration of payments data is not possible. The data governance tools and systems must support these requirements, and violations and breaches must be captured, and alerts carried out.

Ideally, a catalog of all the data assets is created, although quite often planning, classification, and implementation can happen at higher levels of abstraction. To carry out the above governance policy, for example, it is not necessary that you have an explicit catalog of all the possible aggregates of payment data—only that any aggregates that are created are placed in a governance environment with strict boundaries.

Lineage and Quality

As discussed in Chapter 5, data lineage and quality considerations are critical aspects of data governance. Therefore, they need to be part of the protection planning process. It is not enough to consider data protection of only raw data; instead, protection of the data at each stage of its transformation needs to be considered. When aggregates are computed from protected data, those aggregates need some level of protection that is typically equal to or less than the aggregate. When two datasets are joined, the level of protection afforded to the joined data is often the intersection of authentication and authorization permissions. Aggregates and joins affect the data quality, and so governance needs to take this into account as well. If the data protection on the raw data has restrictions on the volume of data that any person or partner is able to access, it might be necessary to revisit what the restriction on the aggregates and joins needs to be.

Lineage and quality checks also offer the capability to catch erroneous or malicious use of data. Corrupt or fraudulent data may be clearer when aggregated. For example, Benford's Law predicts the relative incidence of leading digits on numeric values that span multiple orders of magnitude. The last digits of numeric values are expected to have a normal distribution. Carrying out such statistical checks is easier on aggregated, transformed data. Once such fraud is observed, it is necessary to have the ability to trace back (through data lineage) where the change occurred and whether it was the result of a data protection breach.

It is part of the *data culture* of an organization that data published by the organization and used within the organization is trustworthy. Data quality, as discussed in Chapter 5, remains a fundamental goal of data protection. For this purpose, it is important to have trust-but-verify safeguards built into data pipelines to catch quality errors when they arise.

Level of Protection

The level of protection to be afforded to an asset should reflect the cost and likelihood of a security breach associated with that asset. This requires cataloging the types of security breaches and the costs associated with each breach. Different levels of protection also carry costs, and so it is necessary to identify the likelihood of a breach occurring with the given level of protection. Then a cost analysis that balances risk between different protection levels needs to be carried out, and a protection level chosen.

For example, consider the raw payments-processing information stored in a data lake. Potential security breaches might include individual transaction data being read by a malicious actor, all the transactions within a certain time period being read, all the transactions from a certain store being read, and so on. Similarly, there is a risk of data being modified, corrupted, or deleted.

 When considering the risk of data being modified, corrupted, or deleted, note that this may happen on purpose due to a malicious actor as we've described above, or it may happen unintentionally because of a mistake made by an internal employee. In many of our interviews with companies we have found that both scenarios can and have resulted in unfavorable and at times disastrous outcomes, and thus both warrant your attention and consideration.

The cost of a security breach at a given level of protection needs to include the cost of that data not being available, whether because of data protection or because of a security breach. It is also important to realize that loss of data continuity itself can carry costs, and so the cost of losing, say, an hour of data may affect the company's ability to provide accurate annual reports. The costs can also be quite indirect, such as downtime, legal exposure, loss of goodwill, or poor public relations. Because of all of these factors, the costs will typically be different for different stakeholders, whether they are end users, line-of-business decision makers, or company executives. The costs might also accrue outside the company to customers, suppliers, and shareholders. In cases where a granular-level cost estimate is impractical, a cost level of high/medium/low can be assigned to guide the level of protection that is needed.

There are usually a variety of choices in terms of the data protection that can be applied. At one extreme, we might choose to not store the data at all. At the other extreme, we might choose to make the dataset publicly available. In between are choices such as storing only aggregated data, storing only a subset of the data, or tokenizing certain fields. We can also choose where to store the data, perhaps driven by regulations around geographic locations and by which roles need to be provided access to the data. Risk levels vary between these choices, because the likelihood of a breach, data loss, or corruption is different with each.

Classification

As covered in detail in Chapter 4, implementing data governance requires being able to profile and classify sensitive data. This profile of the data is required to identify the potential security breaches, their cost, and their likelihood. This in turn will allow the data governance practitioner to select the appropriate governance policies and procedures that need to apply to the data.

There may be a number of governance directives associated with data classification, organization, and data protection. To enable data consumers to comply with those directives, there must be a clear definition of the categories (for organizational structure) and classifications (for assessing data sensitivity).

Classification requires properly evaluating a data asset, including the content of its different attributes (e.g., does a free-form text field contain phone numbers?). This process has to take into account both the business use of the data (which parts of the organization need to be able to access the data) and the privacy and sensitivity implications. Each data asset can then be categorized in terms of business roles and in terms of the different levels of data sensitivity, such as personal and private data, confidential data, and intellectual property.

Once the classification is determined and the protection level chosen by cost analysis, the protection level is implemented through two aspects. The first aspect is the provisioning of access to available assets. This can include determining the data services that will allow data consumers to access the data. The second aspect is prevention of unauthorized access. This is done by defining identities, groups, and roles and assigning access rights to each.

Data Protection in the Cloud

Organizations have to rethink data protection when they move data from on-premises to the cloud or when they burst data from on-premises to the cloud for ephemeral hybrid workloads.

Multi-Tenancy

When large enterprises that typically deploy their systems on-premises move to the cloud, one of the biggest changes they must come to terms with is being one of many organizations simultaneously using multi-tenant cloud architecture. This means that it is particularly important not to leak data by leaving it in unsecured locations due to unfounded confidence that malicious actors will not be able to authenticate into the physical infrastructure. Whereas on-premises organizations have physical and network perimeter control, that control may be lost when going to the cloud.

Some cloud providers provide "bare metal" infrastructure or "government cloud," essentially providing data center management to address this change. However, relying on such single-tenant architecture often brings increased costs, greater silos, and technical debt.

Many of the concepts and tools of on-premises security are implemented in the cloud. So it is possible to hew closely to the way data access, categorization, and classification are done on premises. However, such a lift-and-shift approach can involve giving up many of the benefits of a public cloud in terms of elasticity, democratization, and lower operating cost. Instead, we recommend applying cloud-native security policies to data that is held in the cloud, because there are better and more modern ways to achieve data protection goals.

Use cloud identity and access management (IAM) systems rather than the Kerberos-based or directory-based authentication that you may be using on premises. This best practice involves managing access services as well as interoperating with the cloud provider's IAM services by defining roles, specifying access rights, and managing and allocating access keys for ensuring that only authorized and authenticated individuals and systems are able to access data assets according to defined rules. There are tools that simplify migration by providing authentication mapping during the period of migration.

Security Surface

Another big change from on premises to cloud is the sense of vulnerability. At any particular time, there are a number of security threats and breaches in the news, and many of these will involve the public cloud. As we discussed in Chapter 1, much of this is due to the increased security monitoring and auditability that public cloud systems offer—many on-premises breaches can go unnoticed for long periods of time. However, because of this increased media attention, organizations may be concerned that they might be the next victim.

One of the benefits of the public cloud is the availability of dedicated, world-class security teams. For example, data center employees undergo special screening and are specifically trained on security. Also, a dedicated security team actively scans for security threats using commercial and custom tools, penetration tests, quality assurance (QA) measures, and software security reviews. The security team includes world-class researchers, and many software and hardware vulnerabilities are first discovered by these dedicated teams. At Google, for example, a full-time team known as Project Zero (*https://oreil.ly/E3HF0*) aims to prevent targeted attacks by reporting bugs to software vendors and filing them in an external database. The final argument against this sense of vulnerability is that "security by obscurity" was never a good option.

The security surface is also changed by the scale and sophistication of the tools used on the cloud. Whether it is the use of AI-enabled tools to quickly scan datasets for sensitive data or images for unsafe content, or the ability to process petabytes of data or to carry out processing in real time on streaming data, the cloud brings benefits in terms of being able to apply governance practices that may not be possible on premises. Being able to benefit from widely used and well-understood systems also reduces the chances of employee error. Finally, using a common set of tools to be able to comply with regulatory requirements in all the places where an organization does business leads to a dramatically simpler governance structure within that organization.

It is therefore worth having a conversation with your cloud vendor about security best practices, because they vary by public cloud. A public cloud where much of the traffic is on private fiber and where data is encrypted by default will have a different surface than one where traffic is sent over public internet.

Virtual Machine Security

A necessary part of securing your data in the public cloud is to design an architecture that limits the effects of a security compromise on the rest of the system. Because perimeter security is not an option, it is necessary to redesign the architecture to take advantage of shielding and confidential computing capabilities.

For example, Google Cloud offers Shielded VM to provide verifiable integrity of Compute Engine virtual machine (VM) instances. This is a cryptographically protected baseline measurement of the VM's image in order to make the virtual machines tamperproof and provide alerts on changes in their runtime state.

This security precaution allows organizations to be confident that your instances haven't been compromised by boot- or kernel-level malware. It prevents the virtual machine from being booted in a different context than it was originally deployed in—in other words, it prevents theft of VMs through "snapshotting" or other duplication.

Microsoft Azure offers Confidential Compute to allow applications running on Azure to keep data encrypted even when it's in-memory. This allows organizations to keep data secure even if someone is able to hack into the machine that is running the code.

AWS offers Nitro Enclaves to its customers to create isolated compute environments to further protect and securely process highly sensitive data such as PII and healthcare, financial, and intellectual property data within Amazon EC2 instances.

Part of data governance is to establish a strong detection and response infrastructure for data exfiltration events. Such an infrastructure will give you rapid detection of risky or improper activity, limit the "blast radius" of the activity, and minimize the window of opportunity for a malicious actor.

 Though we are discussing "blast radius" in terms of minimizing of the effects caused by a malicious actor, the blast radius concerns also apply to employees mistakenly (or purposefully) sharing data on the public internet. One concern of companies moving from on-premises to the cloud is the increased blast radius of such leaks. Data housed on premises, if leaked, will only leak internally and not publicly. Companies fear that if their data is in the cloud and leaks, it could potentially be accessible to anyone online. While this is a valid concern, we hope that by the end of this book you will be convinced that through the implementation and execution of a well-thought-out governance program you can head off and prevent either scenario. Ideally, you can make your decisions about where your data resides based on your business goals and objectives rather than on apprehension about the safety of cloud versus on-premises data storage and warehousing.

Physical Security

Make sure that data center physical security involves a layered security model using as many safeguards as possible, such as electronic access cards, alarms, vehicle access barriers, perimeter fencing, metal detectors, biometrics, and laser-beam intrusion detection. The data center should be monitored 24/7 by high-resolution interior and exterior cameras that can detect and track intruders.

Besides these automated methods, there needs to be good old-fashioned human security as well. Ensure that the data center is routinely patrolled by experienced security guards who have undergone rigorous background checks and training. Not all employees of the company need access to the data center—so the data center access needs to be limited to a much smaller subset of approved employees with specific roles. Metal detectors and video surveillance need to be implemented to help make sure no equipment leaves the data center floor without authorization.

As you get closer to the data center floor, security measures should increase, with extra multifactor access control in every corridor that leads to the data center floor. Physical security also needs to be concerned with what authorized personnel can do in the data center, and whether they can access only parts of the data center. Access control by sections is important in cases where regulatory compliance requires that all maintenance be performed by citizens of a certain country/countries and/or by personnel who have passed security clearances.

Physical security also includes ensuring an uninterrupted power supply and reducing the chance of damage. The data center needs redundant power systems, with every critical component having a primary and an alternate power source. Environmental controls are also important to ensure smooth running and reduce the chances of machine failure. Cooling systems should maintain a constant operating temperature for servers and other hardware, reducing the risk of service outages. Fire detection and suppression equipment is needed to prevent damage to hardware. It is necessary to tie these systems in with the security operations console so that heat, fire, and smoke detectors trigger audible and visible alarms in the affected zone, at security operations consoles, and at remote monitoring desks.

Access logs, activity records, and camera footage should be made available in case an incident occurs. A rigorous incident management process for security events is required so as to inform customers about data breaches that may affect the confidentiality, integrity, or availability of systems or data. The US National Institute of Standards and Technology (NIST) provides guidance on devising a security incident management program (NIST SP 800–61) (*https://oreil.ly/ahWHi*). Data center staff need to be trained in forensics and handling evidence.

Physical security involves tracking the equipment that is in the data center over its entire life cycle. The location and status of all equipment must be tracked from the time it is acquired, through installation, and all the way to retirement and eventual destruction. Stolen hard drives must be rendered useless by ensuring that all data is encrypted when stored. When a hard drive is retired, the disk should be verifiably erased by writing zeros to the drive and ensuring the drive contains no data. Malfunctioning drives that cannot be erased have to be physically destroyed in a way that prevents any sort of disk recovery—a multistage process that involves crushing, deformation, shredding, breakage, and recycling is recommended.

Finally, it is necessary to routinely exercise all aspects of the data center security system, from disaster recovery to incident management. These tests should take into consideration a variety of scenarios, including insider threats and software vulnerabilities.

If you are using the data center in a public cloud, the public cloud provider should be able to provide you (and any regulatory authorities) with documentation and processes around all of these aspects.

Network Security

The simplest form of network security is a perimeter network security model—all applications and personnel within the network are trusted, and all others outside the network are not. Unfortunately, perimeter security is not sufficient for protecting sensitive data, whether on-premises or in the cloud. First of all, no perimeter is 100% safe. At some point, some malicious actor will break into the system, and, at that point data may become exposed. The second issue with perimeter security is that not all applications within the network can be trusted—an application may have suffered a security breach, or a disgruntled employee may be trying to exfiltrate data or trying to access systems they shouldn't have access to. Therefore, it is important to institute additional methods of data protection to ensure that exposed data cannot be read—this can include encrypting all stored and in-transit data, masking sensitive data, and having processes around deleting data when it is no longer needed.

Security in Transit

Network security is made difficult because application data often must make several journeys between devices, known as "hops," across the public internet. The number of hops depends on the distance between the customer's ISP and the cloud provider's data center. Each additional hop introduces a new opportunity for data to be attacked or intercepted. A cloud provider or network solution that can limit the number of hops on the public internet and carry more of the traffic on private fiber can offer better security than a solution that requires use of the public internet for all hops. Google's IP data network, for instance, consists of its own fiber, public fiber, and undersea cables. This is what allows Google to deliver highly available and low-latency services across the globe. Google Cloud customers can optionally choose to have their traffic on this private network or on the public internet. Choose between these options depending on the speed your use case requires and the sensitivity of the data being transmitted.

Because data is vulnerable to unauthorized access as it travels, it is important to secure data in transit by taking advantage of strong encryption. It is also necessary to protect the endpoints from illegal request structures. One example of this is to use gRPC (Google's high-performance remote procedural call) as the application transport layer. gRPC is based around the idea of defining a service, specifying the methods that can be called remotely with their parameters and return types. gRPC can use protocol buffers as both its interface definition language (IDL) and its underlying message interchange format. Protocol buffers are Google's language-neutral, platform-neutral, extensible mechanism for serializing structured data—think XML, but smaller, faster, and simpler. Protocol buffers allow a program to introspect, that is, to examine the type or properties of an object at runtime, ensuring that only connections with correctly structured data will be allowed.

Regardless of the type of network, it is necessary to make sure applications serve only traffic and protocols that meet security standards. This is usually done by the cloud provider; firewalls, access control lists, and traffic analysis are used to enforce network segregation and to stop distributed denial-of-service (DDoS) attacks. Additionally, it is ideal if servers are allowed to communicate with only a controlled list of servers ("default deny"), rather than allowing access very broadly. Logs should be routinely examined to reveal any exploits and unusual activity.

Zoom Bombing

COVID-19 has changed how many of us work, and we have found ourselves attending a ton of video meetings across Zoom, Google Meet, Webex, and other videoconferencing apps. It's not surprising that this surge in popularity and usage has also brought up many cautionary tales of "Zoom bombings," in which bad actors use open or poorly secured Zoom meetings to post malicious content (*https://oreil.ly/jkLR-*).

First the media and then, in quick succession, regulators and Congress began to scrutinize, publicize, and take legal action with respect to what were perceived as privacy or data security flaws in the products of some technology companies. The premise was that some of these video calls were not as private as you might think, and that customer data was being collected and being used in ways that the customers did not intend. The issues have been a lot more complicated because the California Consumer Privacy Act (CCPA), which took effect on January 1, 2020, instituted many regulations pertaining to consumer data and how it can be used.

When the world changes and companies are forced to react quickly to these dynamics, things are bound to happen, and consumer privacy and data security are usually violated. This is not new. We've seen this with Zoom, Facebook, YouTube, TikTok, and many other large organizations that grow quickly and then get caught up in the limelight. Whenever any organization rises to prominence so quickly, it emerges from obscurity and can no longer treat privacy and data security as anything other than a top priority.

And even with all these violations, these are still difficult conversations to have in light of the immense contributions Zoom is making to advance the greater good by scaling its operations so quickly to allow millions of Americans to communicate with each other during a public health crisis.

This truly reinforces the notion that security and governance should not be an afterthought; they should be baked into the fabric of your organization. This chapter reinforces all the elements your organization should think about when it comes to data protection and ensuring that your data is always protected, in transit and at rest. Happily, Zoom made several security improvements, including alerting organizers of video calls if the link to their meeting is posted online (see Figure 7-1).

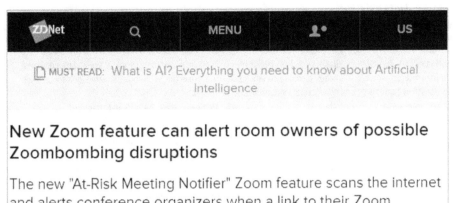

Figure 7-1. Improvements being made after a Zoom security debacle (https://oreil.ly/-EPCf).

Data Exfiltration

Data exfiltration is a scenario in which an authorized person or application extracts the data they are allowed to access and then shares it with unauthorized third parties or moves it to insecure systems. Data exfiltration can occur maliciously or accidentally. It can also happen because the authorized account has been compromised by a malicious actor.

The traditional method of addressing data exfiltration risk relied on hardening the physical perimeter defenses of private networks. In a public cloud, though, the network fabric is shared among multiple tenants, and there is no perimeter in the traditional sense. Securing data in the cloud requires new security approaches and methods of auditing data access.

It is possible to deploy specialized agents that produce telemetry about user and host activity in virtual machines. Cloud providers also support the introduction of explicit chokepoints, such as network proxy servers, network egress servers, and cross-project networks. These measures can reduce the risk of data exfiltration, but they cannot eliminate it completely.

It is important to recognize common data exfiltration mechanisms, identify data at risk of exfiltration through these vectors, and put mitigation mechanisms in place. Table 7-1 summarizes the considerations.

Table 7-1. Data exfiltration vectors and mitigation strategies

Exfiltration vector	Data at risk	Mitigation mechanism
Use business email or mobile devices to transmit sensitive data from secure systems to untrusted third parties or insecure systems.	Contents of organization emails, calendars, databases, images, planning documents, business forecasts, and source code.	Limit volume and frequency of data transmission. Audit email metadata such as from- and to- addresses. Scan email content using automated tools for common threats. Alert on insecure channels and attempts.
Download sensitive data to unmonitored or insecure devices.	Files of sensitive data; any sensitive data accessed via applications that offer a download feature.	Avoid storing sensitive data in files ("data lake"), and instead keep it in managed storage such as an enterprise data warehouse. Establish a policy that prohibits downloads, and keep access logs of data that is requested and served. Regulate connections between authorized clients and cloud services using an access security broker. Implement dynamic watermarking in visualizations to record the user responsible for screenshots or photographs of sensitive information. Add permissions-aware security and encryption on each file using digital rights management (DRM).
Requisition or modify virtual machines (VMs), deploy code, or make requests to cloud storage or computation services. Anyone with sufficient permission can initiate outbound transmission of sensitive data.	Any sensitive data that is accessible to employees in organizations' IT departments.	Maintain precise, narrowly scoped permissions, and comprehensive, immutable audit logs. Maintain separate development and test datasets that consist of simulated or tokenized data, and limit access to production datasets. Provide data access to service accounts with narrow permissions, not to user credentials. Scan all data sent to the broader internet to identify sensitive information. Prohibit outgoing connections to unknown addresses. Avoid giving your VMs public IP addresses. Disable remote management software like remote desktop protocol (RDP).
Employee termination	All types of data, even normally benign data like historical company memos, are at risk of data exfiltration by employees anticipating imminent termination.[a]	Connect logging and monitoring systems to HR software and set more conservative thresholds for alerting security teams to abnormal behavior by these users.

[a] Michael Hanley and Joji Montelibano, "Insider Threat Control: Using Centralized Logging to Detect Data Exfiltration Near Insider Termination" (*https://oreil.ly/UXny3*), Software Engineering Institute, Carnegie Mellon University, 2011.

In summary, because perimeter security is not an option, use of public cloud infrastructure requires increased vigilance and new approaches to secure data from exfiltration. We recommend that organizations:

- Minimize the blast radius of data exfiltration events by compartmentalizing data and permissions to access that data, perhaps through line of business or by common workloads that access that data.

- Use fine-grained access control lists and grant access to sensitive data sparingly and in a time-bound manner.

- Provide only simulated or tokenized data to development teams, because the ability to create cloud infrastructure creates special risks.

- Use immutable logging trails to increase transparency into the access and movement of data in your organization.

- Restrict and monitor ingress and egress to machines in your organization using networking rules, IAM, and bastion hosts.

- Create a baseline of normal data flows, such as amounts of data accessed or transferred, and geographical locations of access against which to compare abnormal behaviors.

Virtual Private Cloud Service Controls (VPC-SC)

Virtual Private Cloud Service Controls (VPC-SC) improves the ability of an organization to mitigate the risk of data exfiltration from cloud-native data lakes and enterprise data warehouses. With VPC-SC, organizations create perimeters that protect the resources and data of an explicitly specified set of services (Figure 7-2).

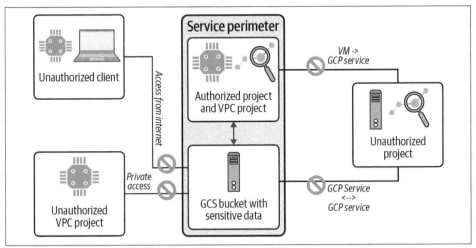

Figure 7-2. VPC-SC creates a perimeter around a set of services and data so that the data is inaccessible from outside the perimeter, even to personnel and applications with valid credentials.

VPC-SC thus extends private access and perimeter security to cloud services and allows unfettered access to data for applications within the perimeter without opening up that data to access from malicious insiders, compromised code, or malicious actors with stolen authentication credentials. Resources within a perimeter can be accessed only from clients within authorized VPC networks (either the public cloud network or an explicitly allowed on-premises one). It is possible to restrict internet access to resources within a perimeter through allowed IP addresses or ranges of addresses.

Clients within a perimeter that have private access to resources do not have access to unauthorized (potentially public) resources outside the perimeter—this is what limits the data exfiltration risk. Data cannot be copied to unauthorized resources outside the perimeter.

VPC-SC, when used in conjunction with a restricted virtual IP, can be used to prevent access from a trusted network to storage services that are not integrated with VPC service controls. The restricted VIP (virtual IP) also allows requests to be made to services supported by VPC Service Controls without exposing those requests to the internet. VPC Service Controls provides an additional layer of security by denying access from unauthorized networks, even if the data is exposed by misconfigured Cloud IAM policies.

We recommend that you use the dry-run features of VPC-SC to monitor requests to protected services without preventing access. This will enable you to monitor requests to gain a better understanding of request traffic to your projects and provide a way to create honeypot perimeters to identify unexpected or malicious attempts to probe accessible services.

Note that VPC-SC limits the movement of data, rather than metadata, across a service perimeter via supported services. While in many cases VPC-SC also controls access to metadata, there may be scenarios in which metadata can be copied and accessed without VPC-SC policy checks. It is necessary to rely on Cloud IAM to ensure appropriate control over access to metadata.

Secure Code

Data lineage is of no effect if the application code that produces or transforms the data is not trusted. Binary authorization mechanisms such as Kritis (*https://oreil.ly/pqoXi*) provide software supply-chain security when deploying container-based applications. The idea is to extend the Kubernetes-managed runtime and enforce security policies at deploy time. In Google Cloud, binary authorization works with container images from Container Registry or another container image registry and extends Google Kubernetes Engine (GKE). This allows the organization to scan built containers for vulnerabilities before deploying to systems that can access sensitive data.

Binary authorization implements a policy model, where a policy is a set of rules that governs the deployment of container images to an operational cluster. Rules in a policy specify the criteria that an image must pass before it can be deployed. A typical policy requires a container image to have a verified digital signature before it is deployed.

In this type of policy, a rule specifies which trusted authorities, called *signers*, must assert that required processes have completed and that an image is ready to move to the next stage of deployment. A signer may be a human user or more often it's a machine process such as a build-and-test system or a part of your continuous deployment pipeline.

During the development life cycle, signers digitally sign globally unique container image descriptors, thereby creating certificated statements called *attestations*. Later, during the deploy phase, Binary Authorization uses *attestors* to verify the certificate indicating that required processes in your pipeline have been completed.

Zero-Trust Model

A perimeter-based security model is problematic, because when that perimeter is breached, an attacker has relatively easy access to a company's privileged intranet. As companies adopt mobile and cloud technologies, the perimeter becomes increasingly difficult to enforce. By shifting access controls from the network perimeter to individual users and devices, a zero-trust security model allows users to access enterprise applications from virtually any location without the need for a traditional VPN.

The zero-trust model assumes that an internal network is untrustworthy and builds enterprise applications based on the assumption that all network traffic emanates from a zero-trust network, i.e., the public internet. Instead of relying on the IP address of the origin, access to an application depends solely on device and user credentials. All access to enterprise resources is authenticated, authorized, and encrypted based on device state and user credentials. Fine-grained access to different parts of enterprise resources is enforced, and the goal is to make the user experience of accessing enterprise resources effectively identical between internal and public networks.

The zero-trust model (*https://oreil.ly/evZSf*) consists of a few specific parts:

- Only a device that is procured and actively managed by the enterprise is allowed to access corporate applications.
- All managed devices need to be uniquely identified using a device certificate that references the record in a *device inventory database*, which needs to be maintained.

- All users are tracked and managed in a *user database* and a *group database* that tightly integrate with HR processes that manage job categorization, usernames, and group memberships for all users.

- A centralized user-authentication portal validates two-factor credentials for users requesting access to enterprise resources.

- An unprivileged network that very closely resembles an external network, although within a private address space, is defined and deployed. The unprivileged network only connects to the internet, and to limited infrastructure and configuration management systems. All managed devices are assigned to this network while physically located in the office, and there needs to be a strictly managed access control list (ACL) between this network and other parts of the network.

- Enterprise applications are exposed via an Internet-facing access proxy that enforces encryption between the client and the application.

- An access control manager interrogates multiple data sources to determine the level of access given to a single user and/or a single device at any point in time. The latter is called *endpoint verification*.

Identity and Access Management

Access control encompasses *authentication*, *authorization*, and *auditing*. Authentication determines who you are, authorization determines what you can do, and auditing logs record what you did.

Authentication

The identity specifies who has access. This could be an end user who is identified by a username, or an application identified by a service account.

User accounts represent a data scientist or business analyst, or an administrator. They are intended for scenarios (e.g., notebooks, dashboard tools, or administration tools) in which an application needs to access resources interactively on behalf of a human user.

Service accounts are managed by Cloud IAM and represent nonhuman users. They are intended for scenarios in which an application needs to access resources automatically. Service accounts are essentially robot accounts that are defined to have a subset of the permissions held by the creator of the service account. Typically, they are created to embody the limited set of permissions required by applications that are run on the account creator's behalf.

Cloud APIs reject requests that do not contain a valid application credential (no anonymous requests are processed). Application credentials need to provide the required information about the caller making the request. Valid credential types are:

API keys
> Note that an API key says only that this is a registered application. If the application requires user-specific data, the user needs to authenticate themselves as well. This can be difficult, and so API keys are often used only to access services (e.g., requests for stock market quotes) that do not need user credentials but just a way to ensure that this is a paid subscriber.

Access tokens such as OAuth 2.0 client credentials
> This credential type involves two-factor authentication and is the recommended approach for authenticating interactive users. The end user allows the application to access data on their behalf.

Service account keys
> Service accounts provide both the application credential and an identity.

Authorization

The role determines what access is allowed to the identity in question. A role consists of a set of permissions. It is possible to create a custom role to provide granular access to a custom list of permissions. For example, the role `roles/bigquery.metadata Viewer`, when assigned to an identity, allows that person to access metadata (and only the metadata, not the table data) of a BigQuery dataset.

To grant multiple roles to allow a particular task, create a group, grant the roles to that group, and then add users or other groups to that group. You might find it helpful to create groups for different job functions within your organization and to give everyone in those groups a set of predefined roles. For example, all members of your data science team might be given `dataViewer` and `jobUser` permissions on data warehousing datasets. This way, if people change jobs, you'll just need to update their membership in the appropriate groups instead of updating their access to datasets and projects one dataset or project at a time.

Another reason to create a custom role is to subtract permissions from the predefined roles. For example, the predefined role `dataEditor` allows the possessor to create, modify, and delete tables. However, you might want to allow your data suppliers to create tables but not to modify or delete any existing tables. In such a case, you would create a new role named `dataSupplier` and provide it with the specific list of permissions.

Normally, access to resources is managed individually, resource by resource. An identity does not get the `dataViewer` role or the `tables.getData` permission on all resources in a project; rather, the permission should be granted on specific datasets or tables. As much as possible, avoid permission/role creep; err on the side of providing the least amount of privileges to identities. This includes restricting both the roles and the resources on which they are provided. Balance this against the burden of updating permissions on new resources as they are created. One reasonable compromise is to set trust boundaries that map projects to your organizational structure and set roles at the project level—IAM policies can then propagate down from projects to resources within the project, thus automatically applying to new datasets in the project. The problem with such individualized access is that it can quickly get out of hand.

Another option for implementing authorization is to use Identity-Aware Proxy (IAP). IAP lets you establish a central authorization layer for applications accessed by HTTPS, so you can use an application-level access control model instead of relying on network-level firewalls. IAP policies scale across your organization. You can define access policies centrally and apply them to all of your applications and resources. When you assign a dedicated team to create and enforce policies, you protect your project from incorrect policy definition or implementation in any application. Use IAP when you want to enforce access control policies for applications and resources. With IAP, you can set up group-based application access: a resource could be accessible for employees and inaccessible for contractors, or accessible only to a specific department.

Policies

Policies are rules or guardrails that enable your developers to move quickly, but within the boundaries of security and compliance. There are policies that apply to users—authentication and security policies, such as two-factor authentication, or authorization policies that determine who can do what on which resources—and there are also policies that apply to resources and are valid for all users.

Where possible, define policies hierarchically. Hierarchical policies allow you to create and enforce a consistent policy across your organization. You can assign hierarchical policies to the organization as a whole or to individual business units, projects, or teams. These policies contain rules that can explicitly deny or allow roles. Lower-level rules cannot override a rule from a higher place in the resource hierarchy. This allows organization-wide admins to manage critical rules in one place. Some hierarchical policy mechanisms allow the ability to delegate evaluation of a rule to lower levels. Monitor the use of the rules to see which one is being applied to a specific network or data resource. This can help with compliance.

Context-Aware Access is an approach that works with the zero-trust network security model to enforce granular access control based on a user's identity and the context of the request. Use Context-Aware Access when you want to establish fine-grained access control based on a wide range of attributes and conditions, including what device is being used and from what IP address. Making your corporate resources context-aware improves your security posture. For example, depending on the policy configuration, it is possible to provide edit access to an employee using a managed device from the corporate network, but provide them only view access to the data if the access is from a device that has not been fully patched.

Instead of securing your resources at the network level, Context-Aware Access puts controls at the level of individual devices and users. Context-Aware Access works by leveraging four key pieces of technology that have all been discussed in this chapter:

Identity-Aware Proxy (IAP)
A service that enables employees to access corporate apps and resources from untrusted networks without the use of a VPN.

Cloud identity and access management (Cloud IAM)
A service that manages permissions for cloud resources

Access context manager
A rules engine that enables fine-grained access control.

Endpoint verification
A way of collecting user device details.

Data Loss Prevention

In some cases, especially when you have free-form text or images (such as with records of support conversations), you might not even know where sensitive data exists. It is possible that the customer has revealed their home address or credit card number. It can therefore be helpful to scan data stores looking for known patterns such as credit card numbers, company confidential project codes, and medical information. The result of a scan can be used as a first step toward ensuring that such sensitive data is properly secured and managed, thus reducing the risk of exposing sensitive details. It can also be important to carry out such scans periodically to keep up with growth in data and changes in use.

AI methods such as Cloud Data Loss Prevention (*https://cloud.google.com/dlp*) can be used to scan tables and files in order to protect your sensitive data (see Figure 7-3). These tools come with built-in information type detectors to identify patterns, formats, and checksums. They may also provide the ability to define custom information type detectors using dictionaries, regular expressions, and contextual elements. Use the tool to de-identify your data, including masking, tokenization, pseudonymization, date shifting, and more, all without replicating customer data.

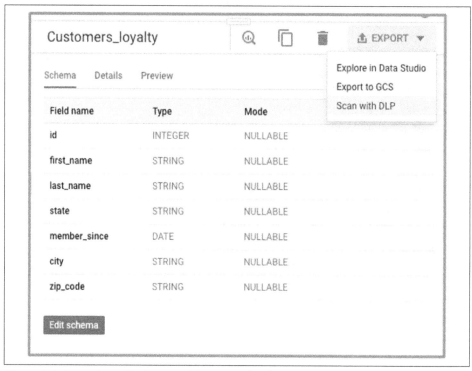

Figure 7-3. Scanning a BigQuery table using Cloud DLP.

To redact or otherwise de-identify sensitive data that the Cloud DLP scan found, protect the data through encryption, as discussed in the next section.

Encryption

Encryption helps to ensure that if the data accidentally falls into an attacker's hands, they cannot access the data without also having access to the encryption keys. Even if an attacker obtains the storage devices containing your data, they won't be able to understand or decrypt it. Encryption also acts as a "chokepoint"—centrally managed encryption keys create a single place where access to data is enforced and can be audited. Finally, encryption contributes to the privacy of customer data—it allows systems to manipulate data, for example, for backup, and it allows engineers to support the infrastructure without providing access to content.

It is possible to use a public cloud provider's encryption-at-rest and encryption-in-transit mechanisms to ensure that low-level infrastructure access (to hard drives or network traffic, for example) does not afford the ability to read your data. Sometimes, however, regulatory compliance might require you to make sure that your data is encrypted with your own keys. In such cases, you can use customer-managed encryption keys (CMEK), and you can manage your keys in a key management system (KMS), even in Cloud KMS, GCP's central key management service. Then you can designate datasets or tables that you want to be encrypted using those keys.

Multiple layers of key wrapping are used so that the master keys aren't exposed outside of KMS (see Figure 7-4). Every CMEK-protected table has a wrapped key as part of the table metadata. When the native cloud tools access the table, they send a request to Cloud KMS to unwrap the key. The unwrapped table key is then used to unwrap separate keys for each record or file. There are a number of advantages to this key-wrapping protocol that reduce the risk should an unwrapped key be leaked. If you have an unwrapped file key, you can't read any other files. If you have an unwrapped table key, you can only unwrap file keys after you pass access control checks. And Cloud KMS never discloses the master key. If you delete the key from KMS, the other keys can never be unwrapped.

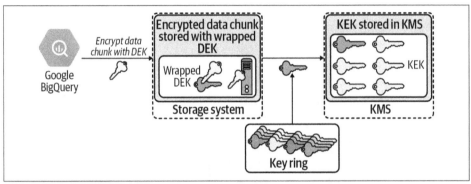

Figure 7-4. Envelope encryption with data encryption key (DEK) and key encryption key (KEK). The KEKs are managed centrally in a KMS, which rotates keys through the use of a key ring.

A common use of encryption is to delete all records associated with a specific user, often in response to a legal request. It is possible to plan for such deletion by assigning a unique encryption key to each userId and encrypting all sensitive data corresponding to a user with that encryption key. In addition to maintaining user privacy, you can remove the records for a user simply by deleting the encryption key. This approach has the advantage of immediately making the user records unusable (as long as the deleted key is not recoverable) in all the tables in your data warehouse, including backups and temporary tables. To query the encrypted table, you need to decrypt the data before querying. This approach is called *crypto-shredding*.

Differential Privacy

Another concept for keeping data secure, especially when discussing private data, is differential privacy. Differential privacy is necessary when you want to share a dataset that contains highly personal or otherwise sensitive information without exposing any of the involved parties to identification. This means describing aggregate data while withholding information about the individuals. However, this is not a simple task—there are ways to statistically re-identify individuals in the dataset by cross-matching different dimensions of aggregate data (and knowing something about the individual). For example, you can extract a particular salary from an aggregate average—if you run multiple averages across the salary recipient's home neighborhood, their age group, and so on, you will eventually be able to compute the salary.

There are common techniques for ensuring differential privacy:

k-anonymity
> k-anonymity means that aggregates returned from queries to the datasets are representing groups of at least k individuals, or are otherwise expanded to include k individuals (Figure 7-5). The value of k is determined by the size of the dataset and other considerations relevant to the particular data represented.

Name	Age	Gender	Religion	Disease
*	$20 < Age \leq 30$	Female	*	Cancer
*	$20 < Age \leq 30$	Female	*	Viral infection
*	$20 < Age \leq 30$	Female	*	TB
*	$20 < Age \leq 30$	Male	*	No illness
*	$20 < Age \leq 30$	Female	*	Heart-related
*	$20 < Age \leq 30$	Male	*	TB
*	$Age \leq 20$	Male	*	Cancer
*	$20 < Age \leq 30$	Male	*	Heart-related
*	$Age \leq 20$	Male	*	Heart-related
*	$Age \leq 20$	Male	*	Viral infection

Figure 7-5. Example of a k-anonymized table in which the age was replaced with a k-anonymized value.

Adding "statistically insignificant noise" to the dataset
> For fields such as age or gender where there is a discrete list of possible values, you can add statistical noise to the dataset so that aggregates are skewed slightly to preserve privacy but the data remains useful. Examples of such techniques that generalize the data and reduce granularity are *l*-diversity and *t*-distance.

Access Transparency

It is important for safeguarding access to the data that any access to the data is *transparent*. Only a small number of on-call engineers should be able to access user data in the production system, and even then it should only be to ensure safe running of the system. Whenever someone in the IT department or cloud provider accesses your data, you should be notified.

In Google Cloud, for example, Access Transparency provides you with logs that capture the actions Google personnel take when accessing your content. Cloud Audit Logs helps you answer questions about "who did what, where, and when?" in your cloud projects. While Cloud Audit Logs provides these logs about the actions taken by members within your own organization, Access Transparency provides logs of the actions taken by personnel who work for the cloud provider.

You might need Access Transparency logs data for the following reasons:

- To verify that cloud provider personnel are accessing your content only for valid business reasons, such as fixing an outage or in response to a support request
- To verify and track compliance with legal or regulatory obligations
- To collect and analyze tracked access events through an automated security information and event management (SIEM) tool

Note that the Access Transparency logs have to be used in conjunction with Cloud Audit Logs because the Access Transparency logs do not include access that originates from a standard workload allowed through Cloud IAM policies.

Keeping Data Protection Agile

Data protection cannot be rigid and unchanging. Instead, it has to be agile to take account of changes in business processes and respond to observed new threats.

Security Health Analytics

It is important to continually monitor the set of permissions given to users to see whether any of those are unnecessarily broad. For example, we can periodically scan user-role combinations to find how many of the granted permissions are being used. In Figure 7-6, the second user has been granted a BigQuery Admin role but is using only 5 of the 31 permissions that the role grants. In such cases, it is better to either reduce the role or create a more granular custom role.

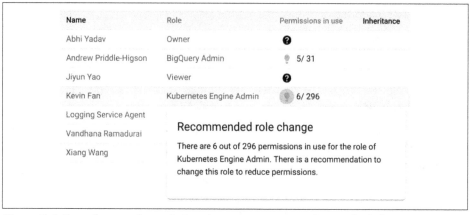

Figure 7-6. Scan the use of permissions by users to narrow down role definitions or provide the users more fine-grained access.

Data Lineage

A key attribute of keeping data protection agile is to understand the lineage of every piece of data. Where did it come from? When was it ingested? What transformations have been carried out? Who carried out these transformations? Were there any errors that resulted in records being skipped?

It is important to ensure that data fusion and transformation tools (see Figure 7-7) provide such lineage information, and that this linear information is used to analyze errors being encountered by production systems.

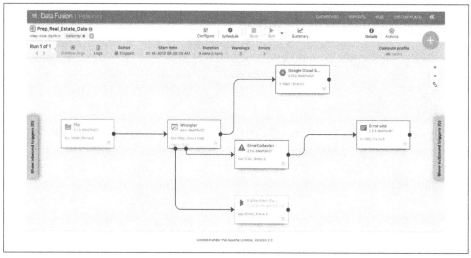

Figure 7-7. It is important to maintain the data lineage of all enterprise data and address errors in ingest processes.

Event Threat Detection

The overall security health needs to be continually monitored as well. Network security logs need to be analyzed to find the most frequent causes of security incidents. Are a number of users trying (and failing) to access a specific file or table? It is possible that the metadata about the file or table has been breached. It is worth searching for the source of the metadata leak and plugging it. It is also advisable to secure the table before one of the attacks succeeds.

Instead of limiting ourselves to scanning security logs, it is worth modeling network traffic and looking for anomalous activity in order to identify suspicious behavior and uncover threats. For example, an unusual number of SSH logins by an authorized employee might be a sign of data exfiltration, and the definition of "unusual" in this case can be learned by an AI model that compares the activity of an employee against their peers who are doing a similar role and working on similar projects.

Data Protection Best Practices

While data protection is top of mind for all industries and users, there are different approaches from one industry to another, including some stricter approaches in industries such as healthcare, government, and financial services that routinely deal in sensitive data.

The healthcare industry has been dealing with medical records for decades. As healthcare providers have moved more and more to digital tools for record keeping, the industry has experienced globally known incidents. The ransomware cyberattack that affected more than 60 trusts within the United Kingdom's National Health Service (NHS) spread to more than 200,000 computer systems in 150 countries, and the list continues to grow.[1]

Similarly, financial institutions have been dealing with cyberattacks. We still remember when Equifax announced a massive cybersecurity breach in 2017 in which cybercriminals accessed the personal data of some 145.5 million Equifax customers, including full names, social security numbers, birth dates, addresses, and driver's license numbers. At least 209,000 customers' credit card credentials were taken in the attack.[2] Since then, a number of more visible data breaches have taken place, and many if not all of them affected managed systems that were part of the companies' own data centers.

---

1 Roger Collier, "NHS Ransomware Attack Spreads Worldwide" (*https://oreil.ly/54shB*), *Canadian Medical Association Journal* 189, no. 22 (June 2017): E786–E787.

2 David Floyd, "Was I Hacked? Find Out If the Equifax Breach Affects You" (*https://oreil.ly/1oJpI*), *Investopedia*, updated June 25, 2019.

The natural question that comes to mind is: why are these data breaches still taking place. even with the effective processes and tools that are available, and despite a concerted focus to protect data? It comes down to how the best practices are implemented, and whether the institutions are staying on top of their data governance processes day in and day out, 24/7, with no complacency. In the previous sections, we have highlighted a comprehensive way of protecting the data; in cloud, with physical and network security, and with advanced IAM.

Professionals in each industry—healthcare, financial institutions, retail, and others—are trying to establish what they believe to be the best practices for their world when it comes to data protection. As an example of those best practices, let's start with what data protection experts in the healthcare industry are suggesting to their users.

A data breach in healthcare can occur in several forms. It could be a criminal cyberattack to access protected health data for the purpose of committing medical identity theft, or it could be an instance of a healthcare employee viewing patient records without authorization.

Organizations in the healthcare industry have to be very diligent in protecting sensitive patient, financial, and other types of datasets, and must stay on top of this 24/7, throughout their entire operations, by educating their employees and by utilizing best-in-class security tools and best practices for the industry. Here are some of the recommended best practices for the healthcare industry.

Separated Network Designs

Hackers utilize various methods to gain access to healthcare organizations' networks. IT departments in the healthcare industry should rigorously deploy tools such as firewalls and antivirus and anti-malware software rigorously. However, focusing on perimeter security is not enough. Healthcare firms should adopt network design approaches that separate networks so that intruders cannot access the patient data even if they are able to obtain access to parts of their network. Some firms are already practicing and benefitting from these practices at the network-design level.

Physical Security

Paper-based record keeping of much of the sensitive data is still a very common practice in the healthcare industry, and it is imperative that healthcare providers provide physical security with locked cabinets and doors, cameras, and so on, while physically securing the IT equipment where sensitive data is stored, including providing cable locks to the laptops within offices.

Physical Data Breach in Texas

Throughout this book we have discussed (and will discuss further) security around your data in on-premises storage systems and/or in cloud-based storage. There are use cases, however, around securing actual physical data (like papers or tapes), as we pointed out in the introduction to this section.

While it's a bit of an older example, an event that occurred in Texas in 2011 (*https://oreil.ly/_3ag-*) illustrates the importance of physical security.

A data contractor was working for Science Applications International Corporation (SAIC), the firm that handles data for TRICARE, the federal government and military healthcare program. In his car, the contractor had the backup tapes of electronic healthcare records for over 4.6 million active and retired military personnel. All of these tapes were stolen from the car, compromising the health information of not only the active and retired military personnel, but also their families.

SAIC clarified in a press release that while the tapes medical record data such as social security numbers, diagnoses, and lab reports), financial data was not included on the tapes and thus was not leaked.

SAIC and TRICARE set up incident response call centers to help patients deal with the security breach and to help them to place a fraud alert on their credit reports if needed, but they also made a statement:

> If you are a citizen in the modern society, if you have a credit card, if you shop online, if you have information stored, you should anticipate that some day your information will get stolen.[3]

This statement isn't wholly inaccurate even a decade later, but what it fails to consider is the role of governance in preventing these sorts of things from happening in the first place—which is likely to be the main reason you are reading this book.

You should be aware of and consider implementing additional security measures for any physical data that you may have. Healthcare, as in this example, is an obvious scenario, but there are many instances in which there may be physical sensitive data that needs to be treated and/or needs to be something that you educate your employees on and build into your data culture (see Chapter 9 for more on this).

As in this example, even the methods by which you transport physical data from one location to another should be considered. Often we think about how data is transferred between applications, where it's stored, whether or not it's encrypted, and so on. But as this example shows, you should also consider how you are physically transporting data, if this is something you or your company will be doing. Will it be by car?

---

3 Jim Forsyth, "Records of 4.9 Million Stolen from Car in Texas Data Breach" (*https://oreil.ly/_3ag-*), *Reuters*, September 29, 2011.

What are the safeguards that are in place to ensure that data is always being watched over or protected? Do you have any safeguards in place in the event of this data being stolen? Is it unreadable? Is it encrypted?

Hopefully, if you note these areas of consideration and generate a plan for how to treat and protect your physical data, what happened to SAIC and TRICARE in 2011 won't happen to you.

Portable Device Encryption and Policy

Data breaches in the healthcare industry in recent years have occurred largely because a laptop or storage device containing protected health information was lost or stolen. A key measure that healthcare organizations should always undertake to prevent a data breach due to a stolen portable device is to encrypt all devices that might hold patient data, including laptops, smartphones, tablets, and portable USB drives. Also, in addition to providing encrypted devices for their employees, healthcare organizations should establish a strong policy against carrying data on an unencrypted personal device. We are seeing more and more bring-your-own-device (BYOD) policies adopted by various institutions, and many healthcare providers are now using mobile device management (MDM) software to enforce those policies.

Data Deletion Process

A key lesson that data-breach victims have learned is the need for a data-deletion policy, because as more data is held by an organization, there is more for intruders to steal. Healthcare institutions should deploy a policy mandating the deletion of patient and other information that's no longer needed, while complying with regulations that require records to be kept for a certain duration. Furthermore, regular audits must be exercised to ensure that policies are followed and that organizations know what data is where, what might be deleted, and when it can be deleted.

Electronic medical device and OS software upgrades

One of the areas that healthcare providers and their IT organizations need to pay closer attention to is medical device software and OS upgrades. Intruders have discovered that healthcare providers were not always so diligent and still utilize outdated OS-based medical devices that become easy targets to hack, despite update recommendations from the healthcare device vendors'. While these updates may seem disruptive to the providers and their employees, a data breach is much worse for a provider. Keeping these devices patched and up to date will minimize these vulnerabilities.

Data breach readiness

There is no such thing as preventing every possible IT security incident; this is exactly why institutions should have a well-established plan to deploy when and if a data breach occurs. Educating employees on what a HIPAA violation is, how to avoid phishing, avoiding target attacks, and choosing strong passwords are among a few simple steps that healthcare institutions can take.

The healthcare industry best practices and suggestions we've highlighted apply to other industries as well. Institutions at large should implement processes and procedures to reduce in-the-moment thinking when it comes to dealing with data breaches. Automation and well-planned and commented response are key in dealing with a potential data breach. Establishing internal data security controls will reduce the risk of data breaches while improving regulatory compliance. In summary, organizations should establish the following steps in their company-wide process:

- Identify systems and data that need to be protected.
- Continuously evaluate possible internal and external threats.
- Establish data security measures to manage identified risks.
- Educate and train employees regularly.
- Monitor, test, and revise—and remember that the IT world risks change all the time.

Why Do Hackers Target the Healthcare Industry?

Every year, we see study after study on the impact of security breaches in the healthcare industry, where hackers demand large ransoms from healthcare vendors and providers. 2019 was no different; in fact, according to a study by Emsisoft, it has reached record levels, costing healthcare industry members over $7.5 billion just in the US, where over 100 state and local government agencies, over 750 providers, nearly 90 universities, and more than 1,200 schools have been affected.[4] The results were not just an inconvenience of expense but a massive disruption to healthcare delivery: surgeries were postponed, and in some cases patients had to be transferred to other hospitals to receive the urgent care they needed—not to mention the disruption to payment systems and collection systems. Even student grades were lost. 2020 was no better in terms of healthcare data breaches, according to *HealthITSecurity* (*https://oreil.ly/Sm7Df*). The World Privacy Forum website has an interactive map

---

4 Emsisoft Malware Lab, "The State of Ransomware in the US: Report and Statistics 2019" (*https://oreil.ly/sPveu*), December 12, 2019.

(*https://oreil.ly/WSNC5*) that is a great resource for getting the latest on medical data breaches (see Figure 7-8).

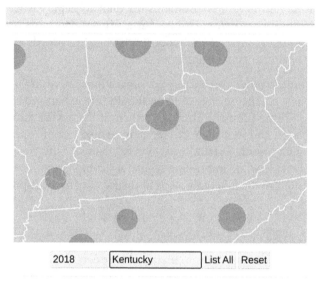

Figure 7-8. An example from the World Privacy Forum website shows medical data breaches in the state of Kentucky in 2018.

Many of us regularly wonder, "Why is this happening, and why is this happening especially in the healthcare industry?" We are alarmed to discover that a large percentage of these institutions did not even know how often these breaches were happening, and only a small fraction had the processes in place to recover and protect their data. It is especially worrying to know that many of the breaches were happening via very smart and digitally connected IoT devices. The industry has to do much better going forward.

Hackers target the healthcare industry largely because it is one of the few industries with legacy operating systems like Microsoft XP or Windows 7 in their medical devices, and it has not been industry practice to stay on top of OS patches when they become available. In fact, some of these older OS-based medical devices will no longer be supported by Microsoft, meaning the vendors need to ensure their users upgrade to a device that is up to date and better prepared for today's security breaches. Failing to patch or renew their devices will continue to increase the risk. Manufacturing a medical device is not easy; it takes many years to build one, and then it is in use for 15 years or longer. So these devices become easy targets during their 20+ years of use, not to mention that many of them are shipped to other countries for secondary and tertiary use. Considering how often the electronics and software in our daily lives change (e.g., cell phones have an average life cycle of two years before we refresh them), you can see why hackers target healthcare devices.

The healthcare industry must be much more proactive in its approach to data protection. It must utilize best practices around data protection; have total control of assets; continuously assess gaps and processes; leverage best practices and experts from NIST, HITRUST, and others in the cybersecurity industry; and ensure that appropriate budgets are allocated for upgrading legacy medical device software and endpoints that are open to hackers. A single weak point is enough for a hacker to impact an entire network.

Summary

In this chapter, we looked at what is perhaps the key concern of data governance—protecting data. A necessary part of planning protection is ensuring that lineage is tracked and quality monitored so that the data remains trustworthy. The planning process should identify the levels of protection and decide the kind of protection afforded at each level. Then the classification process itself—classifying data assets into levels—needs to be planned for.

A key concern with data stored in the public cloud is multi-tenancy. There could be other workloads running on the same machines that are carrying out data processing for your company. Therefore, it is important to consider the security surface and take into account virtual machine security. Typically, physical security is provided by the cloud provider, and your responsibility for network security is limited to getting the data to/from the cloud (security in transit) and configuring the appropriate security controls, such as VPC-SC. Important aspects to consider are data exfiltration, zero trust, and how to set up Cloud IAM. These involve setting up governance of authentication, authorization, and access policies.

Because your data may be used by data science users who need access to all of the data, Cloud IAM and row-based security may be insufficient. You must also determine the need for the masking, tokenization, or anonymization of sensitive information that may not be needed to train machine learning models. A clear understanding of what to encrypt and how to implement differential privacy, comprehensive access monitoring, and the ablity to change security profiles in response to changing risks all become more important the more the data gets used for machine learning.

The data protection governance process should also create policies on when separate network designs are necessary, how portable devices have to be treated, when to delete data, and what to do in the case of a data breach. Finally, data protection needs to be agile, because new threats and attack vectors continue to materialize. So the entire set of policies should be periodically revisited and fine-tuned.

CHAPTER 8

Monitoring

In previous chapters, we explained what governance is; discussed the tools, people, and processes of governance; looked at data governance over a data life cycle; and even did a deeper dive into governance concepts, including data quality and data protection.

In this chapter, we will do a deep dive into *monitoring* as a way to understand how your governance implementations are performing day-to-day, and even on a longer-term basis. You will learn what monitoring is, why it is important, what to look for in a monitoring system, what components of governance to monitor, the benefits of monitoring, and the implications of doing so. You have implemented governance in your organization, so how do you know what's working and what's not? It's important to be able to monitor and track the performance of your governance initiatives so you can report to all the stakeholders the impact the program has had on the organization. This allows you to ask for additional resources, course-correct if/as needed, learn from the wins and failures, and really showcase the impact of the governance program—not to mention making the most of potential growth opportunities that might become more visible to the chief data and digital officers of your organization. So what is monitoring? Let's start by introducing the concept.

What Is Monitoring?

Monitoring allows you to know what is happening as soon as it happens so you can act quickly. We're in a world in which companies and individuals are made and destroyed on social networks; that's how powerful these platforms are. User expectations are fueling complexity in applications and infrastructure, so much so that over 50% of mobile users abandon sites that take more than three seconds to load. Most web pages take a lot longer than that to load, creating a significant gap between consumers' expectations and most businesses' mobile capabilities (*https://oreil.ly/Hxgj9*).

If you're an organization that services customers and you know of this stat, then you must ensure that you have a system that's constantly monitoring your website load times and alerting you when numbers are outside acceptable bounds. You want to make sure that your team can resolve issues before they become bigger problems.

So what is monitoring? In simple terms, monitoring is a comprehensive operations, policies and performance management framework. The aim is to detect and alert about possible errors of a program or a system in a timely manner and deliver value to the business. Organizations use monitoring systems to monitor devices, infrastructure, applications, services, policies, and even business processes. Because monitoring applies to many areas of the business beyond what we can cover, in this chapter we will primarily focus on monitoring as it relates to governance.

Monitoring governance involves capturing and measuring the value generated from data governance initiatives, compliance, and exceptions to defined policies and procedures—and finally, enabling transparency and auditability into datasets across their life cycle.

What's interesting about monitoring is that when everything is working well and there are no issues, efforts usually go unnoticed. When issues arise and things go wrong—for example, with data quality or compliance exceptions—then governance is one of the first areas that gets blamed because these areas fall right within governance areas that should be constantly monitored. (We will do a deeper dive into each of these areas later in the chapter.) Because of this, it's important for you to define metrics that allow you to demonstrate to the business that your efforts and investments in data governance are benefiting the business in reducing costs, increasing revenue, and providing business value. You need to implement metrics that you will track accordingly, enabling you to understand and showcase the improvements you are making to the bottom line. In later sections of this chapter, we will provide you with a list of some of the key metrics you can track to show the efficacy of your governance program.

Why Perform Monitoring?

Monitoring allows you to review and assess performance for your data assets, introduce policy changes within the organization, and learn from what's working and what's not, with the ultimate goal of creating value for the business. If your organization is used to hearing about incidents via its customer base and is spending too much time and money on manual support, then a monitoring system is vital. Monitoring serves many different functions, and for the majority of the use cases, a monitoring system will help you with alerting, accounting, auditing, and compliance. Let's do a deep dive into these core areas:

Alerting

In its simplest terms, an alert warns someone or something of a danger, threat, or problem—typically with the intention of avoiding it or dealing with it. An alert system can help you prevent incidents, and when incidents happen, they are detected earlier and faster. A governance monitoring system that is specifically designed to monitor data quality can alert you when data quality thresholds fall outside the allowable limits, allowing you to avoid falls in service or to minimize the amount of time needed to resolve the issue.

Accounting

An account refers to a report or description of an event or experience. In this core area of monitoring, you want to get an in-depth analysis of your applications, infrastructure, and policies. This enables you to create more appropriate strategies, set realistic goals, and understand where improvements are needed, allowing you to discover the effectiveness and value generated from data governance and stewardship efforts.

Auditing

Auditing refers to a systematic review or assessment of something to ensure that it is performing as designed. Audits also enable transparency into data assets and their life cycle. Auditing allows you to understand the ins and outs of your business so that you can make improvements to processes and internal controls, with the aim of reducing organizational risk and preventing unexpected costs from external auditors.

Compliance

Regulatory compliance refers to the efforts required to help you meet relevant policies, laws, standards, and regulations. When your systems, thresholds, or policies are outside the defined rules, resulting in out-of-compliance processes, monitoring can help you stay in compliance; your business can be alerted as soon as these exceptions are detected, giving you the opportunity to resolve the issues in order to stay compliant.

 Although this is not the first time we're covering this subject, we want to reiterate just how important *alerting* is to your governance program. In countless interviews, and during our research, the lack of sufficient alerting has been mentioned as a top pain point among data scientists, data engineers, and the like. While there are many ingredients we've discussed that are key to a successful governance strategy, proper alerting is something that often gets overlooked. Improvements in this area not only aid in prevention and early detection of incidents but also help to streamline tasks and the time spent on those tasks by your employees.

Monitoring use cases will tend to fall within the four buckets we've just highlighted, and in most cases they will overlap. For example, as you monitor compliance in your organization, this can also help you when it comes to audits and proving that your organization is doing the right things and performing as designed.

Monitoring is often done using a monitoring system that can be built in-house by purchasing a system and configuring it to your other internal systems. It can be outsourced to other vendors as a managed service for ease of setup and expense, or if you're using cloud solutions, it can be embedded within your organization's workflows. Open source tools also provide some monitoring solutions to be considered. We will delve more deeply into monitoring systems later in this chapter; for now, let's focus on what areas of governance you should monitor, why, and how.

Why Alerting Is a Critical Monitoring Function

This is a cautionary tale about a small website management services company that served 50 major hospitals around the country. The story sounds a little too familiar, and honestly, this continues to happen to many organizations that store customer information. For the company, things were going so well that it decided to introduce a new service that allowed patients and partners to do online bill payment.

One day during a maintenance procedure, an employee accidentally turned off the company's firewall, and all of the patient data stored on its online billing service system (for at least five hospitals and approximately 100,000 patients) was left exposed to the world.[1] And because the hospitals reported the breaches as separate incidents, the nature of the error was not immediately apparent.

Unfortunately for this small company, there was no way to recover from such an incident. It simply closed its doors and shut down its website. There's so much to learn from this experience, because if customer data had been properly governed and stored—that is, if the data had been encrypted and the right access controls had been enforced—it would have been easier to catch the incident right when it happened and alert the hospitals as needed. In addition, this reinforces the importance of monitoring and, more specifically, of alerting. It's scary to think that an employee turned off a firewall system without any system alerts being triggered or the right folks being alerted.

---

1 Tim Wilson, "A Cautionary Tale" (*https://oreil.ly/n35j7*), *Dark Reading*, August 17, 2007.

What Should You Monitor?

There are many areas of an organization that are monitored: operating systems and hardware, network and connectivity, servers, processes, governance, and more. In order to stay close to the core of this book and chapter, we will now do a deeper dive into monitoring as it relates to data governance. A lot of the concepts we will explore next have already been covered in previous chapters, and so we will focus on which parts need to be monitored and how to go about it. We will keep referring back to what you've learned in order to solidify these concepts across the key areas.

Data Quality Monitoring

In Chapters 1 and 2, we introduced the concept of data quality, and we went into that in more detail in Chapter 5. Data quality allows the organization to trust the data and the results. High-quality data means that the organization can rely on that data for further calculations/inclusions with other datasets. Because of how important data quality is, it should be monitored proactively, and compliance exceptions should be identified and flagged in real time. This will allow the organization to move quickly to identify and mitigate critical issues that can cause process breakdowns.

There are critical attributes of data quality that should be tracked and measured, including completeness, accuracy, duplication, and conformity. These are outlined in detail in Table 8-1 and should map to specific business requirements you have set forth for your governance initiative. Monitoring can help you create controls for validation and can provide alerts as needed when these are outside the defined thresholds. The attributes in Table 8-1 are common problem areas within the data management space that make it difficult to trust data for analysis.

Table 8-1. Data quality attributes

Attribute	Description
Completeness	This identifies what data is missing and/or not usable.
Accuracy	This identifies the correctness and consistency of the data and whether the correct values are stored for an object.
Duplication	This identifies which data is repeated. Duplicate records make it difficult to know the right data to use for analysis.
Conformity	This identifies which data is stored in a nonstandard format that will not allow analysis.

Process and tools for monitoring data quality

A data quality monitoring system routinely monitors and maintains data quality standards across a data life cycle and ensures they are met. It involves creating controls for validation, enabling quality monitoring and reporting, accessing the level of incident severity, enabling root cause analysis, and providing remedy recommendations.

When setting up a data quality monitoring process, some of the things you need to consider are:

Establishing a baseline
Establish a baseline of the current state of data quality. This will help you identify where quality is failing and help you determine what is "good" quality and what those targets are. These targets must be tied to the business objectives you have set forth for your governance initiatives. Comparing results over time is essential to proactive management of ongoing data quality improvement and governance.

Quality signals
These are usually monitored over a period of time or by the source of the data. The monitoring system will be looking to verify data fields for completeness, accuracy, duplicates, conformity, statistical anomalies, and more. When data quality falls below a specified threshold, an alert would be triggered with more information about the quality issue observed. These quality signal rules are usually set forth by the data governance committee, which ensures compliance with data policies, rules, and standards. More details around this are outlined in Chapter 4. These policy guidelines and procedures ensure that the organization has the data program that was envisioned by the organization.

In order to get started with monitoring data quality, determine a set of baseline metrics for levels of data quality and use this to help you build a business case to justify the investment and, over time, help you make improvements to the governance program.

Data Lineage Monitoring

We introduced the concept of data lineage in Chapter 2 and talked about why tracking lineage is important. The natural life cycle of data is that it is generated/created by multiple different sources and then undergoes various transformations to support organizational insights. There is a lot of valuable context generated from the source of the data and all along the way that is crucial to track. This is what data lineage is all about. Monitoring lineage is important to ensure data integrity, quality, usability, and the security of the resulting analysis and dashboards.

Let's be honest: tracking and monitoring lineage is no simple task; for many organizations, their data life cycle can be quite complex, as data flows from different sources, from files to databases, reports, and dashboards, while going through different transformation processes. Lineage can help you track why a certain dashboard has different results than expected and can help you see the movement of sensitive data classes across the organization.

When looking to track and monitor lineage, it's important to understand certain key areas that you will come across. Table 8-2 has some of these attributes. These are not all encompassing but are just some of the more important ones for you to know.

Table 8-2. Data lineage attributes

Attribute	Description
Data transformations	These are the various changes and hops (aggregates, additionals, removals, functions, and more) as data moves along the data life cycle. Monitoring helps you understand details of the data points and their historical behavior, as data gets transformed along the way.
Technical metadata	Metadata is important for understanding more about the data elements. Enabling automatic tagging of data based on its source can help provide more understanding of the data asset.
Data quality test results	These represent data quality measurements that are tracked at specific points of the data life cycle, in order to take action as/if needed.
Reference data values	Reference data values can be used to understand backward data lineage and transformation from that specific data point, and/or the intermediate transformation following that point with forward data lineage. Understanding reference data values can be useful in performing root cause analysis.
Actor	An actor is an entity that transforms data. It may be a MapReduce job or an entire data pipeline. Actors can sometimes be black boxes, and the inputs and outputs of an actor are tapped to capture lineage in the form of associations.

Process and tools for monitoring data lineage

What makes monitoring lineage so complicated is that it needs to be captured at multiple levels and granularities—this is tedious and time consuming because of all the intricacies and dependencies. As mentioned earlier in this chapter, monitoring serves different purposes; for lineage it can be used to alert, audit, and comply with a set of defined rules and policies. As described in Table 8-2, one of the things you could monitor is the behavior of the actors; when their resulting transformed outputs are incorrect, an alert function can be set up that the inputs are investigated, and the actors are augmented and corrected to behave as expected or are removed from the process flow of the data.

Monitoring lineage can also provide a lineage audit trail, which can be used to determine the who, what, where, and when of a successful or attempted data breach in order to understand which areas of the business were or might have been affected by the breach. In addition, the important details tracked by data lineage are the best way to provide regulatory compliance and improve risk management for businesses.

Lineage is about providing a record of where data came from, how it was used, who viewed it, and whether it was sent, copied, transformed, or received and it is also about ensuring this information is available. You will need to identify the best way to do this for your organization, depending on the use cases and needs of the business. Identify the data elements, track the listed elements back to their origin, create a repository that labels the sources and their elements, and finally, build visual maps for each system and a master map for the whole system.

Compliance Monitoring

Compliance has been covered in great detail in several of the previous chapters. Understanding state and federal regulations, industry standards, and governance policies and staying up to date on any changes ensures that compliance monitoring is effective.

The changing nature of laws and regulations can make monitoring compliance difficult and time consuming. Noncompliance is not an option because it often results in considerable fines—sometimes more than twice the cost of maintaining or meeting compliance requirements. In a study from the Ponemon Institute (*https://oreil.ly/ JJxHl*), the average cost for organizations that experience noncompliance problems is $14.82 million. That includes fines, forced compliance costs, lack of trust from customers, and lost business.

Monitoring compliance means having an internal legal representative (attorney), though at times this task falls on the privacy tsar or someone else in security, who must continually keep up with laws and regulations and how they impact your business. It also requires that changes are made according to the new information gathered in order to stay in compliance. In addition, to stay in compliance requires auditing and tracking access to data and resources within the organization. All of this is done to ensure your business is compliant in case of an audit by the government.

Process and tools for monitoring compliance

To be successful in monitoring regulatory compliance, you need to evaluate which regulations apply to your data governance efforts and what compliance looks like with these regulations. Once this is done, do an audit to understand your current governance structure with regard to the relevant regulations. Consider this a benchmark exercise to understand your current standing, future requirements, and how you can build a plan to get to the end state, and then continuously monitor that end state to ensure compliance.

Once you've completed the audit, you should jump to creating a monitoring plan; here you should address all risks identified in the audit stage and prioritize those that are the greatest threat to the organization. Next, decide how you are going to implement the monitoring program, including roles and responsibilities.

The resulting output will be dependent on the level and frequency of regulatory changes and updates from the relevant regulatory boards. Make sure you have a way to inform the regulatory agencies of failed audits and of how you're looking to mitigate them.

Here are some ways you can be proactive about compliance:

- Keep on top of regulatory changes and make sure that you're checking for up dated standards and regulations. Of course, this is easier said than done.

- Be transparent so your employees understand the importance of compliance and the regulations they are complying with. Offer training sessions to explain the regulations and their significance.

- Build a culture of compliance within the organization—and yes, there must be someone who has the task of staying up to date on regulatory requirements that the company may (or may not) need to be in compliance with. Most big companies have large compliance teams; even if you're a small organization; however, it's still important to designate someone to handle compliance, including monitoring, checking for updates in regulations and standards, and more.

- Cultivate a strong relationship between your compliance person/team and the legal department so that when incidents occur, those teams are in lockstep with each other and are already used to working together.

Monitoring compliance can be a manual process, with checklists and all, but that can also make things even more complicated. There are automated compliance tools that your organization can look at that provide compliance in real time, giving you continuous assurance and minimizing the chance that human error may lead to a gap in compliance.

Program Performance Monitoring

Monitoring and managing the performance of a governance program is integral to demonstrating program success to business leadership. This type of monitoring allows you to track progress against the program's aims and objectives, ensuring the governance program delivers the right outcomes for the organization, accounting for efficient and effective use of funding, and identifying improvement opportunities to continue creating impact for the business.

In order to monitor program performance, some of the items you might want to measure include:

- Number of lines of business, functional areas, and project teams that have committed resources and sponsorship

- Status of all issues that come into the governance function, how they were handled, and what the resulting impact was

- Level of engagement, participation, and influence the governance program is having across the organization, which will help people understand the value of the governance program

- Value-added interactions, including training and project support, and what the impact is to the business
- Business value ROI from data governance investments, including reducing penalties by ensuring regulatory compliance, reducing enterprise risk (e.g., contractual, legal, financial, brand), improving operational efficiencies, increasing top-line revenue growth, and optimizing customer experience and satisfaction

Process and tools for monitoring program performance

Program performance monitoring needs to be continuous and ongoing, helping you identify areas that are not performing to expectations and determining what types of program adjustments are needed. Most performance management frameworks consist of the sets of activities outlined in Figure 8-1.[2]

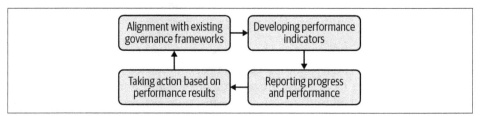

Figure 8-1. Performance management framework

Let's look more closely at each of these areas:

Alignment with existing governance frameworks
    This ensures that your program performance is aligned with the established governance framework. In Chapter 4, we did a deep dive into governance frameworks, groups, and what is needed for effective governance.

Developing performance indicators
    Now that you are aligned with existing governance frameworks, develop key performance indicators (KPIs) for your governance program. These should be well defined, relevant, and informative.

Reporting progress and performance
    Documenting the governance performance objectives and how they're being met and sharing this information with leadership will ensure that people see the value of the program. Providing reports becomes an essential way for people to consume this information.

---

2 Grosvenor Performance Group, "How Is Your Program Going…Really? Performance Monitoring" (*https://oreil.ly/BaX2W*), May 15, 2018.

Taking action based on performance results

It's important to identify ways to ensure that the performance results are used to inform decision making in your organization; otherwise, what is the point?

As you can see in Figure 8-1, this is an ongoing and iterative process, with one area feeding and informing the other.

Security Monitoring

Cyberattacks are becoming bigger than ever before, with new threats from state actors and increasingly sophisticated methods. The damage related to cybercrime is projected to hit $6 trillion annually by 2021, according to Cybersecurity Ventures.[3] In addition, many countries are now taking consumer data privacy and protection more seriously by introducing new legislation to hold businesses accountable.

Attacks cost more than money. They can affect a business's brand and shareholder reputation. In the recent Equifax data breach, in which over 140 million records were exposed, the company most likely incurred a cost of more than $32 billion to resolve the issue.[4] This was reflected in their stock price, which fell more than 30% after the breach. Perhaps even worse, adjacent firms in Equifax's industry who did not get breached felt a 9% stock drop, likely due to loss of confidence in security measures.[5] So even if you're doing everything right, you can still be impacted by a breach.

That's why security monitoring is so important. It is the process of collecting and analyzing information to detect suspicious behavior, or unauthorized system changes on the network in order to take action on alerts as needed. Most companies are routinely exposed to security threats of varying severity; the causes of security breaches include hackers and malware, careless employees, and vulnerable devices and operating systems. Security threats are part of the normal course of conducting business; therefore it's important to be prepared and act on threats and breaches before they cause damage and disruption.

There are many areas of the business where you can monitor security. Table 8-3 highlights some of those areas.

---

3 "29 Must-Know Cybersecurity Statistics for 2020" (*https://oreil.ly/iQ0M_*), *Cyber Observer*, December 27, 2019.

4 "5 Reasons Why You Need 24x7 Cyber Security Monitoring" (*https://oreil.ly/VXyOD*), *Cipher* (blog), May 15, 2018.

5 Paul R. La Monica, "After Equifax Apologizes, Stock Falls Another 15%" (*https://oreil.ly/iNN_C*), *CNNMoney*, September 13, 2017.

Table 8-3. Security monitoring items, showing some areas of the organization that you can monitor security on

Item	Description
Security alerts and incidents	These are any alerts or incidents generated from an IT environment. They could be data exfiltration or unusual port activity, acceptable use policy violations, or privileged user-activity violations.
Network events	This involves the ability to monitor network activity and receive alarms or reports of the occurrence of selected events, including device statuses and their IP addresses, new device alerts, and network status.
Server logs	This involves monitoring and detecting server activities continuously, examining alerts before a server mishap occurs, recording server logs and reports for easy tracking of errors, performing log analysis, and monitoring server performance and capacity.
Application events	This involves monitoring events surrounding your software and applications in their stack, ensuring they are accessible and performing smoothly.
Server patch compliance	This involves installing and patching all the servers in your IT environment and staying compliant. This helps mitigate vulnerabilities, server downtimes and crashes, and slowing down.
Endpoint events	This is a list of all events that can be emitted by an instance of an application, a process, or an event.
Identity access management	This involves defining and managing the roles and access privileges of individual network users and maintaining, modifying, and monitoring this access throughout each user's access life cycle.
Data loss	This involves detecting potential data breaches/data exfiltration transmissions and employing monitoring techniques and prevention when data is in use, in motion, and at rest.

Process and tools for monitoring security

An effective process of monitoring security is continuous security monitoring, providing real-time visibility into an organization's security posture and constantly looking for cyber threats, security misconfigurations, and other vulnerabilities. This allows an organization to stay a step ahead of cyber threats, reducing the time it takes to respond to attacks while complying with industry and regulatory requirements.

Cyber security can be conducted at the network level or the endpoint level. With network security monitoring, tools aggregate and analyze security logs from different sources to detect any failures. Endpoint security technologies, on the other hand, provide security visibility at the host level, allowing for threats to be detected earlier in the process flow.

Security monitoring is an area with many players: from companies that offer solutions you can implement within your organization to full-fledged companies that you can outsource the entire service to. The solution you choose to go with depends on your business, the size of your in-house team, your budget, the technologies at your disposal, and the level of security-monitoring sophistication that you're looking for. Both options have pros and cons that need to be weighed before you can make an effective decision for your business.

You should now have an understanding of what governance items to monitor, the how, and the why. The next section will look more closely at monitoring systems, their features, and which criteria to monitor.

What Is a Monitoring System?

Monitoring systems are the core set of tools, technologies, and processes used to analyze operations and performance in order to alert, account, audit, and maintain the compliance of organizational programs and resources. A robust monitoring system is paramount to the success of a program and needs to be optimal with regard to what the business needs.

Monitoring can be done in-house by purchasing a system and configuring it to your other internal systems; it can be outsourced as a managed service to other vendors because of an internal lack of expertise and expense; or if you're using cloud solutions, it can be embedded within your organization's workflows. Open source tools also provide some monitoring solutions that can be considered as well. Whatever option you choose to go with, here are common features of a good monitoring system.

Analysis in Real Time

Real time is real money. In a world in which things change so fast and people need information at their fingertips, you must have a monitoring system that does analysis in real time. A good system should offer continuous monitoring with minimal delays, allowing you to make changes and improvements on the fly.

System Alerts

A monitoring system needs to have the ability to signal when something is happening so that it can be actioned. A system that allows multiple people to be informed with the right information will go a long way toward ensuring that issues are addressed as quickly as possible. A system should allow configuration for multiple events and have the ability to set different sets of actions depending on the alert. The alert should contain information about what is wrong and where to find additional information.

Notifications

A good monitoring system needs to have a robust, built-in notification system. We're no longer in the age of pagers, so your system needs to be able to send SMS, email, chat, and more to ensure that the message gets to the right folks. And once the message is received, the right people need to be able to communicate back to the team that the alert has been received and that the issue is being investigated—and when issues are resolved, communicate that the system or process is back to normal operations. Notifications could kick off additional processes automatically, where certain systems take an action.

Reporting/Analytics

Monitoring systems are big data collection and aggregation units given all the alerts and trigger events collected over a period of time. Your monitoring system needs to allow for robust reporting that will allow you to present the data to clients or different departments in the organization. Reporting allows you to identify trends, correlate patterns, and even predict future events.

Graphic Visualization

Collecting data should be augmented with the ability to analyze and visualize a situation. Dashboards play a critical role in ensuring that everyone has a place to look to see how things are going, and even to observe trends over time. A visual representation of what's happening is easier for people to understand and absorb and is one of the top customer requests in a data governance solution. A good monitoring system should have friendly and easy-to-understand graphs that allow the organization to make decisions.

Customization

It's no surprise that different organizations have different business requirements. You need to have the ability to be able to customize your monitoring system by function, user type, permissions, and more, allowing you to have the right alerts triggered, and to have them actioned by the right folks.

Monitoring systems need to run independently from production services, and they should not put a burden on the systems they are tracking. This simply allows the monitoring system to continue running in the case of a production outage or other failure event. Otherwise, a failure could take down a monitoring system (when the production environment is down), and that defeats the purpose of its existence. In addition, as you would with any system, ensure you have a failover for your monitoring system in case it is the one that's affected by a blackout or failure. Figure 8-2 highlights a simple monitoring system, given some of the features we've just highlighted.

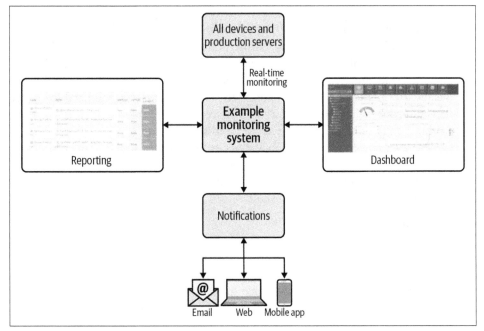

Figure 8-2. Example monitoring system

As you can imagine, monitoring systems are becoming even more sophisticated with the introduction of machine learning capabilities, so even though this list of features is robust, it's not by any measure the be-all and end-all. Use this list as a starting point to select or build the right monitoring system for your organization, and, depending on your use case and company needs, augment your system as needed.

Monitoring Criteria

Now that you have selected a monitoring system, what are the types of criteria that you can set up to monitor? Monitoring systems collect data in two distinct ways: *passive systems,* where the tools observe data created by the application and system under normal conditions (i.e., log files, output messages, etc.); and *active systems*, which are more proactive, use agents and other tools to capture data through a monitoring module, and are often integrated within production systems.

Here's some common criteria you can follow as you set up your monitoring system:

Basic details
Identify basic details for the items you're looking to monitor. Capture a list of rules, their purpose, and a distinct name for each one. If your system has predefined alerts and queries, select the ones you want to monitor and label them accordingly so they can be easily identified.

Notification condition

Program your notification condition. Once the query/criteria you set is identified and the result is evaluated against configurable thresholds, an alert should be set off if there's a violation on the criteria set forth. Users should be identified by email or SMS, and the information should be made available on the monitoring dashboard. In addition, it's not enough to simply send alerts; you need to ensure that someone acknowledges that they've received the alert and that they are working on it. Also, the alert needs to go to someone on call, and if that person, for whatever reason, is not available, it needs to be routed to the right person who can respond to the alert. If the alert is not responded to, the system should send another notification within a specified amount of time as long as the metric continues to remain outside the threshold.

Monitoring times

In this instance, specify the frequency of the running of a certain validation (daily/weekly/monthly), and then how long and how frequently it should occur within the day (business hours within the day and frequency within the day). This is more of a gut check system that looks to make sure processes and systems are operating correctly; it is more useful for passive systems in which things are monitored to ensure ongoing operations.

Given the complexity of all these items and the level of sophistication needed to maintain them, monitoring systems are what make all this possible. The next section offers some reminders and touches on other things you should keep in mind.

Important Reminders for Monitoring

From reading this chapter, you will have discerned some recurring themes when it comes to monitoring. Here are some considerations to keep in mind:

Getting started with a monitoring system

Just like any software development process, monitoring can be done in-house by purchasing a system and configuring it to your systems; it can be outsourced as a managed service to other vendors because of an internal lack of expertise and expense,; or if you're using cloud solutions, it can be embedded within your organization's workflows. Open source tools also provide some monitoring solutions that can be considered as well.

Real-time improves decision making

For the majority of the governance items outlined in the previous section, a continuous, real-time monitoring system is paramount to improving decision-making and staying on top of compliance. In addition, having an alert system that is robust and allows people to take action as needed will ensure that things are remedied within the outlined SLAs.

Data culture is key to success

Employee training needs to be embedded into the fiber of your business—your *data culture*, as discussed in Chapter 9. Many governance concerns are undertaken by employees who might not be aware that they're doing something that will compromise the business. Find ways to make education personal, because people are most likely to apply education when they see it as important to their lives.

Summary

This chapter was designed to give you a foundation on monitoring and how to think about implementing it for your organization. Monitoring is vital to understanding how your governance implementations are performing on both a day-to-day and a longer-term basis. Monitoring is where the rubber meets the road, allowing you to ask for additional resources, course-correct as needed, learn from the wins and failures, and really showcase the impact of your governance program.

Take an audit of your current governance and monitoring initiatives and augment them as needed, because doing this can only reap more benefits for your organization.

CHAPTER 9

Building a Culture of Data Privacy and Security

In this book we have covered a lot: considerations in data governance, the people and processes involved, the data life cycle, tools, and beyond. These are all pieces of a puzzle that need to come together in the end for data governance to be successful.

As alluded to earlier, data governance is not just about the products, tools, and people who carry out the process—there is also the need to build a *data culture*. The careful creation and implementation of a data culture—especially one focused on privacy and security—not only aids in the establishment of a successful data governance program but also ensures that the program is maintained over time.

As we discussed in Chapter 3, the people and processes around data governance—in *conjunction* with data governance tools—are essential components of a data governance program. In this chapter we will go one step further than thatby including the data culture (the culture within a company *around* data) as a key final component in creating a highly successful data governance program.

Data Culture: What It Is and Why It's Important

The data culture is the set of values, goals, attitudes, and practices around data, data collection, and data handling within a company or organization. While many companies or organizations spend quite a bit of time vetting data governance tools and creating processes, they often fail to set up a *culture* within the company around data.

This culture defines and influences things like:

- How data is thought about within the company/organization (Is it an asset? Needed to make decisions? The most important part of the company? Just something to be managed?)

- How data should be collected and handled

- Who should be handling data and when

- Who is responsible for data during its life cycle

- How much money and/or resources will be committed to serving the company/organization's data goals

While this is certainly not an exhaustive list, it begins to show you the vast amount of considerations that go into the definition of a data culture.

Having a set and defined data culture is important for a multitude of reasons, but the most important is that it sets the stage and serves as the glue that holds everything else together within a data governance program.

We will go into more detail in this chapter about what the "North Star" of a data culture should look like and about what considerations you should be making when designing your own.

Starting at the Top—Benefits of Data Governance to the Business

A key aspect of building a successful data culture is getting buy-in from the top down, which generally requires that decision makers within a company see how a data governance program will work and agree on why implementation of a data culture benefits the company's bottom line. An efficient data culture aids in ensuring reliable, high-quality data that not only produces better analytics but also reduces compliance violations and penalties. All of this will result in better business performance, as highlighted in various studies including a 2018 McKinsey report that found that "breakaway companies" are twice as likely to claim they had a strong data governance strategy.[1] In many of our interviews with companies, one of the most common complaints we hear about initiating and implementing a data governance program is getting buy-in from those that have the power to fund data governance initiatives, as well as to support and enforce a data culture.

---

[1] Peter Bisson, Bryce Hall, Brian McCarthy, and Khaled Rifai, "Breaking Away: The Secrets to Scaling Analytics" (*https://oreil.ly/1CYJG*), McKinsey & Company, May 22, 2018.

Often the investment in a data governance program and building a data culture (both in terms of the purchasing of tools and infrastructure and in terms of headcount) is seen as a cost with no ROI other than hoped-for assurance that a company won't be hit with fines for being out of compliance with a regulation. A well-thought-out and well-executed governance program can, however, provide the cost savings of proper data handling, and it also has the ability to increase the value of already existing assets ("old data" that may be sitting around).

We have found and will discuss several areas that can be quite persuasive in helping decision makers to see the value and importance of building a data culture.

Analytics and the Bottom Line

We've discussed in depth the implications of governance and how knowing what data there is, and where it is, not only aids in locking down and handling sensitive data but also helps analysts to run better, more actionable analytics. Better analytics—analytics that are based on higher-quality data or come from a synthesis of data from multiple sources, for example—enable us to make better data-driven decisions. All companies are driven by a desire to increase their profitability, whether by increasing revenue and/or by decreasing waste or expenditure. The entire push to data-driven decision making has at its heart the hope and promise of driving revenue. When decision makers are able to see that a data governance program and data culture generate better analytics, which in turn positively affects the bottom line, they are not only a bit more likely to be passively "bought in," but they may also rise to be champions and drivers of the data culture.

Company Persona and Perception

While not directly related to the bottom line, there is much to be said for the public perception of a company and how it handles data.

In the last five years, there have been several companies that have fallen under great scrutiny regarding the data they collect and how that data is used. The public's perception that these companies have used data unethically carries a host of cascading negative repercussions—ranging from decreased employee morale to financial effects such as dropped sponsors and/or losing customers to a competitor—and these do indeed affect a company's bottom line.

Top-Down Buy-In Success Story

One company we've interviewed has had a particularly successful execution of a data governance program, in large part due to the buy-in it received from the top of the organization. This company works in research and in healthcare and is looking to leverage analytics across data collected on each side of the business. Currently its data resides in separate storage for each line of business. To marry this data together into a central repository, it recognized the need for a comprehensive data governance strategy.

We hope we've impressed upon you in this book that all companies should have a data governance strategy and program, but of course there are certain business types that, due to their high level of regulation, need to be even more conscious of their implementation of governance. Healthcare is one of those. This company knew that a comprehensive governance program would need to be broad and be executed at many different levels within the organization. The company deals almost exclusively in sensitive data, and for this data to be moved, manipulated, joined with other datasets, and so on, the governance on it had to be top-notch.

To achieve the level of buy-in that would be required, the company set out to create a charter that outlined exactly what the governance program within the company should look like: the framework/philosophy that should be followed, tools that would be needed, the headcount needed to execute these tools, and notably, the establishment and ongoing reinforcement of a data culture. Is this exhaustive? Lofty? Idealistic? Perhaps. But through this charter, the company was able to gain that buy-in from the top, and it is now executing one of the most well-thought-out and structured governance programs we've seen (complete with headcount for governance-only related tasks—a true rarity).

We include this example not to imply that every single one of these "boxes" must be ticked or that a smaller-scale or fledgling governance program is not worth it. On the contrary: we hope that this example (while extreme) serves to show you just how much documenting a well-thought-out strategy, including how this strategy will be embedded into the culture of the company, can help you in getting not only initial buy-in, but also the level of buy-in that will maintain and support your governance program in the long run.

Intention, Training, and Communications

Perhaps one of the most important aspects of building a data culture is the internal data literacy, communications, and training. In the overview of this chapter, we mentioned that a key to successful governance and data culture is not just the establishment of a program but maintenance over time to ensure its longevity. Integral to this end is intention, data literacy (a deep understanding of and ability to derive meaningful information from all kinds of data), training, and communications.

A Data Culture Needs to Be Intentional

Just as we discussed that a successful governance program needs to have a set process, the building and maintenance of a data culture is very much the same.

What's important

When creating and establishing a data culture, a company first needs to decide what's important to it—what its tenets are. For example, a company that deals with a lot of sensitive data (like a healthcare company) may decide that the proper treatment and handling of PII is a primary tenet, whereas a small gaming app company may decide that ensuring data quality is its primary focus. Alternatively, a company may decide that many tenets are important to it, which is fine—the key aspect here is that these tenets need to be clearly defined and collectively agreed upon as the rest of the establishment and maintenance of a data culture stems from this step.

Aside from internal tenets, there also exist tenets that are nonnegotiable in nature, such as legal requirements and compliance standards that all or most companies need to integrate as tenets, no matter what.

It's also worth noting here that in addition to tenets and requirements/compliance standards, we would argue that an important and perhaps even crucial tenet is that of caring. This may seem like a strange tenet to have as part of a data governance program, but it is an essential component of a data *culture*. For a governance program to function at its highest level, there must be an intrinsic desire on the part of the company and its employees to do the right thing. The protection of and respect for data has to be an integral part of the fabric of the company and its data-handling ethos. It must be something that is touted and supported from the top so that it cascades down to the rest of the company. Without this concern, the company is one that merely deals with data, and perhaps has a data governance program but has no data culture. While no company wants to rely solely on its employees to do the right thing, fostering a data culture helps to fill in the gaps for when things invariably go sideways.

Training: Who Needs to Know What

A successful implementation of a data culture not only needs to have its tenets well defined; it also needs to identify *who* will be carrying these out, *how* they will do this, and whether or not they have the *knowledge and skills* needed for proper execution.

The "who," the "how," and the "knowledge"

Too often we have seen that one or more of these three areas is glossed over or taken for granted. As when we discussed the different "hats" involved in data governance, there is a high likelihood that several of the folks carrying out these tasks have: little-to-no technical knowledge; some may be doing other tasks as part of their role, leaving little time to dedicate to data governance; and there are often breakdowns around who is responsible for what tasks. Each of these components is important and should not be overlooked. Each component needs to be thoroughly considered when planning and implementing the data culture aspect of a data governance program.

Part of the data governance and data culture execution strategy includes determining who will do what. Not only is this important in terms of defining roles and responsibilities, but it's also important that the people who will be fulfilling these duties have the skills and the knowledge to perform their tasks. It is simply not enough to enlist a person to a task, give them a tool, and hope for the best. A plan for how knowledge and skills will be not only acquired but also *maintained* over time is critical.

A solid plan for what training will be required and how it will be disseminated is essential. Again, this is a place where we've seen companies falter—they may have decided who does what and even provided some initial training to get people up to speed, but they forget that as technology and the data collected grow and change, new skills and knowledge may be necessary. Training is often not a "one-and-done" event —it should be seen as ongoing.

In devising your own training strategy, you should think in terms of what's initially needed to teach your staff and what should continue to be reinforced and/or introduced in subsequent training. For example, we have seen companies have success with setting up events such as "Privacy Week" or "Data Week," in which essential training about proper data handling and governance considerations are reviewed and new considerations and/or regulations are introduced. What makes these "events" so much more successful than simply providing required virtual click-through training is that you can center your event around a particular topic of recent importance (perhaps an internal issue that occurred, a new regulation that's been launched, or even a highly publicized issue from an external company). This event structure gives you some freedom and flexibility around how to go about your training, depending on what's most important to either reinforce or disseminate to your staff.

An example of what this type of event could look like is shown in Table 9-1.

Table 9-1. Sample schedule

Monday	"Basics of Proper Data Handling and Governance" (one hour)
Tuesday	"How to Use Our Governance Tools 101" *or* "Advanced 'How to' on Our Governance Tools. Did You Know You Can Do…?!" (one hour)
Wednesday	"Governance and Ethics: How and Why Governance Is Everyone's Responsibility" (one hour)
Thursday	"How Do I Handle That? A Guide On What to Do When You Encounter a Governance Concern" (one hour)
Friday	Guest speaker on an aspect of governance and/or data culture you find particularly important to your organization (one hour)

Of course you will have to evaluate what sort of training strategy works best for your organization, but the takeaway here should be that you need to have an *ongoing* strategy—a strategy to address not only the initial training and expertise that your staff will need, but also how you're going to continue to reinforce past learning and introduce new learning.

Communication

Another area we often see overlooked is an intentional plan around communication. As mentioned with training, communication is also not a "one-and-done" activity. It is something that should not only be ongoing and consistent but also strategic and exhaustive. In fact, we would argue that proper communication and an intentional strategy around it are what fuels a powerfully effective data culture.

Top-down, bottom-up, and everything in between

When thinking about communication in terms of a data governance program, there are multiple facets to consider. Two common facets of focus are *top-down* communication of the governance program itself and its practices, standards, and expectations, and *bottom-up* communication encompassing breaches and problems in governance being bubbled up for resolution.

These two facets, while clearly important, are only *pieces* of the communication necessary to foster a company-wide data culture. These facets are focused simply on the passage of governance information back and forth, not on how to develop and enrich the *culture* of data privacy and security. For data culture, communication needs to center around the tenets—what the culture for data *is* within the company, and how each of those responsible for its success matter and are a part of it.

Additionally, while not specifically training per se, communication that bolsters a company's data culture can serve as a reminder and reinforcement not only of the information covered in said trainings but also of the company's overall vision and commitment to its data culture.

Beyond Data Literacy

In the previous section we briefly discussed the value and impact of fostering caring within the data culture. Here we will explore that more deeply and expand on why this is such a fundamental part of a successful data culture.

Motivation and Its Cascading Effects

To be sure, education around *what* data is (namely, what different kinds of data are), and *how* data should be treated is essential, but so too is the *why*. The question of why data should be handled and treated with respect is an overlooked component of data culture. Of course it is part and parcel for several of the user hats in the governance space (legal and privacy tsars, to name a few), but it should be so for other hats as well.

Motivation and adoption

This isn't a text on psychology by any means; however, the power of motivation and its impact on people's likeliness to do *this* over *that* influences greatly whether a data culture will be adopted or fall by the wayside.

For a data culture to be fully adopted, the motivation really needs to begin at the top and permeate down from there. Take, for example, a company that needs to put into place a governance program to abide by new data compliance and security laws. Several people (or teams) within the company know that their data collection and handling needs to meet higher standards to be in compliance and bring this need to the C-level. For a governance program to be fully implemented (as we discussed earlier in this chapter), the C-level folks need to buy into the idea that a governance program is important and worth their support (including funding). Without C-level support for a governance program, it's highly likely that the program would fall short due to lack of budgetary support and the absence of an ongoing advocacy of a data culture.

C-level involvement and belief in a governance program and implementation of a data culture has many downstream effects.

First, there is the financial aspect. Without proper funding, a company does not have the resources in terms of both headcount and tools but also in terms of education of the data governance space and how to use said tools effectively. Not only does this influence whether or not a governance program is executed effectively, but it also affects how well people are able to do their jobs and how happy they are doing those jobs. As we discussed in Chapter 3, people in the governance space wearing many different hats and spreading their time across many different tasks—some of which they're ill-equipped to do—can lead to decreased job satisfaction and productivity and ultimately high job turnover (which has its own implications in terms of sunk cost and lost time).

While C-level buy-in is clearly critical for its consequential effects, there is still the need to cultivate motivation for best practices within the rest of the workforce. Here again is where data culture becomes so important. First, the workforce needs to be informed/educated on *why* proper data treatment and handling is not only necessary but ethical. Of note here is that this is not where the reinforcement should stop. A data culture continues to reinforce this value through the behavior of the company— the training that is offered/required (and how often), the communications that are sent out, the behavior of decision makers/those in positions of influence, and finally, even the way the company is structured. A prime example of this would be a company that touts a data culture of privacy and security and yet does not have dedicated teams and/or resources that support that culture. If there is a disconnect between what is internally *marketed* as the data culture and what actually *exists to support* that culture, motivation and adoption of the data culture is not only less likely—it's improbable at best.

Maintaining Agility

Hopefully in the preceding sections we've driven home the need for a very thoughtful, thorough, and structured approach to creating and cultivating a data culture. An important aspect of this, one that should not be ignored in inception and creation of a data culture, is how agility will be maintained. We have seen this be a highly problematic area for many companies and would be remiss if we didn't address its importance, as it's much easier to maintain agility than to create it after the fact.

Agility and Its Benefits on Ever-Changing Regulations

During the course of our research we encountered a very interesting use case relating to the CCPA. While you may not be encountering compliance with this particular regulation, the struggles one company is facing may give you some food for thought.

This company is a large retailer that has many different ingestion streams, as it sells its products in many different locations across the United States. This company has always struggled to keep track of not only the data that it collects itself, but also the data it collects from third parties (e.g., a retailer sells its product directly to consumers on its website but may also sell its product via other retailers, either in their stores or via their websites).

Part of compliance with CCPA is to track down PII data for a California resident regardless of where the item was purchased. For example, Ben lives in California but purchased this company's product at a large retailer while he was on vacation in Florida. The transaction itself occurred in Florida, but because Ben is a California resident, he can request that the product company find his purchase data and delete it.

While many companies are now facing this conundrum, the company in this case study has a highly structured and inflexible governance strategy—one that does not easily lend itself to quickly adapting to these new requirements. As such, it recognizes the need to revise its governance strategy, to allow the company to be more agile. The main way it is spearheading this effort is to focus on building and nurturing a strong data culture. With so many moving parts to its business (i.e., so much data coming from so many different places), and with the likelihood that more regulations like CCPA are on the horizon, this company feels that defining and building a culture that will support (ever-changing) governance initiatives will be the key to its success. In this way the company is creating (and has begun enacting) a comprehensive data culture.

Requirements, Regulations, and Compliance

The most obvious reason for creating a culture around agility is the ever-changing legal requirements and regulations that data must be in compliance with. To be sure, the data regulations of today are likely to be less robust than the regulations of tomorrow. In Chapter 1 we discussed how the explosion of available data and its collection has resulted in heaps and heaps of data just sitting there—much of it uncurated.

It is shortsighted and unfeasible to take an approach of simply "handling" the regulation(s) of the present. The ability to pivot once regulations change or pop up (because they will) is not just a necessity—it can be made much easier if steps are taken at the outset.

The Importance of Data Structure

A key aspect to consider when cultivating agility is to "set yourself up for success"—again, this is a component that can be relied upon and enforced by the data culture. Note that being "set up for success" is an intersection of how the data warehouse is structured (the metadata that's collected, the tags/labels/classification used, etc.) with the culture that supports or enables the structure to run smoothly. These two in conjunction help to make it much easier to pivot when new regulations arise.

This is an area in which we've seen many companies struggle. Take, for example, data that is stored based on the application from which it comes—say, sales data from a specific company's retail stores across the US. In the company's current analytics structure, this data is tagged in a certain way—perhaps with metadata relating to the store, purchase amount, time of purchase, and so on.

Now let's say that a new regulation comes along stating that any data from a customer who lives in a certain state can be retained for only 15 days. How would this company easily *find* all the sales data from customers who *live* in a certain state? Note that the criteria is not *sales* with a certain state but *customers*, so a customer from state X could make a purchase in state Y, and if state X is part of the regulation, then that customer's data will need to be deleted after 15 days. The company in our example will have a hard time complying quickly and easily with this regulation if it doesn't have the data structure set up to record the location of the purchaser (for the sake of simplicity, we are assuming here that these are all credit card or mobile pay transactions that can be traced to each purchaser's state of residence).

A process and culture from the outset to collect this kind of metadata (whether or not it is labeled or tagged initially) will make it that much easier to *find* this class of data and then tag/label it, and thus attach a retention policy.

Scaling the Governance Process Up and Down

While we have touted the importance of not only the right tools and process but also the right players (hopefully provided by the buy-in from C-level), there undeniably are times when things don't go according to plan, and the process needs to scale (usually down, although there is the use case that it could need to scale up).

It could be the case that a company loses headcount due to reorganization, restructuring, an acquisition, or even a change in data collection (in terms of actual data collected and/or in the platform[s] used, tools for transformation, storage types and locations, or analytics tools). Any of these will likely affect how a governance program functions, and that program needs to be elastic to accommodate for such changes. The data culture—agreed upon, supported, and reinforced—will aid in successful elasticity.

One strategy we'd like to mention here is one we touched on in Chapter 2: making sure that the most critical data is tended to first (again, this should be a part of the data culture). It's impossible to predict what requirements and regulations may come in the future, but prioritizing data that is most critical to the business (as well as data that has any relation back to a person or identifiable entity) will aid in your ability to scale to accommodate whatever changes may come. At the absolute minimum there should be a process in place (for example, all types of critical data are always tagged or classified upon ingestion and/or are always stored in a certain location) that can quickly address and tend to this category of data.

Interplay with Legal and Security

In this book we've discussed at length the different roles and/or "hats" involved in data governance. When looking at the data culture specifically, two hats of note are legal and security/privacy tsar, and the interplay between the two and their respective teams is important.

Staying on Top of Regulations

Regardless of how a company is organized in terms of roles and who does what, there must be someone who has the task of staying up to date on regulatory requirements that the company may (or may not) need to be in compliance with. As we've previously discussed, sometimes this is done by an internal legal representative (attorney) and at other times this task falls on the privacy tsar or on someone else in security.

What's important about this task is that it needs to be done early and often, not only to ensure current compliance but also to help aid in the ability to ensure *future* compliance. As we've seen over the past 10 years, data handling standards and regulations have greatly changed—the ability to be aware of what these changes might be and how best to set up a data culture to flex as needed and be in compliance is critical.

As we've discussed several times throughout the book, and especially in Chapter 8, having an auditing system in place will greatly aid you in monitoring your governance strategy over time and also facilitate the task of being on top of compliance and regulations, so that if (or when) you face an external audit, you will know that you are in compliance and that nothing unexpected will be found.

Communication

Staying on top of regulations is, however, only half of the story. There must be a process in place for how changes in regulations will be discovered and how these will be communicated to those who decide on how to proceed. In essence, there needs to be constant communication back to the decision-making body about what regulations might be coming up and/or whether there are any changes that need to be made to current data handling practices in order to be in compliance.

It's easy to see how this is a process that very much should be a part of the data culture within a company.

Interplay in Action

An excellent recent example of this process in action is the reaction to GDPR. All companies in the EU were well aware that this new regulation was coming and that changes were needed in order to be compliant. The story was different for companies in the US, however. During many of our interviews with US companies about their data governance practices and their plans for the future in terms of changing regulations, we heard two different approaches: the first was to simply ignore new regulations until they become a requirement (so in the case of GDPR, not to address compliance until it is a requirement for US companies); the second was to assume that the most restrictive regulations in the world *could* become a requirement and thus work toward being in compliance now, even before it's required.

This takes a strong data culture that includes a robust interplay between the gathering of legal requirements, a group deciding which requirements the company will comply with, and another group actually carrying out the work of ensuring that compliance is being met.

Agility Is Still Key

This point really hearkens back to the previous section on agility. It is likely that new regulations will continue to emerge, and the flexibility of the data structure and system that a company builds would do well to have the potential to be easily modified or to pivot when needed to accommodate such requirements.

Incident Handling

We've talked at length about the importance of process and communication in a successful data culture. One particular process we'd like to spend time unpacking is that of incident handling—how are breaches in data governance handled, and who is held responsible?

When "Everyone" Is Responsible, No One Is Responsible

During some of our initial research into how companies structure their data governance strategy, one of the questions we asked was, "Who, at the end of the day, is responsible for improper governance? Whose job is on the line?" Surprisingly, many companies danced around this question and struggled to give us a direct answer of a particular person and/or group who would be held accountable in the event of something going wrong.

This might seem like an unimportant part of the data culture, but it is actually quite critical. Earlier in this chapter we spoke about the importance of fostering an environment of caring and responsibility (and indeed this is important), but it also needs to have a backbone—there must be a person(s) or group(s) who is culpable when things go wrong. When this structure is lacking, governance becomes "everyone's" and yet "no one's" responsibility. The culture needs to support everyone doing their part in proper data handling and owning their portion of governance responsibilities, and it also needs to identify who is the go-to—the end of the line, so to speak, for specific aspects of the governance strategy.

For example, as part of the data culture, it is on every data analyst in a company to know what is PII data and whether or not it should be accessed, and/or for what purposes it can be accessed. A good data culture will support these analysts with education and reinforcements for proper data handling. In the event that an analyst mistakenly (or malevolently as the case may be) accesses and improperly uses PII data, someone should be held accountable for that breach. It may be a data engineer in charge of enforcing access controls, or even a privacy tsar whose responsibility it is to set up and manage access policies. In any event, there needs to be someone who has, as part of their job, the responsibility for ensuring that things go right and accepting the consequences when things go wrong.

We may be overstating this, but implementing and *enforcing responsibility* is key here. People should also be *trained* in how to be responsible and what this looks like (and what it doesn't look like), and this should also be outlined in specific roles from the outset. Literally listed within a role description's key tasks should be what that role is specifically responsible for in terms of data handling, and what the consequences are for failure to carry out this task. Responsibility should be something that is defined and agreed upon, as well as trained and communicated on, so that people are taught *how to be* responsible and are also *held* responsible.

Importance of Transparency

Transparency is an oft-forgotten (or intentionally sidestepped) ingredient of governance that warrants a deeper dive into not only why it's important, but also why you should keep it in mind and most certainly address it as part of building your data culture.

What It Means to Be Transparent

To be sure, many companies and organizations do not want to disclose everything about the ins and outs of their data governance structure, which is to be expected and is not entirely problematic. There is value, however, in a certain amount of transparency from an organization, in terms of what data it collects, how it uses the data (and what for), and what steps/measures it takes to protect data and ensure proper data handling.

Building Internal Trust

Earlier we touched on the importance of trust in building a data culture, and that trust goes both ways—bottom up and top down. A key aspect of building that trust and truly *showing* employees that it is part of the company's data culture is to have full transparency: transparency not only in the items related to data noted above (what data is collected, how it's used, governance processes, etc.) but also in what the incident-handling strategy is. In the previous section we mentioned how important it is to define the specific person or group that is responsible when things go wrong, and just as there should be consequences for these folks, there should also be consequences (albeit different ones) for improper handling by anyone who touches data. While it may make an organization feel uncomfortable to share so broadly about when something has gone wrong and how it was handled internally, doing so builds incredible trust within the company that what is being touted as the data culture is an integral part of the *entire* company culture.

Another strategy that can help you build internal trust is that of enabling two-way communication via a user forum, wherein users of data within your company are able to voice their concerns and needs. We discussed earlier in this chapter the importance of communication, but this is an additional facet that is not just informational (you get to hear from the people actually using the data about why it might be wrong or what could be better)—it also bolsters the data culture by making *all* in the organization feel that they're being heard and are pieces of the greater whole that keeps the governance program running smoothly.

Building External Trust

In creating a solid and successful data culture, focusing on the internal—the company nuts and bolts—is obviously extremely important, but the data culture does not and should not end there. The external perception and trust of a company/organization should also be considered. Just as showing full transparency internally helps to build and reinforce the data culture, what is communicated externally about data collection, handling, and protection practices is also highly important.

In a sense, the customers of a company or organization are an additional extension of its "culture." Customers or consumers should also be considered when thinking about building a data culture. It's not just the actions and perceptions of your staff or employees; it's also the actions and perceptions of your consumers and/or customers, and it's their actions (generally driven by trust) that dictate whether or not they interact with your company or buy your product.

Providing full transparency externally regarding what data is collected, how it's used, how it's protected, and what has been done to mitigate wrongdoing is critical in building trust in a company/organization. There are, to be sure, cases in which customers/people have no choice but to choose one company or organization for a service/purchase/etc., but in the event that there is choice, customers/people are much more likely to choose a company that they *trust* over one they don't trust or are unsure of.

The data culture in essence should not be just an internally decided-upon practice but one that also includes how the company or organization sits in the world—what it wants the world to know about how it handles data and its commitment to compliance and proper data handling.

Setting an Example

It may sound lofty, but another aspect around the importance and maybe even the *power* of transparency is that it can teach and/or inspire others to adopt similar data governance practices and data culture.

If every company or organization were to create, implement, and enforce the governance principles and practices we've laid out, not only would there be excellent governance and data culture within each organization, but there would also be a cross-company, cross-organizational, cross-product, cross-geographical data culture.

Summary

Throughout the course of this text you have learned about all the aspects and facets to be considered when creating your own successful data governance program. We hope that we have educated you not only on all of the facets and features of data itself, governance tools, and the people and processes to consider, but also on the importance of looking at your governance program in a much broader sense to include things such as long-term monitoring and creating a data culture to ensure governance success.

You should walk away from this book feeling that you know what makes up a governance program (some aspects that you may have already heard of, and hopefully some others that you hadn't considered before) and that you know *how* to put those pieces together to create and *maintain* a powerful, flexible, and enduring program that not only meets but also exceeds regulation, compliance, and ethical and societal standards.

Google's Internal Data Governance

In order to understand data governance, it is good to look at a practical example of a company with a deep investment in the topic. We (the authors) are all Google employees, and we believe that in Google we have a great example of a deeply ingrained process, and a fine example of tooling.

The Business Case for Google's Data Governance

Google has user privacy at the top of its priorities and has published strong privacy principles (*https://oreil.ly/HChOe*) that guide us throughout all product development cycles. These privacy principles include, as top priorities, respect for user's privacy, being transparent about data collection, and taking the utmost care with respecting the protection of users' data, and they have ensured that good data governance is at the core of Google.

Before we dive into the specifics of data governance and management at Google, it is crucial to understand the motivations behind Google's data collection, and the use case. This is a good approach for any undertaking. Google provides access to search results and videos and presents advertisements alongside the search results. Google's income (while more diversified than a few years ago) is largely attributable to ads.

Given the importance of ads, a large portion of the effort in Google is focused on making ads relevant. Google does this by collecting data about end users, indexing this data, and personalizing the ads served for each user.

Google is transparent (*https://oreil.ly/WlbZv*) about this information: when someone uses Google services—for example, when they do a search on Google, get directions on Maps, or watch a video on YouTube—Google collects data to personalize these services. This can include highlighting videos the user has watched in the past, showing ads that are more relevant to the user depending on their location or the websites they frequent, and updating the apps, browsers, and devices they use to access Google services. For example, the results and corresponding ads might be different when a search is made by a user on a mobile device and navigating in Google Maps versus a search made from a desktop using a web browser. The personal information associated with the user's Google account is available if the user is signed in. This can include the user's name, birthday, gender, password, and phone number. Depending on the Google property they are using, this can also include emails they have written and received (if they are using Gmail); photos and videos they have saved (if they are using Google Photos); documents, spreadsheets, and slides they have created (if they are using Google Drive); comments they have made on YouTube; contacts they added in Google Contacts; and/or events on their Google Calendar. It is necessary that all this user information is protected when using Google services.

Google, therefore, provides each user with transparency and control of how their personal information is used. Users can find out how their ads are personalized by going to Google Ad Settings (*https://oreil.ly/p4_QK*) and can control the personalization therein. They can also turn off personalization and even take out their data (*https:// oreil.ly/AglJd*). They can review their activity within Google domains (*https://oreil.ly/ KY3bM*) and delete or control activity collection. This level of transparency and control is something that users expect in order to be comfortable with providing a business with their personal information. Google maintains transparency around what data it collects (*https://oreil.ly/WlbZv*) and how this information is used (*https:// oreil.ly/nr04E*) to generate the revenues mentioned above. If you are collecting personal information and using it to personalize your services, you should provide similar mechanisms for your customers to view, control, and redact your use of their personal data.

Given all the information Google collects, it is not surprising that Google is publicly committed to protecting that information and ensuring privacy (*https://oreil.ly/ W4bPM*). Google is meticulous about external certifications and accreditations (*https://oreil.ly/EzBqd*) and provides tools for individual consumers to control the data collected about them (*https://oreil.ly/M2ol9*).

The Scale of Google's Data Governance

Google keeps some information about itself private—for example, how much data it actually collects and manages. Some public information provides a general sense, such as Google's reported investment of $10 billion in offices and data centers in 2020.[1] A third-party attempt at estimating Google's data storage capacity using public

---

[1] Carrie Mihalcik, "Google to Spend $10 Billion on Offices, Data Centers in US This Year" (*https://oreil.ly/ fK_Wj*), *CNET*, February 26, 2020.

sources of information came up with 10EB (exabytes (*https://oreil.ly/dwprc*)) of information.[2]

Some further information about the Google data cataloging effort, its scale, and the approaches taken to organizing data is described in the Google "Goods" paper.[3] This paper discusses the **Goo**gle **D**ataset **S**earch (GOODS) approach, which does not rely on stakeholder support but works in the background to gather metadata and index that metadata. The resulting catalog can be leveraged to further annotate technical metadata with business information.

So, with this significant amount and variety of information, much of it likely sensitive, how does Google protect the data that it has collected and ensure that privacy while keeping the data usable?

Google has published certain papers about the tools used, and we can discuss these.

Google's Governance Process

There are various privacy commitments Google needs to respect and comply with, in particular around user data: regulations, privacy policies, external communications, and best practices. However, it is generally hard to:

- Make nontrivial global statements (e.g., all data is deleted on time)
- Answer specific questions (e.g., do you never record user location if setting X is switched off?)
- Make informed decisions (e.g., is it OK to add this googler to that group?)
- Consistently assert rules or invariants at all times

The ideal state is one in which we have a comprehensive understanding of Google's data and production systems and automatically enforced data policies and obligations. In the ideal state:

The lives of Google employees are easier
- Taking the privacy- and security-preserving path is easier than taking an insecure path.
- Privacy bureaucracy is reduced via automation.

---

2 James Zetlen, "Google's Datacenters on Punch Cards" (*https://oreil.ly/cXhrr*), *XKCD*.

3 Alon Halevy et al., "Goods: Organizing Google's Dataset" (*https://oreil.ly/Ip_ww*) (presented at SIGMOD/PODS'16: International Conference on Management of Data, San Francisco, CA, June 2016).

Google can do more...
- Developers use data without worrying about introducing security and privacy risks.
- Developers can make privacy a product feature.
- Google can make data-supported external privacy statements with confidence.

...while ensuring security and privacy
- Google can prevent privacy problems before they happen.
- Data obligations (policies, contracts, best practices) are objective and enforceable.

Every single feature Google produces and releases undergoes scrutiny by specialized teams external to the core development team. These teams review the product from the following aspects:

Privacy
- The team looks carefully at any user data collected and reviews justification for the collection of this data. This includes reviewing what data, if collected, is going to be visible to Google employees, and under what constraints. The team also ensures that consent was provided for the data collected, and whether encryption is applied and audit logging is enabled for that data.
- In addition, we look at compliance—we make sure that when users choose to delete data, it is verifiably removed within Google's committed SLAs, and that Google has monitoring on all data retained (so that we can ensure minimal retention is preserved).
- By verifying compliance and policies before even starting the collection of data, we limit a significant number of challenges ahead of time.

Security
This is a technical review targeted at scrutinizing the design and architecture of the code according to best practices to potentially head off future incidents resulting from security flaws. Since most capabilities Google launches are exposed to the web, and despite the fact that there are always multiple layers of security, we always provide for an additional review. Web threats are present and evolving, and a review by subject matter experts is beneficial to all.

Legal
This is a review from a corporate governance standpoint, making sure the product or service launched is compliant with export regulations and explicitly getting a review from a regulation perspective.

(There are other approvers for a release, naturally, but we will focus on those related to data governance.)

Google maintains additional certifications (*https://oreil.ly/sBtRS*), with a common theme of most of those being third-party verified.

How Does Google Handle Data?

Much of the information Google holds goes into a central database, where it is held under strict controls. We have already shared information about the likely contents of this database; now let's focus on the controls around this database.

Privacy Safe—ADH as a Case Study

ADH—or Ads Data Hub (*https://oreil.ly/Lt-Hr*)—is a tool Google provides that allows you to join data you collect yourself (e.g., Google ad campaign events) with Google's own data about the same constituents. Yet it does so without breaching the privacy or trust of the individuals inspected. The ways ADH accomplishes this are indicative of the care Google takes with respect to data. There are several mechanisms working in conjunction to provide multiple layers of protection:

Static checks
> ADH looks for obvious breaches, such as listing out user IDs, and blocks certain analytics functions that can potentially expose user IDs or distill a single user's information.

Aggregations
> ADH makes sure to respond only with aggregates, so that each row in the response to a query corresponds to multiple users, beyond a minimal threshold. This prevents the identification of any individual user. For most queries, you can only receive reporting data on 50 or more users. Filtered rows are those omitted from the results without notification.

Differential requirements
> Differential requirements compare results from the current query operation you're running to your previous results, as well as rows from the same result set. This is designed to help prevent the user from gathering information about individual users by comparing data from multiple sets of users that meet our aggregation requirements. Differential requirement violations can be triggered by changes to your underlying data between two jobs.

ADH Uses Differential Privacy

Businesses that advertise on Google often want to measure how well their marketing is working. To do so, it is essential to be able to measure the performance of their ads. A local restaurant that has advertised on Google will want to know how many people who were served a restaurant ad actually came to the restaurant. How can Google provide advertisers the ability to do customized analysis that aligns with the business (e.g., how many patrons placed an online order after seeing the ad on Google), considering such analysis will require joining information on who the ads are served to with the restaurant's own customer transactions database?

ADH uses differential checks to enable customized analysis while respecting user privacy and upholding Google's high standards of data security. Differential checks are applied to ensure that users can't be identified through the comparison of multiple sufficiently aggregated results. When comparing a job's results to previous results, ADH needs to look for vulnerabilities on the level of individual users. Because of this, even results from different campaigns, or results that report the same number of users, might have to be filtered if they have a large number of overlapping users. On the other hand, two aggregated result sets may have the same number of users—appearing identical—but not share individual users and would therefore be privacy-safe, in which case they wouldn't be filtered. ADH uses data from historical results when considering the vulnerability of a new result. This means that running the same query over and over again creates more data for differential checks to use when considering a new result's vulnerability. Additionally, the underlying data can change, leading to privacy check violations on queries thought to be stable.

These techniques are sometimes referred to as *differential privacy*.[4]

The ADH case study exemplifies Google's cultural approach to handling data: beyond the process part mentioned previously, Google has built a system that provides value while at the same time ensuring safeguards and prevention techniques that put user privacy at the forefront. Google has captured some of the capabilities in a "differential privacy library" (*https://oreil.ly/9mjo9*).

For another case study, consider the capabilities of Gmail. Google has built tools to extract structured data from emails. These tools enable assistive experiences, such as reminding the user when a bill payment is due or answering queries about the departure time of a booked flight. They can also be combined with other information to do seemingly magical things like proactively surfacing an emailed discount coupon

---

4 Some of the these techniques are described in a paper Google published entitled "Differentially Private SQL with Bounded User Contribution" (*https://oreil.ly/AH8Sp*).

while the user is at that store. All of the above is accomplished by scanning the user's personal email while still maintaining that user's privacy. Remember, Google personnel are not allowed to view any single email. This is presented in the paper "Anatomy of a Privacy-Safe Large-Scale Information Extraction System over Email" (*https://oreil.ly/tvW8A*). This capability to scan information and make it accessible to the information's owner, while at the same time maintaining privacy, is accomplished through the fact that most emails are business-to-consumer emails, and those emails from a single business to many consumers share the same template. You can, without human intervention, backtrack groups of emails to the business, generate a template that is devoid of any potential information (differentiating between the boilerplate portions and the transient section), and then build an extraction template. The paper goes into more detail.

Additional Resources

The following are some of the works we consulted while writing this book. This is not intended to be a complete list of the resources we used, but we hope that some of you will find this selection helpful as you learn more about data governance.

Chapter 4: Data Governance over a Data Life Cycke

- Association Analytics. "How to Develop a Data Governance Policy" (*https://oreil.ly/kootb*). September 27, 2016.

- Australian Catholic University. "Data and Information Governance Policy" (*https://oreil.ly/vkb3I*). Revised January 1, 2018.

- Michener, William K. "Ten Simple Rules for Creating a Good Data Management Plan" (*https://oreil.ly/q1b4X*). *PLOS Computational Biology* 11, no. 10 (October 2015): e1004525.

- Mohan, Sanjeev. "Applying Effective Data Governance to Secure Your Data Lake" (*https://oreil.ly/9-8Ps*). Gartner, Inc. April 17, 2018.

- Pratt, Mary K. "What Is a Data Governance Policy?" (*https://oreil.ly/sFlcd*). Tech-Target. Updated February 2020.

- Profisee Group, Inc. "Data Governance—What, Why, How, Who & 15 Best Practices" (*https://oreil.ly/zqcRx*). April 12, 2019.

- Smartsheet, Inc. "How to Create a Data Governance Plan to Gain Control of Your Data Assets" (*https://oreil.ly/Gf8z5*). Accessed February 26, 2021.

- TechTarget. "What Is Data Life Cycle Management (DLM)?" (*https://oreil.ly/RWaAp*). Updated August 2010.

- USGS. "Data Management Plans" (*https://oreil.ly/4u6uG*). Accessed February 26, 2021.

- Watts, Stephen. "Data Lifecycle Management (DLM) Explained" (*https://oreil.ly/pW-Z1*). *The Business of IT* (blog). BMC. June 26, 2018.

- Wikipedia. "Data governance" (*https://oreil.ly/SVmnR*). Last modified February 4, 2021.

- Wing, Jeannette M. "The Data Life Cycle" (*https://oreil.ly/DHUVV*). *Harvard Data Science Review* 1, no. 1 (Summer 2019).

Chapter 8: Monitoring

- Alm, Jens, ed. *Action for Good Governance in International Sport Organisations*. Copenhagen: Play the Game/Danish Institute for Sports Studies (*https://oreil.ly/GJ4KR*). March 2013.

- Cyborg Institute."Infrastructure Monitoring for Everyone" (*https://oreil.ly/YrV5x*). Accessed February 26, 2020.

- Ellingwood, Justin. "An Introduction to Metrics, Monitoring, and Alerting" (*https://oreil.ly/Ap2DK*). DigitalOcean. December 5, 2017.

- Goldman, Todd. "LESSON—Data Quality Monitoring: The Basis for Ongoing Information Quality Management" (*https://oreil.ly/t96TV*). Transforming Data with Intelligence. May 8, 2007.

- Grosvenor Performance Group. "How Is Your Program Going…Really? Performance Monitoring" (*https://oreil.ly/P-ZQj*). MAy 15, 2018.

- Henderson, Liz. "35 Metrics You Should Use to Monitor Data Governance" (*https://oreil.ly/CvScL*). Datafloq. October 28, 2015.

- Karel, Rob. "Monitoring Data with Data Monitoring Tools | Informatica US" (*https://oreil.ly/Xrpib*). *Informatica* (blog). January 2, 2014.

- Pandora FMS. "The Importance of Having a Good Monitoring System? Offer the Best Service for Your Clients" (*https://oreil.ly/95ZAW*) (blog post). September 19, 2017.

- Redscan. "Cyber Security Monitoring" (*https://oreil.ly/jMury*). Accessed February 26, 2021.

- Wells, Charles. "Leveraging Monitoring Governance: How Service Providers Can Boost Operational Efficiency and Scalability…" (*https://oreil.ly/ISmaC*). CA Technologies. January 19, 2018.

- Wikipedia. "Data Lineage" (*https://oreil.ly/HCZni*). Last modified November 17, 2020.

Index

Customer Managed Encryption Keys (CMEK), 163
customer support specialists, 64
customers, as extension of company culture, 207
customization, of monitoring system, 188

D

data
    in business context, 75
    decision-making and, 14-16
    enhancing trust in, 5
    evolution of access methods, 75
    use case expansion, 14-16
data access management, xv
data accumulation, 30
data acquisition
    defined, 87
    identity and access management, 52
    workflow management for, 52
data analysis
    data quality in big data analytics, 116
    tension between data governance and
        democratizing data analysis, 24
data analyst, 63
data archiving
    automated data protection plan, 97
    as data life cycle phase, 89
    in practice, 96
data assessment, 45
data breaches
    Equifax, 167
    healthcare industry, 171-173
    physical data breach in Texas, 169
    portable devices and, 170
    readiness, 171
data capture, 87
data catalog, 25
data cataloging, xiv, 44
data change management, 141
data classes
    in enterprise dictionary, 38-40
    policies and, 40-43
data classification and organization, 43
    access control and, 6-8
    automation of, 43
    data classification and organization, 43
    data protection and, 146
    in framework, xiv

data collection
    advances in methods of, 10
    increase in types of data collected, 13
    in sports, 11-13
data completeness, 129
data corruption, 26
data creation
    as data life cycle phase, 87
    defining type of data, 95
    in practice, 95
data culture
    analytics and bottom line, 195
    benefits of data governance to the business,
        194-196
    building a, 193-208
    caring and, 200-201
    communication planning, 199
    data governance policy, 110
    definition/importance of, 193
    incident handling, 205
    as intentional, 197
    interplay with legal and security, 203
    maintaining agility, 201-203
    monitoring and, 191
    motivation and adoption, 200
    motivation and its cascading effects, 200
    privacy/security and, 83, 193-208
    staying on top of regulations, 204
    training for, 197-199
    transparency and, 206
data deduplication, 124
data deletion, 50-52
    best practices, 170
    regulatory compliance and, 28
data democratization, 24
data destruction
    compliance policy/timeline for, 97
    as data life cycle phase, 89
    in practice, 97
data discovery and assessment, xiv
data enablement, 8
data encryption (see encryption)
data enrichment, 65
    cloud dataset, 78
    manual process of, 75
data entry, 87
data exfiltration, 153-158
    secure code, 156
    virtual private cloud service controls, 155

guiding principles, developing/documenting, 106

H

"hats"
   and company structure, 74
Health Insurance Portability and Accountability Act of 1996 (HIPAA), 16
healthcare industry
   cascading data quality problems with tribal knowledge, 124
   data protection best practices, 167
   need for comprehensive data governance, 196
   security breaches, 171-173
Herzberg, Elaine, 16
highly regulated companies, 69-71

I

identity and access management (IAM) systems, 52, 147
identity-aware proxy (IAP), 160
IMPACT (teacher ranking system), 76
incident handling, 205
infotypes, 37
inheritance, 141
innovation, fostering with data governance, 24
internal data governance, at Google, 209-215
internal trust, building, 206

J

Jacob, Oren, 50

K

k-anonymity, 164
key management, 47-49
key management system (KMS), 163
knowledge workers, 8

L

labeling of resources in public cloud, 34
laptops, 170
large companies, 72
legacy companies, 66
legal "hat", 58
legal issues (see regulations; compliance)
life cycle (see data life cycle)
lineage (see data lineage)

lineage graph, 136
lineage tracking, 128
   in enterprise dictionary, 46
   time/cost of, 47
location of data, 110

M

machine learning (ML)
   data governance and, 4
   data quality in, 117-120
management buy-in, 107
maritime domain awareness (MDA), 21
Mars Climate Orbiter, 100
MaxMind, 115
medical records, 167
mergers and acquisitions, large companies and, 73
metadata
   analytics in legacy companies and, 66
   data enrichment and, 65
   data lineage and, 135
metadata catalog, 25
metadata management
   in enterprise dictionary, 44
   as part of framework, xiv
metrics, gaming of, 76
Microsoft Azure, 148
misuse of data, 26
ML (machine learning)
   data governance and, 4
   data quality in, 117-120
monitoring, 175-191
   compliance monitoring, 182
   criteria for, 189
   data lineage monitoring, 180
   data quality monitoring, 179
   defined, 175
   important reminders for, 190
   key areas to monitor, 179-187
   program performance monitoring, 183-185
   reasons to perform, 176-178
   security monitoring, 185
   system features, 187-189
monitoring system
   analysis in real-time, 187
   customization in, 188
   features of, 187-189
   graphic visualization in, 188
   notifications in, 187

About the Authors

Evren Eryurek, PhD, is the leader of the data analytics and data management portfolio of Google Cloud, covering Streaming Analytics, Dataflow, Beam, Messaging (Pub/Sub & Confluent Kafka), Data Governance, Data Catalog & Discovery, and Data Marketplace as the director of product management.

He joined Google Cloud as the technical director in the CTO Office of Google Cloud, leading Google Cloud in its efforts toward Industrial Enterprise Solutions. Google Cloud business established the CTO Office and is still building a team of the world's foremost experts on cloud computing, analytics, AI, and machine learning to work with global companies as trusted advisors and partners. Evren joined Google as the first external member to take a leadership role as a technical director within the CTO Office of Google Cloud.

Prior to joining Google, he was the SVP & software chief technology officer for GE Healthcare, a nearly $20 billion segment of GE. GE Healthcare is a global leader in delivering clinical, business, and operational solutions, with its medical equipment, information technologies, and life science and service technologies covering settings from physician offices to integrated delivery networks.

Evren began his GE career at GE Transportation, where he served as general manager of the software and solutions business. Evren was with Emerson Process Management group for over 11 years, where he held several leadership positions and was responsible for developing new software-based growth technologies for process control systems and field devices, and coordinating cross-divisional product execution and implementation.

A graduate of the University of Tennessee, Evren holds master's and doctorate degrees in nuclear engineering. Evren holds over 60 US patents.

Uri Gilad is leading data governance efforts for the data analytics within Google Cloud. As part of his role, Uri is spearheading a cross-functional effort to create the relevant controls, management tools, and policy workflows that enable a GCP customer to apply data governance policies in a unified fashion wherever their data may be in their GCP deployment.

Prior to Google, Uri served as an executive in multiple data security companies, most recently as the VP of product in MobileIron, a public zero trust/endpoint security platform. Uri was an early employee and a manager in CheckPoint and Forescout, two well-known security brands. Uri holds an MS from Tel Aviv University and a BS from the Technion—Israel Institute of Technology.

Valliappa (Lak) Lakshmanan is a tech lead for Big Data and Machine Learning Professional Services on Google Cloud Platform. His mission is to democratize machine learning so that it can be done by anyone anywhere using Google's amazing infrastructure (i.e., without deep knowledge of statistics or programming or ownership of lots of hardware).

Anita Kibunguchy-Grant is a product marketing manager for Google Cloud, specifically focusing on BigQuery, Google's data warehousing solution. She also led thought-leadership marketing content for Data Security & Governance at Google Cloud. Before Google, she worked for VMware, where she managed awareness and go-to market programs for VMware's core Hyper-Converged Infrastructure (HCI) product, vSAN.

She has an MBA from MIT Sloan School of Management and is passionate about helping customers use technology to transform their businesses.

Jessi Ashdown is a user experience researcher for Google Cloud specifically focused on data governance. She conducts user studies with Google Cloud customers from all over the world and uses the findings and feedback from these studies to help inform and shape Google's data governance products to best serve the users' needs.

Prior to joining Google, Jessi led the enterprise user experience research team at T-Mobile, which was focused on bringing best-in-class user experiences to T-Mobile retail and customer care employees.

A graduate of both the University of Washington and Iowa State University, Jessi holds a bachelor's in psychology and a master's in human computer interaction.

Colophon

The animal on the cover of *Data Governance: The Definitive Guide* is the Pakistan tawny owl (*Strix aluco biddulphi*). While tawny owls are common throughout Europe, Asia, and northern Africa, this subspecies is specifically found in the northern parts of Afghanistan, Pakistan, and India, as well as in Tajikistan and Kyrgyzstan. These owls prefer temperate deciduous forests, or mixed forests with some clearings. They may also roost in shrub land, orchards, pastures, or urban parks with large trees—anywhere with enough foliage to keep them well hidden during the day.

Tawny owls tend to have medium-sized brown or brown-gray bodies with large round heads and deep black eyes. Pakistan tawny owls have a distinctive gray coloring with a whitish base and strong herringbone pattern below the head and mantle. They are also believed to be the largest subspecies, with wingspans around 11 to 13 inches; females are often slightly larger than their male counterparts. These owls are strictly nocturnal and are not often seen in daylight. They are carnivorous and hunt for small mammals, rodents, reptiles, birds, insects, and fish from dusk to dawn. They do not migrate and are considered mature at the end of their first year.

Tawny owls are monogamous and pair for life. Breeding season is from February to July, and they nest in tree holes, among rocks, or in the crevices of old buildings. The female incubates two to four eggs for a month. New hatchlings are altricial and cannot fend for themselves or leave the nest for the first 35 to 40 days; they are fed by the mother with food brought by the father. Juveniles stay with their parents for about three months after fledging, at which point they may disperse after breeding to establish new territory within their local range. Pakistan tawny owls can be highly territorial and defend an area of about one thousand square meters year-round.

Tawny owls are excellent hunters, and while their eyesight may not be much better than a human's, they have excellent directional hearing and can swivel their heads almost 360 degrees when tracking prey. They typically live 4 years in the wild—the oldest wild tawny owl ever recorded lived more than 21 years! Tawny owls are considered a species of least concern by the IUCN. Many of the animals on O'Reilly covers are endangered; all of them are important to the world.

The cover illustration is by Karen Montgomery, based on a black and white engraving from *Meyers Kleines Lexicon*. The cover fonts are Gilroy Semibold and Guardian Sans. The text font is Adobe Minion Pro; the heading font is Adobe Myriad Condensed; and the code font is Dalton Maag's Ubuntu Mono.

O'REILLY®

There's much more
where this came from.

Experience books, videos, live online
training courses, and more from O'Reilly
and our 200+ partners—all in one place.

Learn more at oreilly.com/online-learning

CPSIA information can be obtained
at www.ICGtesting.com
Printed in the USA
JSHW061534180523
41912JS00005B/211